Frances Noble

Gertrude Mannering: A tale of sacrifice

Frances Noble

Gertrude Mannering: A tale of sacrifice

ISBN/EAN: 9783741178009

Manufactured in Europe, USA, Canada, Australia, Japa

Cover: Foto ©Andreas Hilbeck / pixelio.de

Manufactured and distributed by brebook publishing software (www.brebook.com)

Frances Noble

Gertrude Mannering: A tale of sacrifice

GERTRUDE MANNERING.

A Tale of Sacrifice.

By FRANCES NOBLE.

LONDON: BURNS AND OATES,
Portman Street and Paternoster Row.
1875.

TO THE

LADY GEORGIANA FULLERTON,

This little Volume,

BY

HER LADYSHIP'S KIND PERMISSION,

IS MOST

RESPECTFULLY INSCRIBED.

GERTRUDE MANNERING.

CHAPTER I.

'LET me have just two minutes in the chapel before I go, sister;' and a pair of beautiful brown eyes, just then glistening with tears, looked up very earnestly into Sister Teresa's face.

'Poor Gerty! It would not be easy to refuse that request, would it, dear? But do not be long, or papa will be impatient, and perhaps think we are going to keep you for good and all.'

The young girl lingered yet a moment.

'Ah, sister, it doesn't seem five years, does it, since I first came, and when I was crying after papa had left me, you came and took me to the chapel, to ask our Lord to welcome me, you said,—don't you remember? And now it is like going to say good-bye to Him, isn't it?'

'Not good-bye, Gerty dear, but to ask Him to go with you out into the world, and never to let you send Him away by sin.'

Gerty sighed as she looked again into the nun's calm sweet face, and then ran quickly but softly along the corridor and up the stairs which led to the convent chapel.

Five years before, Gertrude Mannering had first

come to school, a little girl of twelve; and now the happy peaceful time was over, and she was going home to begin her life in the world, of which yet she had seen so little, going half in joy and half in sorrow, —joy at the prospect of being always with her dear father, who was everything to her—for mother she had none—and sorrow at leaving her beloved convent and its still more beloved inmates. Gertrude, or 'Gerty,' as her companions liked better to call her, had always been a favourite in the school; and even the good nuns themselves, though they would not *show* any partiality, could hardly help feeling it for the child whose bright sweet face took all hearts by storm almost at once, if it were only by the very beautiful eyes, which could look so laughingly bewitching or so mournfully sympathetic, as the feelings of their possessor prompted. And the sweet yet bright intelligent face was a true mirror to the young girl's character; to the keen clear intellect and warm loving heart; to the generous and forgiving, if at times somewhat quick, sensitive temper. Gertrude had never been what might be called one of the model girls in the convent; she had had her share of scrapes and misdemeanours; she had always been among those who looked forward with girlish delight to their entrance into the world and its untasted pleasures, but she had ever been sincerely good and pious withal, ever really prizing her holy religion above all things, and her very faults had been lovable, as it were.

And now they were going to lose her; she was going to be emancipated from the happy innocent convent life, with its wise and gentle restraint, to go home to be once more her father's spoiled darling, to receive the admiration which the world was sure to give to one on whom nature had bestowed so many outward as well as inward gifts.

For two or three minutes she knelt there in the chapel, on the floor just outside the altar-rails, with her face buried in her hands and the tears still flowing.

'O Jesus! take care of me always; never let me forget Thee or cease to love Thee in the midst of the world. I am very young and weak; give me always grace to resist temptation, to be firm always in our holy faith, whatever trials may come!'

Did she know—that young girl, little more than child as she was—did she understand, in her sweet innocence and heart freedom, the full power of the 'temptation' against which she prayed so simply and earnestly? could she realise in her inexperience the 'trials' which might be in store, while everything looked so bright? Hardly, perhaps, and sad would it have been could she have done so; but surely none the less acceptable to Jesus' Heart was the innocent prayer; none the less surely would He give her the strength she asked for as she stood trembling, as it were, on the threshold of the busy perilously-fascinating world.

Her prayer over, Gertrude rose and went quickly with Sister Teresa to the reception-room, where her father awaited her. He came forward at once and kissed her with a yearning fondness, which showed how much she was to him, and what a happy day this was on which he could claim her again entirely for his own. He was a tall, slender, fine-looking man of sixty, but seeming older than that from his very white hair and venerable aspect. The Rev. Mother, who was with him, seeing the tear-traces still on Gertrude's face, took her hand with a kind smile.

'What, Gerty! tears again, when the day has come for which our little girl used to long so much?'

'Ah, Rev. Mother, that was two or three years ago, when I was always in scrapes; not so much latterly.

Besides, now that it has really come, the saying good-bye to you all, and the girls too, it seems so—so queer, to think I shall never be here again in the old way;' and her lips quivered as the tears glistened again in the bright eyes. 'If it were not for papa, I might want to stay another year; but he would be afraid I was going to stay altogether; and I couldn't do that: you could never spare me, papa, could you?' and putting her little hand in his arm, she gave him another fond kiss.

'No, I couldn't spare Gerty, Rev. Mother,' said Mr. Mannering, as a sad shadow passed across his face, brought there by the thought of the *dead*—of Gerty's mother, his beautiful girl-wife, his bright darling, who had blessed his life for three short years and had then been taken from him, leaving him the little babe of scarce two days old to be her own namesake, and to fill up the heavy void in his heart.

'No, Rev. Mother,' he continued after a pause, 'I have given Rupert to God freely and willingly, proud that my boy is destined to such a high vocation; but may He forgive me if I say that I cannot spare Gerty, my little girl; or rather if I say that I do not think I shall be called on to make the sacrifice—that I do not think He will want her to serve Him in that way;' and the wish for resignation to God's will of the earnest Catholic seemed struggling in his heart with the father's human feelings as he looked with an almost anxious inquiry at the Rev. Mother, who readily replied with a sweet smile, 'I think with you, Mr. Mannering, that God will not call Gerty to our life. We cannot tell yet, of course, but it seems to me that she is a flower that will bloom best in the world, and that God will give her grace to help others on with her, if she asks for it and corresponds with it when it comes.

Eh, Gerty?' she added tenderly, turning to the young girl for the last kiss and embrace.

'Don't expect anything too good from me, Rev. Mother, for I'm afraid I'm not likely ever to do anything very great or wonderful. Only pray that I may not have grown into a stiff worldly young lady when I come to see you next year,—for I *am* to come, you know; papa has promised;' and trying to laugh, to keep back a sob, Gertrude tore herself away from her two dear nuns, and followed her father out to the vehicle that waited to take them to the nearest station, some two miles off.

It was but two days from Christmas, and the snow lay thick everywhere as they drove out of the convent grounds. Gertrude gazed lingeringly at the white peaceful scene.

'I wonder how it will look to me when I see it again, papa,—whether it will seem changed. I wonder if *I* shall be changed at all when I come again. I suppose I shall look a little older and more of a young lady, that's all. O papa, it *is* nice to be coming back to be always with you again.' And as she sat there by him her father drew her still closer, and stroked the pretty bright hair that escaped from the little convent bonnet.

Ay, well might she wonder! She would see her dear convent home again perhaps, and in no very long time; but would it be with the same joyous childlike heart? would she bring back with her no heavier trouble than that she now carried away? would the eyes that looked again upon the familiar spots be dimmed by no more bitter tears than those which glistened in their bright depths to-day?

CHAPTER II.

WHITEWELL GRANGE, Gertrude Mannering's home, was situated in B——shire, seventy or eighty miles from N——, the nearest town to the convent she had just quitted. The Grange stood in a small park, which was quite a miniature of rural beauty of every kind. It had belonged to the Mannerings for centuries— indeed, before the Reformation the family had been a notable one in the county; but since then, despoiled of the greater part of their possessions, often fined and otherwise persecuted for their firm adherence to the ancient faith, they had sunk into comparative obscurity and insignificance, content to keep that which was more precious than all their worldly goods and prosperity—the priceless treasure of the holy Catholic religion. Family pride the Mannerings may have had, perhaps; and who could blame them, for they boasted a long and stainless pedigree? but prouder still were they to have 'suffered persecution for justice' sake,' to have been thought worthy in the most troublous times to give the shelter of their mansion to many a hunted priest and religious, happy to brave peril in such holy cause, and to receive in return from their saintly visitors the blessed ministrations for which the poor Catholics of those days had to hunger so often and so long. There was a priests' hiding-hole in the old dining-room of the Grange, and in its dark recess, in the worst days of persecution, when once staying in the house for two or three days, the great Jesuit,

Father Gerard, had lain concealed for a night, until the baffled search of the priest-hunters was over, and the trembling household might breathe in peace for another short space. This hiding-hole had always been a favourite spot with Gertrude and her only brother, Rupert, in their childhood, when they used to play there together for hours, Rupert being always the hidden priest, and his little sister the baffled pursuivant, searching vainly and sounding the innocent-looking panels, and then changing into the gentle lady of the house who came to bring refreshment to the half-faint prisoner, or to announce to him that he might now come forth in safety.

A portion of the pretty innocent play had now become earnest, for Rupert Mannering had already finished his novitiate in the Society of Jesus, and he always laughingly said that he felt sure the first seeds of his vocation had been sown in his childhood during the hours he had played in the hiding-place which had once for a whole night contained the blessed confessor, Father Gerard.

'You ought to have let me out quicker always, Gerty,' he had said one day to his sister, when she was crying at the thought of parting with him; not that she was not very proud to think that her idolised Rupert would one day be a Jesuit priest. 'You ought to have let me out sooner if you did not want me to go and be a Jesuit. You always kept me in so long, that I have caught some of the graces that Father Gerard left behind him wherever he went. I take no credit for it at all; it is all you, Gerty;' and the youth would try merrily to laugh his dear sister out of her sorrow for his temporary loss.

Rupert Mannering was just a year older than his sister, and was now close upon nineteen. He had been sent early to one of the great Jesuit colleges, and from the age of fifteen had never swerved from his desire to be admitted into the Society. Not three years later—before he was eighteen, when he left college—his father, after a brief and painful struggle with himself, let him go at once to the novitiate, instead of remaining two or three years in the world, as he, Mr. Mannering, had at first wished.

'It would be no use, papa,' the boy had pleaded; 'it would only be so much time lost, and I should want to go all the same at the end of it. Let me go now, while you are used to me being away, while it will only seem as if I were at college still.'

'Then you shall, my boy,' the father had said at last; 'I ought to be ashamed to let you be more courageous than I am, Rupert. God knows it is not that I am not proud to think that my son will be a priest of such a glorious order; but you see, Rupert, I always get thinking of your mother more than ever at these times. If she were alive, it might be easier to part with you, and give up the hope of knowing that the old home will pass to you when I die; but I ought to remember how happy she must be to know what a life her boy has chosen. She used to wonder so much what you would grow up to be, Rupert; she used to talk about it so often when you were a little thing in her arms, before Gerty came and *she* died. She used to pray so often that you might always be kept good and pure amid the temptations of the world. Perhaps God has sent you this vocation in answer to her prayers, Rupert.'

'Poor mamma!' said the boy sadly. 'If it is so, you know you will not only be willing to let me go, papa, but glad as well.' Then seeing that sad remembrances were crowding on his father's mind, he linked his arm in his in boyish fashion, and led him away out into the grounds, talking merrily. 'Don't forget to give Father Gerard a share in the business too, papa, whatever Gerty says to the contrary.'

This had all happened more than a year previously, and now Rupert had just finished his noviceship, as we said before. He was a tall graceful youth, whose face had more of the beauty of expression than merely of feature, and his father was rewarded for his sacrifice every time he saw the sweet heavenly look which was becoming habitual now on the boyish face.

And after all, even in an earthly sense, what had Mr. Mannering to desire more, now that he was to have Gertrude once again with him entirely, his little girl, loved with a more peculiar yearning tenderness than even his idolised boy? During her earliest years, when she was quite a child, he had never intended to part with her, never meant to send her to school at all. He must keep her always in his sight, he told himself, and let her be educated entirely at home, his precious darling, his Gertrude's dying gift. And until she was twelve years old he had kept his resolution. Gerty was kept at home under the care of a governess, as there was no convent sufficiently near for her to attend as a day-scholar; but as the time passed on, Mr. Mannering saw clearly, much as he tried to shut his eyes to the fact, that the child's education would make but little progress if conducted in this fashion. To know that she was in the house and not have her near him, her father found impossible most days out of the seven. He was continually invading the schoolroom on some pretext or other, and fancying Gerty looked pale, would carry her off for a walk, or a ride, or a drive with him, or would give her a whole holiday, so that she might go with him on some little pleasure trip or other, until the poor governess was often on the verge of distraction. And then, too, the child had no companions of her own age, for the Mannerings only associated intimately with one or two families in the neighbourhood, and her brother's holidays came but once a year. It was but a lonely life for a child, for Mr. Mannering saw little company since his young wife's death, and lived almost entirely among his books, and works of charity and piety. Not that little Gerty ever found it lonely; she was as happy as a queen, a bright sunbeam in the grave old house, wanting nothing but to be always with papa.

'If her mother had lived,' Mr. Mannering used to say to himself as he looked at her, 'it would have been different. I should not have been so weak. We might have kept her at home without interfering in this way with her education; we could have had children here oftener of her own age; she might, perhaps—have had sisters;' and the tear came into the poor father's eye as he gazed on his little one, and as he was forced to admit that it was selfish to keep her with him, to let her grow up perhaps peculiar and too old-fashioned, without the incentives to emulation which she would have at school.

And so, soon after Gertrude had turned twelve years old, her father called her to him one day, and they held together one of the loving chats to which they were accustomed in the deep peculiar relationship which was with them almost stronger than the ordinary tie between father and daughter, more familiar, more confidential. Mr. Mannering explained everything to the little girl, making it quite clear to her childish understanding; and she listened very gravely, hating the plan in itself, crying very much while she saw the wisdom of it, but never once thinking of demurring if darling papa wished it and thought it best. If any one else had suggested the separation, Gerty's bright eyes would have looked quick rebellion and defiance; but as it was, she put her arms round her father's neck and kissed him.

'Yes, papa, I'll go to school, if you really, really want me to. Poor papa, how lonely you'll be! But there will be holidays, won't there, where I shall go? I *won't* go where there aren't long holidays, papa, every year.'

And so it had been settled; and Gerty had stolen quietly up to the chapel, to tell this her first trouble to our Lady, asking her to help her not to rebel and feel too sad about it, but to make the years pass quickly, and bring her home safely again to papa at the end.

Then the governess had been dismissed from the Grange, and Mr. Mannering and Gerty, foolishly perhaps, some would say, had given themselves a good long holiday together of three or four months, while a convent was agreed upon to which to send the latter.

It was no difficult task to find one, even for so anxious a father as Mr. Mannering, and the convent of the Sacred Heart at N—— was fixed on as the temporary home of his precious little girl. When the dreaded day came, he himself took her there; and even in his terrible loneliness he could not feel unhappy at leaving her in such a healthy beautiful spot, in the care of the good nuns, who had seen at once what a very precious charge had been committed to them, and who soon grew to love his little Gertrude for other reasons in addition to those of their sacred duty.

CHAPTER III.

AND now the long years were over, and Mr. Mannering had got his darling safe back again; he would never need to feel lonely any more, with the bright loving sunbeam that had come to shine again in the old ancestral home. People had wondered sometimes why he had never married again, why he had not taken another wife to cheer his solitude; but into his own heart the thought or wish to do so had never once entered, not even for his children's sake, or as a method by which he could have kept Gertrude always at home. Such love as he would wish to give to a wife could never dwell in his heart again; it had been given once, and was buried with his dead Gertrude; and without love he could never put another in her place; he could never ask any one to come and be mistress of his home and a second mother to his children unless he could give her his love in return, and that he could never do.

So little Gerty was spared a stepmother, and came back to reign sole mistress of her father's house as well as of his heart. How delicious were her awakenings now every morning, when she remembered where she was, and rising early as was her wont, dressed quickly, so as to be down-stairs in the cosy old breakfast-room before her father, ready to welcome him with her warm kisses, warmer to him than the bright fire she always stirred up so vigorously for his benefit!

Mr. Mannering seemed hardly able to realise it sometimes that he had got his little girl back for good, as he would tell her often, stroking her bright hair as she stood by him. 'It is like a dream, Gerty, still, but it has made me feel younger again already.'

And then, however cold it was, they set out together every morning to Mass at the village church, for they could only have it in their own little chapel when there was an extra priest at hand to come and say it for them. The honest simple country folk themselves felt a personal interest in Miss Mannering's return, for her father's sake as well as because they liked to see her bright face smiling on them outside the church every morning, or as she passed among them riding or driving with Mr. Mannering, as they remembered her doing as a child. And she began to go amongst them at once, not in any systematically benevolent way, but unaffectedly and impulsively, giving to them often out of the well-filled purse her father always provided— so impulsively, indeed, as often to bring upon herself a gentle remonstrance and prohibition from the good priest of the mission, Father Walmsley. The latter was a secular priest, but the custom of his loving parishioners and his own holiness of life had long given to him the title of 'Father,' so typical of his character. He was a man of no mean learning and eloquence, but he joined to these gifts such a simplicity and earnest humility as caused him to be revered as a saint by all hearts. His very face was a sermon, as Gertrude Mannering often said to her father; one of those countenances whose beauty is all of heaven, hardly at all of earth, which Protestants so often cannot understand or admire, shrinking from them even as 'cadaverous' and 'ungenial,' seeing not that in them is mirrored forth God's own holiness, or that they are, as it were, blessed portraits, if but weak human ones, of Jesus' sweet love and mercy, shown to a cold unbelieving world. Father Walmsley had been many years at Whitewell, and, next to her father and brother, was Gertrude's best friend on earth, known and reverenced long even before her dear nuns at N—— convent. He generally dined once a week at the Grange, or rather came to dinner, for, as Gertrude always laughingly told her father when he had gone, she could never see that he *ate* anything. He was persuaded to come now an extra evening or two to honour Gertrude on her return home, to listen to all her convent adventures, and the plans she was laying down for her future life.

'Don't ask me to have a *rule* of life, please, Father Walmsley,' she said laughingly, 'unless you want to kill me straight away. It was all very well at the convent to have rules and regulations, but I've come home to run wild and do just as I like, haven't I, papa?' and she played with her father's white hair.

'You have come home to be his sunbeam, I hope, Gerty, my child; to brighten his lonely life and reward him for parting with you for so long; and sunbeams are not expected to be under very strict control, you know;' and the priest's saintly countenance relaxed into his own sweet smile.

And a sunbeam Gerty was in the old house, singing up and down, early and late, often snatches of some of the sweet convent hymns, or now again some merry bird-like song, brightening up her father's quiet life, until he not only felt younger, but even looked it, as the villagers remarked every time he passed among them, and as Gertrude joyfully wrote to her dear convent friends in the letters she sent to them so often. It was a sweet innocent existence, dull, perhaps, according to worldly ideas, but not dull to the loving father and daughter, who asked no pleasure beyond each other's society, and that of doing good and living as became the representatives of the noble confessors of their ancient house. Would it be always so? would nothing change the simple desires which now filled Gertrude's girlish heart? would her present life always seem to her the best and happiest this world could give? would she for ever be content to live secluded from the world with her father in the quiet old Grange? These questions occurred more than once to the young Jesuit aspirant, Rupert Mannering, when he came before Lent to spend a week with his father and sister, who welcomed him with idolising delight.

'I hope you've not grown *too* holy, you know, Rupert,' Gerty said to him, 'or else I shall be frightened of you, as I used to tell the girls at school.'

A bright smile lighted up the youth's sweet heavenly face.

'If I'm ever holy *enough*, Gerty, I promise you you shall begin to be frightened of me,' he said. 'Who knows but that the case may be reversed, and *I* may have to be afraid of *you* as a very saintly nun, or some other wonderful character, who will make my poor efforts seem very small indeed?'

Gerty shook her head. 'Not the least fear of such a thing. You're as bad as Reverend Mother at the convent, imagining I might perhaps be going to do all sorts of grand things in the world. You see, Rupert, I was never hidden so long in the priests' hole as you were, so the blessings in it have not stuck to me like they have to you.'

But, unknown to his dear sister, Rupert prayed for her, so earnestly, more especially in his daily visits to the Blessed Sacrament whilst he was at home with them—prayed that when Gertrude should go out into the world she might prove strong and steadfast; that the day might never come when she would despise the sweet innocent life which she so loved now.,

CHAPTER IV.

WINTER and spring had passed, and the park round Whitewell Grange looked very green and beautiful in its early summer garb, so beautiful indeed that Gertrude did not care to leave it to go away to the seaside during the coming warm weather, as her father had proposed they should do, thinking she would like a change after these first quiet six months.

'Let us stay at home now, papa,' she said, 'and go away to the sea in September. You see, it is so long since I was at home on these nice long evenings, with the holidays always being in August, papa, that it seems quite delicious to sit out here in the park till bedtime, mooning away under the trees or teasing you, papa. So you will let us stay, won't you? you won't mind, papa?'

'Mind, my darling! *I* would rather be always at home; but I thought you would like a change. Next year, Gerty, I want to take you to London, you know. This year it is getting rather late, and we both seem so lazy; besides, there is plenty of time—you are only eighteen, Gerty;' and her father looked at her with a wistful fondness, trying perhaps to drive away the thought of how soon she might be stolen from him when once her bright sweet face looked out into the great world. 'I have never been since the year before you were born, Gerty, when your mother and I went up together for two months. But you must go in due time, for it won't do to make my little girl into an old hermit like her father, though as yet she seems to care for nothing better.'

'Nothing better! I should think not, papa!' and Gerty threw her arms round his neck as the tears came to her eyes, 'I didn't come home to go to London—I came home to be with you, papa;' and she shook her finger playfully at him as she sank back again on her grassy seat and began to trill out a merry song, while her father's eyes rested on her with a yearning love, though an unconscious sigh, unheard by Gerty, escaped him as he gazed at her.

And so it had been settled, as they thought; when, not two days later, their plans were entirely and most unexpectedly changed. A letter came for Mr. Mannering from a cousin of his wife's, a Lady Hunter, of whom he had seen but little lately, but who had been very fond of Mrs. Mannering, and who had once or twice visited at the Grange during her lifetime. Lady Hunter was a Protestant, and a thorough woman of the world, but very kind-hearted and generous, and a universal favourite. She and her husband, Sir Robert Hunter, owned a splendid house in Park-lane, and went up to London every season without fail; for though they had no daughters or children of their own to introduce into fashionable life, they—at least Lady Hunter—none the less enjoyed partaking of its gaieties and dispensing them to a large and brilliant circle of acquaintance. The object of her letter now to Mr. Mannering was to ask him to allow Gertrude to come to her immediately for the remainder of the season, to make her *début* under her auspices, and get at least 'a glimpse,' as she called it, of the gay world before its gaieties were over for the year.

'I should have asked her before,' she wrote, 'but our plans were so unsettled. Sir Robert was not well, and we thought we could not stay in London, but should have to go abroad again this year at once; however, he has improved so much since we came—indeed, I may say he is quite well—so that we shall stay, as usual, until the beginning of August. So that if Gertrude could come to us in a fortnight from now, she would have a good month to enjoy herself and see life a little. I can hardly expect you will care to stay in town so long, as I know how painful it is for you to come since poor dear Gertrude's death; but you will bring the child of course, and see her safely launched, as we may say. Now I will take no refusal; you must not deny me the pleasure of bringing out poor Gertrude's daughter, as I have none of my own, and I will take as much care of her as you would yourself. Besides, she is eighteen now, and ought to see the world a little; for, as heiress of Whitewell Grange, she holds some position of her own, and it is wrong to keep her still as secluded as if she were in the convent. I shall hardly know her, I daresay, after these four years (for it is just that time since I stayed a night at the Grange, you know), but I shall welcome her most heartily all the same, tell her. This is quite a long letter for me; so if it does not bring Gerty as a reward, you must expect a scolding from

'Your affectionate cousin,   JULIA HUNTER.'

'P.S. How is poor Rupert? I never shall understand what bewitched the boy to choose his present life, though he did look so indignant at me for saying so when he called on me for those few minutes last year on his way through London.'

Mr. Mannering put down the letter for a moment, and

looked across at Gertrude, who met his gaze with a merry smile.

'What a long letter, papa! And how solemn you look over it!'

'Read it, Gerty, and see what grand things are in store for my little country girl.' Then he gave her the letter, watching her face eagerly as she read.

He had already made up his mind that she must accept the invitation; that he must not let her see for a moment that there was a possibility of refusing it, though there was a strange chill in his heart just then at the thought of the change in their happy plan of the long quiet summer in the old home together, at the idea that she was not to be entirely his own any longer, that the world was beginning to claim her sooner than he had looked for. 'She must not see for an instant that it gives me any pain,' he said to himself, with the almost womanly unselfishness of his character, ' or she will not hear of going; and it is only right she should go, and not refuse such an opportunity. She is of the age now to be introduced, and who can tell what may happen to me before next year? And it is only for a month, and she will enjoy it so.'

Another minute, and Gertrude looked up from the letter.

'O papa!' she said, with a mixture of pleasure and dismay which made him smile.

'Well, Gerty, isn't Lady Hunter very kind, and isn't it a grand prospect? I shall not know my little girl when she comes back.'

'But, papa, our plan is all upset: we shall not have the nice long summer together. When you leave me in London, you'll come back to be all alone here again. Am I obliged to go, papa? Couldn't we say that—that it would be better to wait till next year?' she asked, in her tender unwillingness to leave her father, and that half-frightened shrinking which comes on the eve of any great and much-coveted pleasure, which looks less alluring when the reality of it comes very near.

'I don't see how we possibly can refuse, Gerty. You see what Lady Hunter says; and besides, I want my little girl to go and enjoy herself. I shall be disappointed if you don't care to go, Gerty. I shall take you, you know, and stay a few days. And then another good plan has struck me. When I leave you, I will go to the college and pay Rupert my long-promised visit, and make my retreat while I am there. By that time you will have been away three weeks, and I shall only be back in time to welcome you home.'

Gertrude's face brightened, and she came and stood by her father, putting her arm round his neck.

'And we shall go away to the sea together then, shall we not, papa, to be quiet and blow away all the London smoke from me?'

'Of course, Gerty. Why, you'll want the sea-air more than ever after such a round of gaieties; and I shall want to carry you off somewhere where I can have you all to myself after having parted with you for so long. I have got spoiled, you see, during these six months. Our selfish plan of staying at home together all summer was all very well while no one else wanted us, but now it would be downright unkind to refuse Lady Hunter's invitation, for she has evidently set her heart on having you, Gerty. You must remember her quite well; it is only four years since she stayed the night here during your holidays on her way home from London.'

'Yes, papa—a handsome, showy-looking person, isn't she?'

'Handsome certainly, but a very estimable, kind-hearted woman too, as you will find when you know her. She was so fond of your mother, Gerty; and they were as great friends as a good pious Catholic and a worldly though very good-hearted Protestant could be. Your mother used to say that Lady Hunter would make a grand Catholic, Gerty. She is always so much in earnest in whatever she does, that if the energy she devotes now to fashion and amusement were bestowed on religion and her own soul, she would outstrip a great many of us in sanctity. What a grand thing it would be if you were to convert her, Gerty! What a glorious exchange you would be giving her then for her kindness to you! She has simply no religion at all that I ever heard of, except that of kindness and benevolence, poor thing. But of this I am sure—that if ever she did come to think seriously or be convinced of religious need at all, no half-measures would satisfy her; she would turn instinctively to the Catholic faith, which so many of them feel in their hearts to be the *only* one, though they are not generous or in earnest enough to listen to the voice that is calling them to it.' And Mr. Mannering sighed, thinking perhaps of friends of his own, men of intellect and learning, who were thus, with a wilful cowardly blindness, refusing to see the *one* way which the *one* Lord was pointing out to them.

'Poor Lady Hunter!' said Gerty, after a pause. 'It would be a grand thing to be able to convert her—so grand that *I* dare not aspire to the honour. No wonder, papa, she can't understand Rupert, is it?'

'No wonder indeed, Gerty. It must seem like madness for a boy of eighteen, as he was, to give up all — possessions, comforts, home, and a dear little sister's society — to become one of those maligned, dreaded Jesuits. May God help her to understand it all some day, Gerty, so that she may not be among those who at the end of all things will cry out, "We fools esteemed their life madness!"'

If Lady Hunter could have heard the kind of conversation called forth by her letter, so different from what she had pictured of anticipations of the gaieties she was holding out to Gertrude, she would either have laughed good-naturedly, or else have listened in incredulous amazement, understanding not how fitting and natural it was to those two scions of an old Catholic house, whose glory had been so long to suffer persecution for conscience' sake and God's honour—a house which only now was venturing forth shyly to its place in the great world.

They were silent for a minute or two, and then Gertrude said, laughing again:

'I must go and see Father Walmsley this morning, papa, to tell him he is going to be rid of me for a while, so he needn't get ready any more sermons on vanity and worldliness just yet. I shall want them all when I come back; so he had better keep them till then, instead of wasting them on you and the country people, poor things. O papa,' she added suddenly, the soft brown eyes changing all at once to sadness, 'I wish the London visit were over, and we were both safe again here together! I don't know why, but I *do*. Of course I shall enjoy it, and I shall like to see the world; but now the time is coming, I would rather stay at home, papa, with you.'

But her father, hiding his own emotion, drew her to his side, and smilingly began to tell her of the glories of London, of its places of interest and antiquity as well as of amusement and fashion, until she grew merry again, and delighted at the prospect before her.

Gertrude was to go up to London in a fortnight, as Lady Hunter had asked, so that her days began to be very busy now with preparations. Lady Hunter herself sent down two or three dresses as presents, with orders as to how they were to be made. 'And,' she wrote, 'your papa must let me present you with some more on your arrival, when I see what best suits you. It is quite a delight to me to have a young girl to dress and look after. Sir Robert says it is making me a girl again myself, so your papa must not spoil my pleasure by being angry with me for my dubious opinion of country taste and style, dear.'

And when the dresses came home, made as Lady Hunter had directed, Gertrude tried them on for her father with a girlish delight, unconscious of the inward sigh in his heart as he gazed smilingly on her bright fresh loveliness.

'If she looks so beautiful to me, her old father, what will my darling appear to other, younger hearts? Well, God help me to bear it,' he thought, 'if it is His will that I must give her up to a husband. If she only keeps good and innocent, firm and steadfast in her faith, if she does not lose her heart to one whom I could not see her marry! Poor little Gerty, she never thinks of anything like that herself; it is all girlish excitement and amusement she looks forward to, and then to come back to me! But what wonder if I think of it, in my fears for my little sunbeam!' Only to his spiritual adviser and friend, Father Walmsley, were these fears and anxieties confided, and the good priest spoke hopefully and with a cheerful confidence when he had listened to all.

'Trust her to God, Mr. Mannering,' he said; 'He is calling her into the world, and He will take care of her there; perhaps make her even the instrument of good to others. Do not fear that I shall omit to pray for her, poor child; but I have great confidence in Gertrude. She is no weak silly girl, bright and lively as she is; but strong, and brave at heart, with a spirit worthy of her persecuted ancestors, as I feel we shall one day discover, Mr. Mannering.'

And the anxious father came away calm and confident, for the good priest's words seemed to him almost prophetic. The evening before their departure for London arrived—the last evening they would have alone together for several weeks. It was a Sunday, and they walked down together to church for Benediction, sauntering slowly after the heat of the bright summer day.

'What a shame it seems to be going away, doesn't it, papa, just now, when the park is so lovely and everything looks so green and bright!' exclaimed Gertrude. 'How I shall miss Benediction in London, papa, for I shall never get it, shall I, even on Sundays, and perhaps never to Mass in the mornings? Dear me! what a heathen life it will seem! I wrote to Sister Teresa to-day, papa, and told her I would send her a photograph of the dress I am to be presented in, just to shock her, you know, for fun. I'm sure she is praying for me to-day as if I were to be launched into a lions' den to-morrow! You don't know what a horror she has of the world, papa; we girls used often to laugh at the way she used to shudder at the very name of it, and at the earnest way she always said how thankful she was to have escaped from it.'

'Perhaps, Gerty, she knew it too well—better than any of you school-girls yet could do,' replied Mr. Mannering, thinking of the nun's calm sweet face, which perhaps had known many a tear before it had attained to its present happy rest.

Never had the Benediction seemed so sweet and solemn to Gertrude as on this the eve of her going out into the world; never had the moments seemed so precious as when to-night the sacred Host was raised on high, and all heads were bent low to receive Jesus' blessing. Gertrude knelt on still, bowed in adoration and supplication, long after the rest had risen to leave the church. She had been to Communion that morning, and the prayer which had been a custom with her ever since she went to the convent came now from her very heart, the petition to Jesus, whom she had that day received really and sacramentally, that He would stay with her still spiritually, even in the midst of the world 'Let me not grow to love pleasure more than Thee; never let me offend Thee by any mortal sin!' was the girl's simple prayer as she rose at last from her knees and joined her father, who was standing outside in the little grassy churchyard with Father Walmsley.

'Good-bye, my child,' said the latter to her, very kindly, as he shook hands with her. 'Enjoy yourself, and come back not looking too pale and worn out.'

'Good-bye, Father Walmsley,' she answered brightly. 'I'll try and not get too worldly and fashionable, I will really;' and with a merry laugh she turned to her father, and they walked away together.

'Papa, what do you think I dreamt last night?' she said, as they neared home again. 'Rather a strange thing to dream just now, papa. I thought it was the days of persecution again; but somehow it was still you and I who were living here; and we had a priest hidden in the house, a Jesuit, who somehow was a mixture of Rupert and Father Gerard. We were just going to have Mass secretly in the chapel, when the pursuivants came to search the house, and I went down to try and keep them quiet while the priest hid himself.

But they insisted on coming in and seemed to be going straight to the chapel, and I remember thinking that after all the poor priest would be a glorious martyr and that we should have to suffer for harbouring him; but I didn't feel a bit afraid, but glad, somehow. Just as we got near the chapel, I woke, papa; and you can't think what a queer shock it was—almost comical—to remember that, instead of a holy persecuted Catholic of the days of Queen Elizabeth, I was only a very ordinary nineteenth-century one, just on the eve of going to London for the season. I declare I was quite disappointed for the minute, papa, I was really, and felt quite envious of those ancient Miss Mannerings, with the large ruffs and solemn faces, who are hanging up and down the house. How they must despise their degenerate representative, papa!' And Gertrude laughed merrily.

'Not so degenerate either, Gerty, so long as you keep up the martyr's *spirit*, ready to show itself if occasion should offer. And we never can tell how soon we may be called on to suffer, Gerty, if not in a bodily way, in another quite as painful one; for though our country is kinder to us now, though England allows us to flourish again in her midst unmolested, still bigotry is alive, and what is worse, utter irreligion is gaining rapid ground, and we Catholics have a battle to fight yet, if a different one to the old one.'

'Yes indeed, papa, I know; but I don't think I shall ever be called on to do anything much in it; I am not half good enough; I wish I were, if only half as good and holy as Rupert even. I'm not a bit of a heroine, papa; it would be terribly hard to me if I had to die and leave you and the bright world—so hard that I dare not think of it, papa.'

'Who talks of you dying, sunbeam? You're getting melancholy now when the leaving home is coming so near. You will be all right, my darling, when we get to London and you have fallen in love, as every one does, with Lady Hunter.' And they were soon laughing and chatting merrily together in the old Grange drawing-room, prolonging the evening later than usual because it was to be their last quiet one for a whole month or more.

CHAPTER V.

Mr. and Miss Mannering had been in London two days, and already Gertrude felt quite at home with Sir Robert and Lady Hunter—more so than she thought she ever should be with all the novelties that surrounded her, or with the modern, luxurious, fashionably conducted house itself, so different from her own quiet old home, with its antique furniture and the solemn memories of the past clinging to its very walls. She was to be presented by Lady Hunter at the next Drawing-room, which was to be held on the third day after her arrival in London; for, as her ladyship told her laughingly, she might as well get the ordeal over at once, as, until she had done so, she could not be considered to have any proper standing in the fashionable world. It had been arranged on the evening of their arrival that Mr. Mannering was to stay in London until the day after Gertrude's presentation, and to witness her *début* at the ball which Lady Hunter was to give the same evening.

'You must see Gertrude in her court dress, Mr. Mannering; I insist upon it,' her ladyship had said to him the day of their arrival, when he had tried to bargain to escape from London after a stay of only two nights. 'I have set my heart too on you being here for my ball that evening; the child will feel more at home among so many strangers if you are present.' And when Gertrude joined her persuasions to her cousin's, Mr. Mannering laughingly consented to remain a third night, telling Lady Hunter, however, that she would find him but a poor old addition to her ball.

'Now, as a reward, Mr. Mannering,' she had replied, 'I will not ask either of you to go to a single place for these two first days; you shall have them free to go where you like, and to show Gerty all the London sights, and the evenings to rest together; because, after you are gone, I shall want her always with me for sights of a different kind, you know.' Her ladyship had been charmed by Gertrude at once, as she told Mr. Mannering on the very first opportunity, when they chanced to be alone together for a few minutes: 'She is a little treasure, Mr. Mannering. I never saw a sweeter face or such a lovely pair of brown eyes. And I shall really begin to have a better opinion of a convent education, now that I see what unaffected winning manners a girl may learn there. I am only afraid, Mr. Mannering, that when the world sees her, some one will want to steal her from you very soon.' Then seeing the painful look which came over her listener's face, she added kindly: 'Nay, I do not want to frighten you, Mr. Mannering; I did not ask her here with any intention like that, so do not be afraid. I shall take care of her as if she were my own, Mr. Mannering; I should do so for her own sake now that I have seen her again, even if I did not mean to do it for yours and poor Gertrude's.'

And for her part, Gerty had fallen in love, as her father had predicted, with Lady Hunter. The latter was a woman of thirty-eight or forty, but appeared fully five years younger than that age, from her elegant youthful figure and sprightly manners.

'I know I shall love her, papa,' Gertrude had contrived to whisper to her father. 'I knew I should at once, from the very way she kissed me. What a pity such a sweet woman should be so very worldly, papa!'

With Sir Robert too Gertrude soon felt quite at home. He was an elderly man, twenty years older than his wife, a little quiet and reserved at first, but so courteous and really kind that Gertrude was not long in getting over the shyness with which the first sight of his eminently high-bred face and bearing had inspired her. He was very attentive to the young girl, behaving towards her with that kind of old-world gallantry and politeness which is so rarely seen nowadays, and which somehow made Gertrude think of Louis Quatorze and the old *régime*, and of how well Sir Robert would look in a flowing periwig, with a laced coat and high-heeled shoes.

Lady Hunter kept her promise. For the first two days Mr. Mannering and Gertrude had a carriage to take them where they pleased, away from Park-lane and the Park itself with its fashionable throng, out to Westminster, where Gertrude revelled in the glorious old Abbey with mixed feelings of delight and sorrow—sorrow which came naturally to the descendant of an old persecuted house like her own; then on later into the City and to the Tower, where Gertrude felt even more emotion than in the old Abbey at Westminster. She spoke hardly a word as they wandered through the old fortress, in and out its dreary chambers, full of thoughts of poor sainted Henry VI. and the innocent little murdered princes, of hapless Lady Jane Grey, beautiful penitent Anne Boleyn, and a host of others; but perhaps as much or more than all of their own blessed guest of the past, the great confessor, Father Gerard, and his wonderful, almost miraculous, escape from one of these very windows.

Then, both evenings after their long day of sight-seeing, Mr. Mannering and Gertrude stayed quietly indoors to rest, only going out for a short stroll in the Park for a breath of the sweet evening air. Lady Hunter had guessed they would like best to be quiet and alone these two evenings before their temporary separation, and so had given way to their persuasions that she would not consider herself bound to remain at home and give up her own engagements.

'We shall feel you are making strangers of us, if you do that, you know,' Mr. Mannering had said to her.

'Papa,' said Gertrude suddenly, as they sat together in the gathering dusk, 'I can't believe we have only been in London two days. Why, it seems ten, doesn't it, papa?'

'Because we've done so much, eh, Gerty? Our quiet life at home does not fit us for so much sight-seeing, certainly. We seem to have come quite into a new world, don't we?'

'I should think so indeed, papa. But I'm not sure that when the month is over I shall be sorry to leave it all again and go back to the old world. Indeed, I shall be *glad*, I know. I don't mean only to go back to you, because that is of course, but to get back to the country and the quiet. You see I've never lived before in a grand modern house like this, and it doesn't feel homely; I long for the dear old solemn Grange.'

Mr. Mannering laughed kindly.

' Poor little sunbeam! You don't feel nervous about to-morrow, do you, Gerty? You don't intend to stay awake all night practising your curtsy, eh?'

'I don't intend to stay awake at all if I can help it, papa; but of course I feel nervous a bit, you know. Suppose I do anything awkward—O, dear! But Lady Hunter is going to make me practise for a whole hour in the morning, she says, before we begin to dress, so that I may get quite perfect at it. You'll not know me, papa, when I come down to you in my grand dress.'

Gertrude was awake early next morning, being unable to sleep very soundly in her excitement, spite of her protestations to the contrary. It was to be such an eventful day, not merely that of her presentation at court, but also that of her first ball, and such a brilliant ball too as she knew Lady Hunter was about to give.

'If I could only take it all so easily as you do, Lady Hunter,' she said laughingly, as they were engaged on the practising of which she had spoken to her father the night before. 'Were you ever nervous about it, like I am?'

'Like you, my dear? I was about a hundred times worse. I believe I cried over my dressing for my first Drawing-room, and begged to be let off. They said I did; but I was not in a rational state at all that day, and so remember nothing of what happened, except that I got through it somehow and came back alive. But I want you to be more sensible, my love, and to enjoy the sight, if you can.'

'If I can! Indeed I will, if it's only to please you, Lady Hunter. It is so good of you to take all this trouble!'

'Then reward me by not calling me "Lady Hunter" any more, but by my name "Julia," like a dear girl. I'm not so dreadfully old, and I am only your cousin after all; so I mean to claim the privilege of cousinship and to hear you call me "Julia." We shall get on better if we drive away every bit of stiffness, sha'n't we, dear?' she added, with her sweet fascinating smile.

'Thank you, Julia,' Gertrude said, with an eloquent

look of her soft eyes, as they separated to dress for the great event, Gertrude putting herself into the hands of the maid Lady Hunter had assigned to her.

The little country girl hardly knew herself when the operation was over, and she stood up fully arrayed in the elegant tasteful costume chosen for her. With an innocent vanity she took two or three turns up and down before the full-length mirror, trying to appear quite unconcerned and composed before the maid, but her very eyes dancing all the time with excitement.

'Suppose Sister Teresa could see me now,' she thought, 'what a lecture I should get on vanity, to be sure! If she could only see my hair in all these plaits and puffs! And it seems only the other day since I was at school, and she would never let me do my hair in any but the old plain way, because, she said, I was vain enough, without having anything to be vain of either. Dear Sister Teresa! I don't think I *am* quite so plain as she wanted me to think;' and she took another glance at the sweet bewitching face reflected in the glass, then suddenly turned away with a blush on discovering what her thoughts were. 'How silly of me! I really didn't know I was admiring myself like that. How silly of me!' she repeated almost aloud, quite ashamed of her own folly, innocent as it was. 'Perhaps I am beginning to get vain and worldly already, as I soon shall do, with all this dressing and gaiety, and never doing a single good thing all day, except saying my morning and night prayers. O, dear! And still I can't help enjoying it, and liking the dressing and the excitement, because, after all, it is no harm;' and the convent girl made a quiet sign of the Cross on her heart, unseen by the maid, so that she might not be too engrossed by the coming gaieties, but might enjoy them only in moderation. In another minute Lady Hunter came into the room, dressed, and looking, as she always did, graceful and elegant.

'My dear!' she exclaimed at once as she saw Gertrude, 'you're perfection. If it were not for spoiling your dress I should like to give you a good hug. Only look like that to-night, and always, Gerty, and you'll make a sensation; people will all envy me my little country *débutante*.' And placing Gertrude's arm in her own she led her down-stairs, where Sir Robert and Mr. Mannering were waiting to 'see them off,' as her ladyship called it.

'Now, Mr. Mannering, wasn't she worth waiting to see?' And she brought Gertrude forward for him to look at.

The proud father could not hide the almost startled admiration which came to his face as he looked at his daughter.

'Well, she is indeed!' he said smilingly. 'But I hardly know my little country girl,' he added almost ruefully.

'Never mind, papa; I shall not look like this always, you know. I shall be your little country girl again in a month, so don't be afraid.' And she went to his arms and kissed him so heartily, that Lady Hunter was in dismay for fear of the damage to her elaborate costume.

'And don't make rash promises, Gerty,' she laughed, as she led her away, returning herself a minute to whisper to Mr. Mannering, 'Doesn't she look lovely? Wouldn't it have been a shame to have kept her much longer buried away in the country? Mr. Mannering, she is brighter and more beautiful even than her poor mother,' she added in a still lower and more earnest whisper as she left him.

Gertrude never could tell exactly or minutely afterwards how she got through that day's ceremony—her inauguration, as it were, into fashionable life. From the minute she stepped from the carriage with Lady Hunter at the entrance to the Palace, to the time when she found herself seated in it again, it seemed one brilliant maze of gorgeous dresses, young beautiful faces, and elderly bedizened ones. She felt so bewildered with the sight and the genteel crushing, that she was hardly so nervous as she had been in the anticipation. She knew that the Queen seemed to smile very graciously, but looked weary, she thought; and she did not think that she herself was so very awkward over her curtsy; but that was all she seemed to know about it.

'O, I'm so glad it is over!' she exclaimed when they were again seated in the carriage, and she leant back half exhausted among the cushions.

'Of course you are, dear. I don't know who isn't. I really think none exactly enjoy their first attendance at a Drawing-room, unless they are very brave and self-possessed indeed. But you'll remember all about it later, and be able to tell us your first impressions of " life ;" for you are only beginning really to *live* to-day, you know;' and her ladyship laughed kindly. 'It is an importnt day for you to-day, Gerty, the most important yet in your life, though many more important ones are still to come, we hope, dear;' and she patted her young companion's cheek caressingly.

Gertrude smiled, but was silent for a minute. She was thinking of the convent, and of that occasion other than this, which *she* knew to have been what Lady Hunter called to-day's—the most important, the most blessed too yet of her life—the day of her first Communion; and as the thought deepened in her heart, her face grew serious, until the smile faded altogether.

'Why do you look so solemn, Gerty? Don't you agree with me, love?' asked her ladyship.

Then Gertrude smiled again, and hesitated a moment. Could she tell her thoughts, could she explain her inner feelings, to her worldly though kindly companion? For an instant she felt she could not speak freely to one so devoid of religion, to whom the very word was as a sealed book; and then again it seemed like being ashamed of the thought not to own it, and she spoke out of the fulness of her heart.

'I don't know whether you will know what I mean if I tell you, Julia,' she said, using the familiar name timidly as yet; 'but though I know this occasion has been a very important one, it is not *the* most important yet—O, no! And I was thinking of the day that *I* think to have been so, that I *know* was so, that I *must* know, as—as a—Catholic, Julia. You won't think I am making light of to-day, I know, because of course it *is* the most important occasion, in a worldly sense, that I have had yet; but the one I mean was a different one—a religious, spiritual one; and of course, with us, that is above the other—above everything in the world. That is what I was thinking of, Julia.'

'But what was it, the occasion you speak of, Gerty, if you don't mind telling me, dear?' And Lady Hunter listened eagerly for the reply.

'Well, I meant the day of my first Communion, Julia. You know what that is, don't you? You will have heard poor mamma speak of it, have you not?'

'Yes, of course, I must have done, Gerty; and I know it is the same as receiving the Sacrament is to Protestants; but I know little more, for your mamma never liked to speak much of her religion to me, because I was very giddy in those days, and always made great fun of her about it, and never cared to listen to her explanations. I think at last she got to keep it as something quite sacred from me, Gerty. I'm afraid I don't care very much more about it all now, love, though you'll be shocked at me for saying so; but still I could not *laugh* at it now in any one who is earnest about it, like you are, dear.'

'I wish *you* could be in earnest about it too; you would be if you only knew, if you got grace from God!' exclaimed Gertrude impulsively, almost unconsciously, while Lady Hunter looked at her kindly, half in admiration, half in wonderment as to her meaning.

'And our Communion is not like what you think— like the Protestant one,' Gertrude went on quietly, but so earnestly as to be careless of what Lady Hunter might be thinking of her. 'It is so infinitely greater, that —that it cannot be compared to it at all, we cannot speak of them together. If you have ever been to the Sacrament in your life, Lady Hunter, you only thought, didn't you, that you received bread? But we—we Catholics—know that in our Communion it is our Lord Himself—Jesus Christ I mean—who comes to us in the form of bread, becomes our very food, and is one with us for the time. Of course no one can pretend to understand it—it is a mystery; but we believe it just as firmly as if we saw it all plainly with our own eyes, because God Himself instituted it and taught the doctrine to His Church, the Catholic Church—the only true one, *we* know, Julia, though you don't. You're not offended, are you?' she asked affectionately. 'You see you are so kind that I can talk to you quite easily, as if I had known you all my life. And you see now why I think my first Communion day more important than to-day; why I know it to have been the grandest and best altogether that has been in my life, don't you, Julia?'

'Of course, dear, of course; and thanks to you for

telling me all about it. I'm afraid you must think me very irreligious, Gerty, very—what shall I say?—worldly altogether; but you see, I have never been brought up to it at all. I have never thought of such things. I have never read a Catholic book in my life. But I wish well to all religions; I think them all good, and suppose some day I must choose one myself, Gerty.'

'There is but the one, Julia; for don't you see that two opposites cannot be true? O, I wonder how every one does not see it, that there *can* only be *one* Truth, and that God has given it to His Church, the Catholic Church, to teach!' Then, blushing as she became conscious of her own earnestness, she added more calmly, 'I'm afraid you must think me tiresome talking in this way to you, Julia; but you see *I* feel it all so much, it seems so plain to me, as to all Catholics, that—I—can't help wishing it could be the same with you. And you see I have always lived among Catholics; our very home, our dear old Grange, is a relic of the days when our family suffered so much for the faith, that it seems strange at first that it is not the same everywhere —that I must get used to being with Protestants, and mustn't be surprised if they don't care to hear about us. You don't mind me, Julia, do you? you are not offended at me for talking so plainly to you, are you?'

'Offended, Gerty dear! How could I be? I like to hear you speak so earnestly; I envy you, love—I do really. I envy you your faith, though I cannot understand it, or hope that I could ever partake of it; I never could, Gerty. But some day you must let me come and stay with you at the Grange, and you shall show me all the old nooks and corners you are so fond and proud of. I shall be able to appreciate them better now than when I stayed there with your poor mother; though I prefer to *live* in a more modern world, for it is a very pleasant world too, Gerty, and I should not like to leave it.' And its brilliant though kind-hearted votary sighed rather sadly.

'Nor I either, Julia, I'm afraid, though I *am* a Catholic. I'm always afraid of getting too fond of the world, because I *know* it is pleasant. I have to pray against that more than anything. A worldly Catholic is so much worse than a worldly Protestant—I mean, will have so very, very much more to answer for, because *we* know so much better, O, so much more than you can!'

'What a strange girl you are, Gerty!' and Lady Hunter looked curiously, but very kindly, at Gertrude, who noticed that she became silent and abstracted until they reached home again.

'How very solemn we have both got, Gerty!' she said as they entered the house. 'No one would think we had been to a Drawing-room, would they? Now you must have a good rest when you have got rid of your finery, so as to be ready for to-night, you know; and I can promise you, dear, rather more enjoyment than you have had this afternoon.'

And so the great event was over, and the simple convent girl was fairly launched now into the great world.

CHAPTER VI.

LADY HUNTER'S ball that night was a brilliant scene, and Gertrude, who had quite recovered from her fatigue, felt almost in fairy-land in the splendid room with its almost dazzling maze of wax-lights, watching the elegant dresses as they swept in, one seeming more gorgeous than another, until Gertrude gave up in despair trying to decide which she admired the most. Lady Hunter, graceful as ever, and dressed, as she always was, to perfection, was seen to special advantage in the part of hostess, so well suited to her sweet fascinating manners; and so Gertrude thought as she watched her receive her guests. Whatever of serious impression or reflection had occasioned her temporary abstraction that afternoon in the carriage after her conversation with Gertrude, it had completely passed away now, and she was again the brilliant woman of the world, whose highest and most important business just now was to secure the entertainment and enjoyment of her fashionable guests. Gertrude, herself attired in a beautiful but simple dress of white and cerise, which latter suited well with her dark hair and complexion, sat as yet by the side of her father, amusing him with her delight at the novel scene, and her remarks on the company.

'After all, papa, Lady Hunter herself looks as well as any one, doesn't she? and no one would think her to be more than thirty, I'm sure. I always feel as if she were quite a young person, when I am talking to her. What a dear she is, isn't she, papa? And Sir Robert is so noble-looking too; he always reminds me of an old picture, somehow; and none of these young men seem to come up to him, *I* think, papa, or to you either,' she added, stealing her hand into his caressingly, and looking up into his face with fond admiration.

'I'm afraid we are behaving in a very unfashionable manner, Gerty,' laughed her father, very fondly returning her gaze. 'Some of these people would be quite horrified at us.'

'What would it matter, papa? Besides, they are not minding us. What dandies some of the young men are! I suppose I shall be dancing with some of them later on. What ever shall we talk about, I wonder? Ah, to be sure, the Drawing-room to-day will do, won't it, papa—it will be fashionable conversation enough, won't it? But I was in such a stupid state all the time, I'm afraid I can't tell very much about it. O, dear! I wish the dancing would begin, though I rather dread just the first getting up, too. Fancy, papa, when you are at the college, making your retreat, I shall be here still, among all this gaiety, with never time to say an extra prayer, perhaps!'

'Well, never mind, Gerty; it is your holiday, you know, and it is but for a month. Only bring your *heart* safe back with you, instead of leaving it with all this gaiety and fashion, and you will be all the better for having enjoyed them for the time.'

Their chat was soon interrupted now by the partners for the dance, whom Sir Robert and Lady Hunter began to introduce to Gertrude, who was soon borne away from her father's side, and in another minute was treading the mazes of a quadrille, her very heart seeming to dance too to the fascinating music.

'Who was your partner, Gerty? I did not quite catch the name,' asked her father when that first dance was over, and he could get near her once more.

'That was Lord William Southgate, papa, son to the Marquis of—I forget where, though Lady Hunter told me. He was really very pleasant indeed, papa, though he has such a ferocious moustache, and I got on all right. He seemed so much amused to hear how nervous I was about the Drawing-room to-day (for of course we talked about that, you know), and he did so envy me being at my first ball, he said. It must all seem so fresh and enjoyable to me, he said, and he gave such a sentimental kind of sigh that I really couldn't help laughing; and then he began to be cheerful and pleasant again, though I was afraid at first I had offended him, papa.' And Gertrude was still laughing at the recollection, when she was again claimed for the dance.

Her father saw very little of her for the rest of the evening, for she was constantly engaged, enjoying the dancing and the novelty around her, as she did everything, with her whole heart; enjoying it too genuinely to be conscious of the admiration she was attracting on all sides. Most of Lady Hunter's guests were perfectly charmed with her 'pretty little cousin from the country,' whose sweet face and engaging manners quite fascinated the gentlemen who danced with her, when once her first shyness wore off. Lady Hunter was delighted at the favourable impression created by her *protégée* among her brilliant and fashionable company, and kept finding out Mr. Mannering, who perhaps hardly appreciated the fact as such an important one as she did, to tell him her satisfaction.

'Mr. Mannering, Gerty is quite making a sensation in her own way,' she whispered to him in the course of the evening. 'Fancy that for your little convent girl!

I was half afraid she would be too shy at first, especially as there are two or three noted belles here to-night; but Gerty is too genuine and artless to be *awkwardly* shy, and holds her own against them all. Are you not proud of her now, Mr. Mannering?'

Mr. Mannering smiled at her eagerness.

'Proud of her? Too much so, I am afraid, Lady Hunter. But perhaps not so much in the sense you mean—perhaps not enough so for you; for I was just as proud of my little girl on the day I brought her from the convent as I am when I see her looking so lovely and attracting admiration as she does to-night. Not that I do not appreciate your great kindness, Lady Hunter, and know how much she owes you; do not for a moment think I do not.' And he looked at her anxiously, and was soon reassured by her bright smile.

'Do you think I know you so little as that, Mr. Mannering?' she said. 'Don't I know how little you always cared for gaiety, even in poor Gertrude's lifetime? I know you only cared to come to London even then more on account of the intellectual part of the society you could meet there, than for the gay and pleasant one. But you really ought to move on a little more with the times, Mr. Mannering,' she added, laughing. 'You are like one of the stones of your old Grange, I declare. I believe you would like to have lived three hundred years ago—in those days you are so proud of, you Catholics, though I really am too earthly to understand why, I'm afraid. Even little Gerty gets quite eloquent on the subject, Mr. Mannering.'

'May she always keep so, Lady Hunter! I'm afraid I am prouder of her for that than for being so much admired to-night,' he said with a smile.

'O you incorrigible Papist! It is quite waste of time trying to convert such an old antiquarian to my worldly views, I see;' and laughingly shaking her fan at him, she left him, and was soon mingling again in the brilliant crowd.

The ball came to an end, as all things must, pleasant or otherwise,—much too soon, it seemed, for Gertrude, as she told her father as they sat chatting with Sir Robert and Lady Hunter before going to bed.

'O, I *have* enjoyed it so, papa! I'm not a bit tired, and shall be quite ready to go out again to-night.'

'Well said, Gerty!' exclaimed Lady Hunter; 'she is a more hopeful pupil than you, you see, Mr. Mannering.'

Mr. Mannering was to leave very early, before Gertrude would be up, after the night's fatigue; so they said 'Good-bye' before they separated.

'I wish you would let me get up to see you before you go, papa. I could, I know.'

'No, no, my darling; I would rather you did not—I would rather you rested.'

'Very well, then; good-bye, you dear, dear old papa, and be *sure* to be looking quite well when I come home. O, I don't like you leaving me, somehow! But you will pray for me when you are in retreat, won't you, papa? because the world *is* so pleasant, *so* fascinating, and I might get too fond of it, after all, mightn't I? And you must give my very best love to Rupert—I do envy you going to see him—and you can tell him to pray for his worldly sister. Perhaps he'll be really alarmed if you tell him that, dear old saint as he is!' Then with another close embrace and another lingering kiss, Gertrude tore herself away and went up-stairs with her maid, to undress and go to bed by daylight, for the first time in her life.

Gertrude hardly kept count of the days now for the next week, so rapidly they flew on in one round of pleasure and brilliant scenes of gaiety. A dinner-party or the theatre every evening, and then some ball or reception afterwards, was always the end of a day spent in making or receiving calls with Lady Hunter, or driving out with her on some errand of fashion or pleasure. Then on two or three days Sir Robert took her to ride with him in Rotten Row; and though at first she felt somewhat nervous at appearing among the fashionable crowd of equestrians, she soon grew excited with the spectacle, and felt quite at home on the beautiful specially-chosen horse which had been lent her for the occasion.

'You *must* ride in the Row, you know, Gerty,' Lady Hunter said to her; 'or else you won't have done your duty properly in London.'

And so Gerty went, and was quite proud of her elderly escort, Sir Robert, who looked so noble on horseback, and who took as much care of her and was as attentive to her as if she were a princess, with that old-fashioned courtesy which Gertrude admired in him so much. He was never tired of answering her eager questions, or of telling her the names of the riders, until she came to know them as well almost as he did; and he was always so proud to introduce his pretty little companion to the numerous acquaintances he met in the ride.

'I hope you don't object to your elderly beau, Gerty dear,' Lady Hunter said to her one day on their return. 'I must find you a younger one, I think, in a day or two.'

'Indeed you need not, Julia,' laughed Gerty. 'I would rather have Sir Robert than twenty of the young men we speak to in the Row. I am quite proud to be with him, I assure you, Julia; and he is so very kind that my awe of him has quite gone. You see I've always been used to being so much with papa, that I think I feel most at home with elderly gentlemen.'

'If we only had Rupert here too, Gerty! Poor boy! I *can't* understand it at all, his going off to be a priest—and a Jesuit too; giving up his rights to the Grange and all hope of perpetuating your name; going off to bury himself in a college for ever so many years, and then to come out only to work wherever he may be sent! What ever bewitched him, Gerty? And such a dear boy as he is, so graceful-looking and so clever! They have plenty without wanting him—an only son too!'

Gertrude smiled brightly.

'And do you think only stupid ugly boys ought to be priests, Julia? Do you think that the Jesuits should have refused to take Rupert because he is clever and handsome, and because we idolise him, papa and I? I really think you do, Julia. And I daresay it does seem hard for you to understand why he should give up his heirship and everything, to live a life like that; I daresay it quite annoys you, Julia; but, you see, *we* know that when God sends any one what we call a vocation (that means a call to serve Him in a special way), it is so great a favour, such a great grace, that it is not only quite worth while throwing away everything else for it, but we are *obliged* to do so; we have no choice in the matter, and could only be really happy in following God's will in the way He chooses. So don't you see, Julia, Rupert had that kind of call, and has only followed his vocation: he would not have been happy or useful in any other life. And if you knew what a grand order the Jesuits' order is, you would not wonder at us for being so proud that he has joined it, though of course, it was hard at first to part with him. You cannot see that it is a higher life than to be married and succeeding to the property would be; but it is very easy to see, after all, to any one who is even a Christian, don't you think so? because a priest's or a religious' life is what God's was when He was on earth, you know; and He said that whoever loved father or mother more than Him was not worthy of Him; and that if we wished to follow Him, we must take up our cross, like He did. Of course only a few are called to follow Him so closely as to become priests and nuns; but those who feel they *are* called would be defying God if they stayed in the world after that. I wish I could tell you better, Julia. I wish you had some one who could explain it all to you more clearly than I can, for I'm afraid I only tire you, Julia.'

'Indeed you don't, dear. I would rather hear it from you than ever such a learned priest, Gerty. I'm afraid I should not listen half so well to a bishop as to you, love. But what a tremendous business it must be to any one who becomes a Catholic to have to learn all that—and much more, I suppose! Every time you talk to me like this, dear, I always feel what a grand religion it is, indeed the *only* one, as you say, if only I could believe or care for any; but somehow I can't—it frightens me. The doctrine of hell, for instance, I *couldn't* believe it, dear; it is too horrible. You think you believe it, Gerty, of course; but you don't really—you could not, if you come to think of it.'

But Gertrude laughed outright now.

'O Julia! not believe it! How could I be a Catholic at all if I did not? It is not for us to choose what to believe, but to take all that God teaches by His Church, don't you see; and the Church most certainly bids us believe in hell; so, horrible or not, we know it is true. Why, Julia, if it came to the point, I should have to *die* rather than deny it for a minute. Suppose it were made against the law to-day to believe in hell, and some one came now to shoot me straight away if I would persist in professing it, well—of course I shouldn't like to be shot, Julia, I would rather live a little longer; but I should pray for courage, and let them shoot me at once, and then I should be a martyr, you know. I declare, if you won't believe me, I shall almost wish it would happen so, just to show you that I am really in earnest; for you don't know a bit what real faith is, Julia; how can you know as yet, when you have never been taught?'

'And I'm afraid I never shall be, Gerty. It is very grand, very wonderful, is your faith, and I do admire it, dear; but it demands too much. I never could embrace a doctrine like that, and so I never could have real faith, I suppose. To believe in an eternal hell, or a hell at all, would destroy all my ideas of God's goodness and beneficence, and is like ascribing to Him the human attributes of anger and revenge. Now I believe God to be all good, incapable of taking such an awful revenge on poor human creatures who offend Him in their weakness. Why, Gerty, no *man*, however bad and cruel, could take an *eternal* revenge on an enemy, and of such a kind too; and can you believe that God is less merciful than the worst of His creatures? No, no, dear; or else the God you worship is inferior to *my* idea of Him.'

Gertrude paused a moment, and then fixing her eyes very earnestly on her cousin's face, she answered:

'Julia, if God were like what you think, He would not be just; and He *is* both just and merciful. There would be no difference between good and bad, if He took no notice, but treated both the same. Why did He come on earth to redeem us, if there was no hell to be redeemed from? why did He preach and teach so much, if it was to make so little matter in the end how we lived—if the good were not to be rewarded and the wicked punished? We must believe that He hates sin,

E

that it cannot come near Him; and how could He have sinners for ever in heaven with Him—persons who have despised and disobeyed Him on earth all their lives? And don't you see that our idea of God is higher than yours, because we believe that whatever He teaches and ordains *must* be good and for the best, however little we can understand it, or however little we may like the idea of it? We do not judge God by our human rules, but believe that whatever He wills is the wisest and best thing that can be, *because* He has willed it, and He is all good and just. Hell even, terrible as it seems, is no harder to believe in than heaven, when once you are convinced that God created both, and that it is presumption to judge or find fault with His actions, as if *we* could know what was best—*we* whom He created and who are less than worms compared to Him!' And the colour mounted to Gerty's face in her earnestness.

Lady Hunter looked at her in admiration for a minute.

'What a good little preacher you'd make, Gerty! And you *do* really believe it all, I think too, or you could not tell it so well and earnestly.'

Gertrude blushed deeper still.

'I wish I could tell you better, Julia. Any Catholic could tell you as much as I have done. We grow up with the knowledge, you see; and we feel, or we should do, more strongly on the subject than on any other; and it would be strange if we did not speak about it too a little warmly, wouldn't it, Julia?'

'But, Gerty, you must be dreadfully shocked at me, and Sir Robert too, and every one you meet here, for that matter, dear. You see, I've always been so content with my own wide views on these subjects. It never struck me before to think of God in that way, or to feel that there was any presumption in my idea of

Him. But your view is a very beautiful one, very sublime; there must be such a feeling of rest and certainty in it, as well as in your religion altogether. I could almost wish I had been *born* a Catholic, Gerty;' and Lady Hunter sighed, while a troubled puzzled look came over her face.

Gertrude said no more, but took her cousin's hand, and smiled as she caressed it, breathing a silent inward prayer that if her poor words should be the means of bringing any whisper of grace to Lady Hunter's heart she might not be prevented from listening to it by any worldliness or self-deception. But she did not weary her now by speaking any more on the subject, as she saw that Lady Hunter seemed to wish to change the conversation; for she soon banished the anxious look from her face, and began smilingly to talk on some less serious and, alas, to her, more congenial topic.

And when the Sunday had come round—Gertrude's first Sunday away from all her old accustomed Catholic surroundings—Lady Hunter was quite surprised to hear that she could not miss going to Mass because she had been up very late the night before and was very tired after rather an exciting day. Gertrude wanted to go to Mass at the Jesuits' church in Farm-street, because she had heard Rupert speak so often of it; and as she was ready long before the time, though the carriage was ordered to take her, she stood talking a few minutes with her cousin and Sir Robert as she waited for it. They were only commencing breakfast, Gertrude having had hers early by herself.

'You are sure, dear, you do not mind going alone?' Lady Hunter asked.

Gertrude laughed merrily at the idea.

'I shall be quite at home when I get into the church, you know, Julia.'

'Yes, I know Catholics always seem to feel that. I remember your poor mamma once saying so to me, but I had forgotten that you never could miss going on any account on Sundays. I had a vague idea that the Mass on Sundays was a kind of obligation; but it never came home to me before, because on the two Sundays I stayed at the Grange, in your mamma's lifetime, the going to church only seemed part and parcel of their religious way of going on altogether, and I did not trouble to think or ask anything about it; besides, as I told you, Gerty, I always laughed so in those days at anything of the kind, that my poor cousin gave up speaking at all on the subject.'

'I am afraid my wife shocks you very much, Gertrude,' said Sir Robert, with his courteous smile; 'but she is not so irreligious as she appears, I assure you.'

'*You* think me an angel, dear, of course; and I am afraid I return the compliment, for you are certainly the chief article in my religion;' and her ladyship smiled fondly at her husband. 'But here is the carriage, love,' she added to Gertrude, 'and I don't want to make you late with listening to my heresy, you know;' and she rose for a minute to kiss Gerty as she left the room.

That afternoon Gerty found at last a spare hour or two, and devoted them to writing to her father and to her dear Sister Teresa at the convent.

'You cannot think,' she wrote to the latter, 'how glad I was to be at Mass again after these few days in London, which have seemed more like a month; I have seen so much, and am getting quite used to all this dressing and visiting and gaiety. I should feel dreadfully strange alone here without papa, if I had any time to think of it, but I have not; and Lady Hunter is so kind, quite a "duck," as we used to say at school. I did so pray for her this morning at Mass, because I think she sometimes puts away the thought of religion out of her head just because it frightens her; and she *would* be a grand Catholic, if such a thing could happen as her conversion. You will pray for her, I know, if only for my sake, won't you? And don't forget me either, your poor giddy child, for I really do like the world, I am afraid, after all. If you saw how I dance and how I enjoy it, and how I delight in looking nice to go out, how I catch myself gazing in the glass so often at my finery, O sister, you would scold your silly Gerty! But still I shall not be a bit sorry to leave it all to go back to papa and the dear old Grange; I shall even be good enough to be quite anxious by then to get to Mass every day again, and see all my poor people again; for, after all, it is a queer sort of life this for a Catholic, to have time for nothing but pleasure, isn't it? I shall not get to Benediction to-night, of course, though it is Sunday; for two or three gentlemen are coming to dinner, and I shall have to stay and eat my dinner and flirt (don't be horrified, sister dear!) with the gentlemen. I will promise not to do much at the last accomplishment; indeed, I would rather flirt with dear old Sir Robert himself than any gentleman I have seen yet; so, you see, you need not be afraid. By the bye, I met Agnes White at church this morning, and have promised to call on her. We hardly knew each other at first. She has grown taller and is very elegant-looking now, and she said she would never have known that the fashionable young lady who tapped her on the shoulder was her old friend Gerty Mannering. I am going to write to papa now such a long letter. You know he is with Rupert at the college, and is going into retreat on Wednesday, the very evening that I am going to a terribly grand ball at the Duchess of N——'s, the grandest, most likely, that I shall go to during my stay in London.

'Give my love to Rev. Mother and every one—the girls too, though I have not time to name them specially. Tell them all how I am enjoying my visit, and how worldly I am getting; and *don't* forget, sister dear, to pray for

'Your ever-loving child,
'GERTY MARY MANNERING,
'*Enfant de Marie.*'

CHAPTER VII.

THE ball at the Duchess of N——'s, of which Gerty wrote in her letter to the convent, was to be one of the largest and most magnificent affairs of the season, and was to be her grace's farewell entertainment, as she was leaving London a few days later. Lady Hunter told Gerty she must consider herself specially fortunate to be in town for it.

'And,' she added, 'Sir Robert and I shall enjoy it twice as much as we should have done without you, you know, love, in watching you enjoy it. Poor Sir Robert! I know he only goes out half the times to please me; but it really makes him feel young again to have a girl like you under his protection, especially such a famous little dancer as you are, Gerty.'

And Gerty herself looked forward with great pleasure and excitement to the evening, though she was getting used, as she had told Sister Teresa, to gaiety and visiting. She was quite unconscious of the interest and admiration she herself excited, being so delighted and amused with the novelty of her new existence that, save for a little girlish passing vanity, it seldom occurred to her to think of herself or the impression she was likely to make on society. Perhaps, in her sweet genuine unconsciousness, she would have laughed if she had been told that she had made any impression at all in her cousin's fashionable circle; but it was so. Already she was spoken of everywhere as 'that sweet little Miss

Mannering;' and her artless engaging manners and beautiful brown eyes had gained her no small number of admirers, of whom, however, she thought very little beyond eht passing moment.

Unconscious and heart-free, she set out with her cousin and Sir Robert to the Duchess of N——'s on the appointed evening, laughing merrily in girlish glee at the anticipation of the grandest entertainment she had yet been present at, and at Lady Hunter's enthusiastic admiration of her appearance.

'Don't make me vain, Julia, please,' she laughed. 'It really is this lovely dress that does it all, don't you see?' and she talked on gaily as the carriage drove on, bearing her to her fate, dreaming not that the knell was sounding of her careless girlish happiness, of her simple desires and freedom of heart; little dreaming that, after to-night, all these would be hers as they had been, never—never more!

Two or three dances were over, and Gerty was sitting down during an interval next to a lady friend of her cousin's, talking to her now and then, but more occupied in admiring the brilliant room afresh, now that she had time to take breath and notice more particularly its splendid decorations and appointments. Her eyes wandered over the dazzling scene for some minutes, until they were arrested suddenly and lingered almost unconsciously, fascinated by a face which attracted them. It was that of a gentleman who was leaning against one of the pillars of the room, a complete stranger to Gerty, for she knew at once that she had never seen that pale proud face anywhere before, and she gazed at it as she might have done at a beautiful picture or statue.

'What a splendid face!' she thought; 'I never saw one like it before! It would do for the picture of a Crusader, or some chivalrous knight in armour; a shade too calm and scornful, perhaps, hardly fiery enough; but—I don't know, it looks as if it *could* look fiery too, sometimes;' and Gerty went on dreaming away quite a string of romantic fancies about the face of the hero on whom she had suddenly lighted, forgetting herself entirely in her innocent poetical admiration. She was recalled to consciousness by her companion, who turned to her with some question about the music, which was just commencing again for the next dance. Gerty started, blushing violently, and replied to the question as well as she could, her companion wondering for a minute what ailed her.

'O, what ever have I been doing?' she asked herself, quite in an agony of confusion. 'Surely he cannot have noticed me looking at him so long! O, no, he never looked this way at all; what a blessing! If I could only get out of my habit of dreaming and romancing so! It didn't matter much to be so often in scrapes for it at school, but here in the world, what would people think of me!' And poor Gerty resolutely kept her eyes away from the part of the room where they had been led into the offence for which she was blushing still.

She had danced again, and was again sitting down, talking to her recent partner and trying to forget the impression which had been made upon her and its consequent annoyance, when, looking up, she saw Lady Hunter advancing towards her, and with her the very gentleman whose face had so attracted Gerty—her 'Crusader,' her 'knight in armour,' as her romantic fancy had suggested.

Almost before she was aware of it, Lady Hunter came close up to her, and was introducing the gentleman to her, Gerty blushing again the while, partly with the natural schoolgirl shyness and modesty which clung to her still, and partly with the recollection of her own 'foolishness,' as she called it. She would have been still more confused could she have known that the gentleman had, unseen, been watching *her* intently all through the last dance and for the last five minutes, and that on discovering she was a *protégée* of Lady Hunter's, he had sought out her ladyship and specially requested an introduction to her cousin.

'Gerty,' began her ladyship with a bright smile, 'I want to introduce you to a particular friend of ours, Mr. Graham. My cousin, Miss Mannering,' she added to the gentleman. 'There now, Stanley, you are acquainted. It is quite a treat to get you back again, you truant. I thought you had sworn love to Italy for the next three months at least, and here we meet you, like a ghost, in London. You had not the heart, Stanley, I see, to let a whole season pass quite without your presence;' and she tapped his arm playfully with her fan.

'I must plead guilty to the weakness, if it is one, Lady Hunter;' and Stanley Graham smiled as he spoke, his smile enhancing the beauty of his countenance, relieving it from the somewhat haughty scornful expression it wore generally in repose. 'It is hardly a week since I discovered that I was tired of Italy, even though I was at the very time enjoying the beauty of Lake Como, and I resolved that before many days were over I should be once more in the great Babylon;' and he smiled again. 'There is no place like home, after all; don't you think so, Miss Mannering?' he added, turning to Gerty.

A vision of her own dear home, the old Grange, deserted just now by the two who loved it so, rose to Gerty's mind as she answered very earnestly, though somewhat shyly:

'Indeed I do,' looking up at the same time with such a world of expression in her soft eyes, that if Stanley Graham had regarded her with interest before, he did so doubly now, and took a seat by her side.

'Well, Stanley,' said Lady Hunter, 'I won't stay now to hear all your news, for you will have to reward us for doing so long without you by giving us a great deal of your society for the next fortnight, remember;' and with her bright sweet smile, she moved slowly away.

Gerty was engaged for the ensuing dance to the young man with whom she had also danced the previous one; but he, having seen the introduction between her and Stanley Graham, and guessing it was a specially requested one, though Gerty did not, hardly liked to claim her just then, but went off to console himself if he could with some other young lady in less requisition. So Gerty was left there with Stanley Graham, a strange new feeling of contentment, which she did not stop to analyse, pervading her heart in spite of the nervousness which she could not wholly drive away as she found herself powerless to escape from such a complete *tête-à-tête* with this stranger, whose grand-seigneur-like air somewhat frightened Gerty, even while it attracted her romantic admiration.

'This is your first visit to London, is it not, Miss Mannering?' he began; and the rich low voice was so very kind and gentle that Gerty's shy alarm vanished entirely, and she looked up again with her own engaging smile into her companion's face.

'O, yes,' she answered: 'I only left school last Christmas; and my own home is in B——shire, quite in the country. I should not have come up to London at all this year, only that Lady Hunter was so very kind and insisted on it.'

Her companion had seen her shyness and girlish alarm of himself, and it pleased him to see how soon he had been able to dispel both, and make her quite at her ease with him.

'But you have been here since the beginning of the season, have you not, Miss Mannering?'

'O, no, not ten days yet. But it seems like ten weeks, because at home I am always so quiet.'

'And in London you are so—what shall I say—*unquiet*, eh, Miss Mannering?' and he laughed, but so very kindly that Gerty laughed too as she continued:

'Well, for *me*, you know, I have been very gay, because at home there are only papa and myself, and it is a very quiet old-fashioned place where we live, where it is quite an event to go out even to a dinner or to a small party.'

'Dear me! How ever do you manage to exist?'

'O, very easily, without any managing at all, Mr. Graham. If you knew how sorry I was to leave it all!'

'How I envy you, Miss Mannering!' and Stanley Graham looked serious again now as he tossed back the dark, somewhat long hair from his forehead. '*I* have been trying for the last ten years to find contentment like yours, and have been half over the world in search of it, and have never found it yet.'

Something in his manner made Gerty serious too, and she said rather timidly once more, but with a gentle sympathy in her tone,

'Perhaps you go too far; perhaps, if you stayed at home, it would be easier for you to be contented when once you got accustomed to it. I—am sorry for you, Mr. Graham; it must be—dreadful for any one to feel like that.'

He looked at her so quickly and suddenly that

Gerty was afraid she had annoyed him by seeming to lecture him; but he only said very earnestly,

'Thank you, Miss Mannering. You are right, I know; but unfortunately one does not always do what is right at once, until one has tried the wrong. I have only come back to England now from a kind of home-sickness, I believe; and because, after all, though I *think* I am weary of it, London in the season has a charm I cannot always find elsewhere, a charm of its own for me.'

'Yes, indeed, I am sure it must be like that for any one who knows it so well and has so many friends here as I suppose you have, Mr. Graham,' Gerty replied gently. 'Even *I* see how fascinating it is. I'm getting quite used to it now, and quite fond of it, really.'

'Quite hardened in the ways of the world, are you not?' and Stanley Graham smiled once more as he spoke with that gentle persuasive voice which stole its way so surely to the girlish heart of his companion. 'You have been to the opera, Miss Mannering, of course?' he added.

'No, not yet. I have been twice to the theatre; but we have always had some other engagement for the first part of the evening ever since I came, and this is only my sixth evening out, you know; because for the first two days in London I did nothing but go about sight-seeing with papa, and in the evenings we stayed in to rest. But we are going to the opera to-morrow night, I know, to see *La Sonnambula.*'

'With Patti as *prima donna.* How you will enjoy it!' and the speaker's eyes were bent upon her again with that look of interest which lent such a softening expression to his somewhat stern intellectual type of beauty.

'O, I hope so!' she replied enthusiastically. 'I have always longed to go to the opera more than anywhere else. Even at school I used to do, because there were one or two of the older girls who had been, and they used to give such glowing descriptions that I used to be perfectly wild to go sometimes. We always considered those girls who had been, quite heroines, you know, Mr. Graham;' and Gerty laughed so artlessly and genuinely at the recollection, that proud scornful Stanley Graham was unable to resist joining in her mirth, and being quite interested in the schoolgirl episode. Gerty was perfectly at home with him now, and he drew her on to talk to him of her short experience of London life, and give him her opinions on everything which she had seen, which she did in her own winning way, knowing not that her fresh girlish enthusiasm was as a breath of pure sweet country air coming into this brilliant London ballroom to the weary restless heart of her listener.

They were still talking when the music stopped and the dance came to an end, and a minute later their hostess, the duchess herself, came up to speak to Stanley Graham.

'I shall have to scold you, Mr. Graham, if you persist in your resolution of being a wall-flower all the evening, really.'

'Won't you have pity on me as a weary traveller, scarcely two days returned to England?' replied Stanley, rising with a smile. 'I really should not have been out at all to-night, most likely, only that I could not resist the temptation of your grace's card, which I found awaiting me.'

The duchess bowed smilingly.

'Well, then, I must blame Miss Mannering, I suppose, since you will not bear any reproaches. I assure you,

Miss Mannering, you have done what few young ladies are able to accomplish, in keeping Mr. Graham so long at your side in animated conversation.'

The duchess spoke merely in jest, or partly so, certainly never intending any meaning which could make her young guest feel uncomfortable for a moment; but poor Gerty in her innocent inexperience fancied there must be something of real earnest in the polite smiling speech, and she blushed painfully, feeling as though she would have liked the earth to open and swallow her just then. Had she really been guilty of monopolising Mr. Graham? had she kept him there at her side by talking so that he could not escape? Her own conscience acquitted her, for it was Mr. Graham who had sought her, and had drawn her on to talk to him; but still her confusion was hardly the less for the knowledge.

The young man saw her embarrassment, though the duchess did not, and came to the rescue at once, saying with a smile,

'Pardon me, your grace. It is *I* who am to blame entirely, and I must apologise to Miss Mannering for having kept her from the last dance. I am afraid I thought only of my own pleasure, forgetting yours, Miss Mannering.'

'Do not say so, please; indeed I did not mind; I did not care about the dance,' said Gerty, thanking him with an earnest look of her soft eyes, but wishing the while that she knew just the proper thing to say at such times as these—that she had at hand some of those careless complimentary replies which she heard every night given by girls little older than herself.

Poor Gerty! poor little convent flower! Perhaps she would hardly have had such a wish if she could have known that the very embarrassment of which she was ashamed was a fresh charm in the eyes of her companion, who sat down again by her side as the duchess left them.

'Then prove it to me, Miss Mannering; prove your forgiveness by giving me a dance, if you have one to spare. I owe you one, you know, for the one I have robbed you of;' and he tried gently to take her card from her hand.

She prevented him a moment, for she knew he had not intended dancing at all to-night.

'Indeed I did not mind, Mr. Graham, I assure you, and I do not care at all about having missed it.'

'But *I* care, Miss Mannering, and I am particularly fond of my own way;' and he laughed kindly as he succeeded in getting the card, where he wrote his own name in one of the few spare places. Soon again now Gerty was claimed for the next dance, and Stanley Graham left her with a bow.

He came to her promptly when the time arrived, and Gerty's heart beat with that strange new feeling which had been over her for the last hour, making everything seem still brighter and more joyous than before; and still with a kind of restless wonder pervading it all, which clung to her through her dance with Mr. Graham, and which somehow made her rather silent and abstracted during the succeeding ones with her other partners.

She did not see much more of him for the rest of the evening, until the ball was coming to an end and she left with her cousin and Sir Robert. The latter gave her his arm, and Stanley Graham, who came forward quickly, took Lady Hunter, who said to him as they reached the carriage,

'Then I shall expect you to dinner, Stanley, and you must be our escort to the opera.'

'I will try my very best to come, Lady Hunter, you

may be assured; but I will let you know decidedly to-morrow,' Gerty heard him reply as he followed close behind her with Lady Hunter.

'Good-night, or good-morning, rather,' he said, as he held out his hand to Gerty, who placed hers in it for a moment; and the next he was gone, and they were once more driving home. Sir Robert was tired, and dozed back in a corner of the carriage; but Lady Hunter leaned forwards to talk to Gerty.

'Well, you've enjoyed it, love; have you not?'

'Yes, indeed, Julia. It was almost like a dream, all evening;' and she sighed, without knowing why.

'And I was so glad for you to make Stanley Graham's acquaintance, Gerty, especially as you seemed to get on so well together. He asked to be introduced to you, love, do you know—quite an honour from him, I assure you. He is a special friend of ours, and it was quite a treat to meet him to-night, when we thought he was not to return for three months. I have never named him to you, because I thought he was so hope-lessly out of the way that it was no use making you wish to see him—my prime favourite among young men, and Sir Robert's too, Gerty. Indeed, he might be a great favourite with everybody if he would, but he is so very exclusive, and as proud as Lucifer himself; and most people, after running after him for a time, give him up as cold and hopelessly unimpressionable. He is considered a great catch, you know; for besides being so very attractive, he is very wealthy, and owns a large property in W——shire, where his family seat is situated, a beautiful place, though he is very seldom at it. He was an only son, and it was thought he would marry at once when he came of age, eight years ago; but he is quite an impervious old bachelor, and often drives his friends wild by taking himself off to the

Continent right in the middle of the season, and not always coming back to his duty as he has done this time. He is highly intellectual, you see, Gerty, and has never cared for mere pleasure or frivolous amusements; indeed, I think his very pride has always kept him from the vices and follies of most other young men in his position. I hope you liked him, and did not find him formidable at all; for, you see, Gerty, I feel almost a motherly or, rather, elder-sisterly interest in him. I knew his mother when I was a girl, and remember how proud she used to be of her beautiful boy. Poor thing! she only lived until he was eighteen.'

'I did not find him at all formidable, just after the first, Julia; he was very kind and polite,' said Gerty, stooping a moment to hide the blush which her cousin might have seen even by the dim morning light.

'That's right, dear, for we are sure to have a great deal of his company during the rest of our stay in London. I have asked him to dine with us to-morrow, and be our escort to the opera. But here we are, love, at home, and I daresay you are tired and quite ready for sleep, aren't you?'

Gerty smiled in reply, feeling very far from sleepy, or tired either, just then, as was proved when she was quiet and alone in her bedroom.

She had dismissed the maid as soon as she was divested of her dress and outer finery, and now, instead of undressing further and going to bed as she had done on all previous occasions, she threw a soft shawl about her and sat down on the couch, to dream away another hour or two of the new existence which she had unconsciously begun that night. Without any deliberation in the matter she began to think over the last few hours, until she had gone over again every word of her conversation with Stanley Graham, conjuring up his face in her imagination—the pale beardless face with its piercing eyes and haughty features, and the dark hair thrown back from it, showing its perfect classical outline. As she thought of him and the strange new fascination which had come with his presence, it came naturally to Gerty to wonder what religion he professed, if any at all. Instinctively she knew he could not be a Catholic: she felt that, even from her own slight acquaintance with him, apart from anything her cousin had told her of his history.

'I dare say he has no religion at all, like Julia herself,' she sighed. 'I could fancy it is so. I wonder what he would have been like if he had been a Catholic. He might have done like Rupert, and have given up everything for God.'

Then somehow the thought of her brother roused her from her reverie, and she started up, seeing by the timepiece that it was close upon four o'clock.

'It will never do for me to sit up like this every time,' she said to herself as she undressed hurriedly and knelt down to say her prayers, which somehow were said less heartily and earnestly than usual, not with any wilful carelessness, O, no, but with a kind of weariness, which she fought against as she did against the ever-recurring image of Stanley Graham which haunted her thoughts. Even after she fell asleep at last, his pale face and rich low voice mingled with her dreams, not only of that evening's brilliant scene, but of her father and her own quiet home.

CHAPTER VIII.

LADY HUNTER and Gertrude went out driving on the following afternoon, and on their return learnt that Mr. Graham had called during their absence. As Sir Robert had been out too, he had left a note for her ladyship to say that he would come to dinner that evening as requested, and accompany them afterwards to the opera. Gerty tried to look calm and unconcerned as her cousin showed her the note; but could not as easily repress the inward feeling of undefined joy, which was so different from the peaceful happiness which had always been hers before.

She tried hard to think of nothing during her dressing but home and the convent, of Rupert, and of her father in his retreat, praying perhaps for her; but the task was almost a vain one: she could not be peaceful and calm; her heart would beat joyously in the anticipation of what was coming, and she knew it was not *all* the thought of the opera, delightful as the prospect of it was. Then when she was dressed she stood before the mirror for a minute, until she found *why* she was looking at herself so anxiously, *why* the reflection of the sweet bewitching face pleased her to-night more than it had ever done before, when she turned resolutely away with a blush, making the sign of the cross quietly on her heart, the old convent custom in any little trial or danger.

'I must not go back to papa vain and silly like

that,' she sighed; and she took not another look in the
glass, though she lingered still some time longer in the
room, unconsciously dreading the going down-stairs,
though she dare not pause to confess the reason even
to herself.

She went down at last, and found Stanley Graham
in the drawing-room with her cousin and Sir Robert.
He rose and came forward to meet her, with a kindly
inquiry as to whether she was fatigued, as he took her
hand, with that tender yet respectful look which went
so dangerously straight to Gerty's heart.

'You are quite ready to enjoy the opera, I hope,
Miss Mannering?'

'O, yes, indeed!' she replied earnestly, looking up
with a smile as she recovered from her first embarrassment.

'It was really very good of you to come, Stanley,'
Lady Hunter said to him, as they sat down to dinner.
'I am afraid you have put off some other engagement
for us. However, I hope it was not anything very
fascinating.'

'Ah, no, Lady Hunter, don't be at all uneasy on my
account. It was only a promise to Major Leigh to
dine with them at the mess; but I saw him this morning and made it all right. I much prefer renewing my
acquaintance with Mademoiselle Patti as Amina in
your company and Miss Mannering's.'

'Thank you, Stanley; we are highly honoured,'
laughed her ladyship.

Gerty was somewhat quiet during dinner, for though
Mr. Graham was very attentive and constantly addressed her, she did not feel able to talk to him quite
so freely before her cousin and Sir Robert as she had
done during their *tête-à-tête* the previous evening. Sir
Robert was remaining at home that night; and Gerty

was very quiet too in the carriage as they drove to the opera, letting Lady Hunter and Mr. Graham almost entirely monopolise the conversation, though her heart was beating fast in its new vague satisfaction, and with the excitement of being so near to beholding the sight she had longed for so often. When they were fairly in the theatre, in Lady Hunter's box, Gerty's excitement quite overcame her shyness; and as her cousin was engaged in talking with three or four other gentlemen who had made their way to the box, she turned to Stanley Graham, and began to ask him several questions concerning the opera so earnestly, and listening so intently to his answers, that he felt as though he had never known what it was to enjoy a visit to the theatre before.

'You have seen *Sonnambula* before, of course, Mr. Graham, have you not?'

'Many times, Miss Mannering.'

'And you are not tired of it? You could not be, I should think, for the music *is* so lovely; even I know that much about it.'

'Well, no, I am not tired of it exactly; but if I were, I should resolve to try and enjoy it all fresh over again for your sake, because I should not like to be a kill-joy to your pleasure, you know,' he said with a smile.

'You are very kind,' she said, blushing slightly, but with a frank look up into his face; and in another minute the overture began.

Then from the moment of the opening of the opera Gerty had eyes and ears for nothing else, almost forgetting the presence of Stanley Graham, as she leaned forwards, motionless, gazing fixedly at the stage, entranced with the delicious music. Perhaps, unknown to herself, something in her own heart responded sympathetically to the warblings of the love-lorn Amina, making them touch her as they might not have done a few nights before. She spoke very little during the intervals between the acts, feeling too impatient for a continuance of the opera, but sat gazing anxiously before her, unconscious of the almost tender admiration depicted on the pale proud face so near her, as its deep eyes rested ever on her rather than on the stage.

And when it came to the joyous ending, the glorious 'Ah, non giunge!' in which the heroine pours forth her whole soul in such delicious song, Gerty's eyes filled with tears so rapidly that she was obliged to brush them away, and she drew back in her seat, ashamed of having thus betrayed her emotion.

'Why, Gerty,' whispered Lady Hunter, smiling, 'this is a real tribute to Patti's genius!'

'It is very silly, I know, Julia;' and poor Gerty blushed dreadfully. 'I'm afraid I must look very foolish, Mr. Graham,' she added, turning to him; 'but I couldn't help it, really. It was so delicious altogether, the singing and everything; and I have never seen anything of the kind before, you know;' and she tried to laugh away her emotion.

'Don't apologise, please, Miss Mannering;' and Stanley Graham's voice was very, very gentle as he smiled at the upturned tear-stained face. 'If I might come with you to the opera every night, I should learn to enjoy it again, perhaps;' and he sighed almost imperceptibly.

'How I wish *I* could cry at the opera, Stanley!' said Lady Hunter, as they rose to leave the box; Gerty feeling as though just awakened from a delicious dream, and wondering why all these people seemed to take it so coolly—what they came for, if they did not enjoy it as she had done.

'I should not care to come if I could not enjoy it,' she thought. 'But I suppose they are so used to it that many of them come only to meet their friends and show themselves off. But they can do that just as well and better at a ball. And what does Mr. Graham come for, I wonder; for he can have no frivolous reason, I know.'

For how could Gerty guess that Stanley Graham, intellectual and world-weary as he was, had come here tonight for nothing else than the pleasure of seeing *her* enjoy the opera; of revelling, as it were, in her fresh unaffected delight and enthusiasm? How could she know that his proud heart was moved as it had not been for years, when she had turned to him with the tears still glistening in her soft eyes, trying to smile as she apologised for her 'foolishness,' as she called it?

'Stanley, will you give your arm to my cousin?' Lady Hunter said to him, as they joined him on leaving the cloak-room. 'I can take care of myself, you know.'

The young man did as requested; and, taking his arm rather nervously, Gerty let him lead her to the carriage, unconscious of the pure sweet happiness it gave him to have that little hand resting on his arm, that its very touch was to him like a revelation from a better, simpler world than the one he had known so long. And Gerty walked by his side as if in a dream from which she did not care to awake, but which was dispelled in another minute or two as they found their carriage, and Lady Hunter turned to shake hands with Stanley Graham, who had handed Gerty in before her.

'Well, we must say "Good-night," I suppose, Stanley, with many thanks for your escort. I wish you were coming with us to Lady A——'s; we shall only stay an hour or two.'

'I wish so too; but I *must* show myself at Mrs. Banerstock's reception to-night, or I shall give serious offence. I met her this afternoon in the Park, and made a solemn promise not to disappoint her,' he replied, with a smile which was somewhat sarcastic, Gerty thought.

'Ah, one of her literary receptions, isn't it? Well, Gerty, we won't keep him any longer, for he is going into such a terribly intellectual company that we must seem very frivolous indeed by comparison;' and her ladyship laughed a musical little laugh.

'That is a very unkind speech, Lady Hunter;' and as Stanley Graham spoke, taking off his hat with a farewell smile, the carriage began to drive away.

For the next few minutes Gertrude would have given anything to be alone, free even from the kindly affectionate presence of her cousin, so as to be able to collect her thoughts and calm the bewildering feeling—half joy, half pain—with which her brain and heart were throbbing. Ah, it was a beautiful world, she knew now only too surely, all *too* fascinating and alluring perhaps! No wonder she had been warned against it; no wonder she had been taught to pray for strength to resist its charms if ever they should prove perilous, to pray that she might not grow to love it too much.

And she could not pause to think quietly and try to define her feelings, for Lady Hunter began at once to talk as usual of the opera, of the house to which they were going, and of Stanley Graham; and Gerty had to listen and reply, thinking as she did so what a strange whirl was this, the fashionable life of a London season.

'Julia,' she said rather abruptly, after her cousin had finished some remark about Stanley Graham, 'is Mr. Graham a Protestant, or has he any religion at all?'

And though she tried to speak carelessly, Lady Hunter looked at her somewhat with surprise as she asked smilingly:

'Whatever made you think of that, Gerty?'

'Well, I was only wondering, Julia, because I can fancy somehow that he does not think much of anything of the kind;' and Gerty blushed slightly under her cousin's gaze.

'Well, you're right, Gerty; he does not. I am afraid he is worse than myself in that respect; for while I tolerate all religions, he has no patience with any. Indeed, he is known as a professed infidel.'

'O Julia!' escaped from Gerty almost involuntarily.

'Well, perhaps not quite so bad as that, dear; for he does just believe in the existence of God, but no more. I expect he will be rather shocked if he hears *you* are a Roman Catholic, though of course he is so much accustomed to them, having been so much abroad. As to a boy doing as Rupert has done, it would make him bitter and scornful even to hear of it; so you must be prepared with the nice explanation of his conduct which you gave me the other day, love.'

Lady Hunter spoke lightly and smilingly, knowing not the strange feeling of chilly desolation her words had cast over her listener's heart as she sat there so quietly. Gerty said no more, but tried to smile, as she fanned herself quickly in her agitation. That Stanley Graham should be proved to be like that, his splendid intellect employed chiefly, perhaps, in hatred of religion, in scornful contempt of its very name!

She seemed able to think of nothing else all through the next hour or two while they were at Lady A——'s, and yet the knowledge did not drive away the new joy and wonder in her heart, only mixed it with a vague foreboding and sense of pain.

Only when they were at home again and she was alone did she seem able to pause and face the thoughts and feelings in her heart. She could not sleep, so she sat up in bed, with her long hair all about her shoulders, and her face buried in her hands.

'O, what am I doing? What does it all mean?' was her inward cry. 'What is Mr. Graham to me? O, if he would only go away, or if I could never see him any more! He does not think of *me;* it is only because he sees I am shy that he is so kind, and, O, so unlike anyone else I have ever seen! Wouldn't I rather die than he should know that *I* have thought of *him* like this? I thought I never could feel this way towards any one; I thought I was so strong; and now—! Perhaps I felt too secure; perhaps I did not pray enough; but it is not too late. I can forget it; I can ask our Lord to take the feeling out of my heart before it grows too strong. But, O, if only the time were over, and I could be safe back again with papa!'

But even in the thought, the idea that in little more than a fortnight she must leave her present life, with its fascinations, which already had taken such hold of her heart, she shrank with a kind of dismay from the prospect, knowing, alas, too surely, what it was that held her so enchained—that it was the presence of him whom she tried to wish never to see more. Only a few days before, the thought of returning to her quiet home, with its sweet religious atmosphere, to her dear father and his fond idolising embrace, had given her unspeakable delight; and now was it really chilling her heart with its prospect, because that heart, which could never feel or love but strongly and with all its depth, had learned to thrill and palpitate at the sight of the face and the sound of the voice of one who after all was a mere stranger, who had certainly been very kind and attentive, but who would forget her, of course, when he ceased to meet her daily. An infidel too, one who held religion in contempt—most and more than all, the *one true* religion, which holy possession she, descendant of martyrs and glorious confessors, had ever guarded as her most precious treasure!

Gerty turned round at last and threw herself face downwards on the pillow, weeping sadly alone there, in the silence of the night, tears so bitter as she shed then for the first time, which almost seemed in their bitterness to drive away the image of Stanley Graham and make it abhorrent to her.

'O papa, if I were only going back to you to-morrow! If I had only never come here at all, but could wake and find it all a dream, with the crucifix looking down at me in my own little room at home!'

But not so easily was her trial to be ended—not so soon; not until her feet had trod wearily but patiently in the way of the Cross, was the young girlish heart to find peace.

CHAPTER IX.

WHEN Gerty rose next morning, she hardly looked or felt so refreshed as she had always done previously from her peaceful healthy sleep. When she had fallen asleep at last, with the tear-traces still on her cheeks, she had been haunted by uneasy dreams, which changed vaguely and rapidly, until she dreamed that she herself was the heroine of the opera she had that night witnessed. She was Amina walking across the broken bridge, when it gave way entirely, and she fell into the abyss below, calling out wildly to Stanley Graham to help her, for somehow he seemed near at hand among the spectators, and the shock awoke her too rudely to allow of her trying to sleep again.

With the bright summer sun streaming into her room, and the long cheerful day before her, her anguish of the previous night hardly seemed so sharp or so heavy to the still buoyant young heart, but yet her morning prayers were almost one long petition for strength and guidance in the new existence to which she seemed tending, for help in the trials which she felt vaguely, yet certainly, were in store. For the dim foreboding was upon her still, much as she tried to shake off the feeling, striving to tell herself how she longed for the day of her return home, where she would soon forget all her silly fancies, and the fascinations which now seemed at times too strong for her.

Lady Hunter noticed Gerty's weary looks at breakfast.

'But a good canter in the "Row" this morning will set you all right, dear, won't it? We can't expect your country roses to be quite so perpetual in London, after all, can we? But they will soon bloom again in their native air, all the better, perhaps, for a short absence. The only thing is, I hope your papa won't scold me for their loss, love.'

Gertrude tried to laugh gaily.

'I must take a pot of rouge home, Julia, if you're so afraid, shall I?' and the very effort to be gay brought back the colour to her cheeks for the time, and her cousin could not guess at the pain the brave little heart was suffering even while she laughed so merrily.

They went out to ride at the usual hour, about noon, and Gerty tried to talk to Sir Robert with her customary ease and gaiety, the open air and bright sunshine kindly helping her in the effort. They had taken but two or three turns up and down the 'Row,' and were now stopping for a minute to speak to some acquaintances, when Gerty, looking up, saw Stanley Graham ride in on to the ground, accompanied by two other young men. Alas for her resolutions, for the strength she fancied she had gained by the discovery of where her heart and thoughts were tending! At the sight of him that poor little heart beat with a tell-tale joy; and had any close or interested observers been at hand, they must have seen the rosy colour mount quickly to her face as the brown eyes sparkled with the new light that had come so often to them during these last two days.

Mr. Graham rode up at once to where Sir Robert and Gerty were halting, and when he had spoken to them, was seized upon by the friends to whom they were speaking.

'If one *may* venture to scold you, Mr. Graham,' said a young lady amongst them, a handsome fast-looking girl, 'I think you ought to apologise to us all for having made us sigh in vain for you so long;' and she laughed, somewhat boldly, Gerty thought.

Stanley Graham's lips curled slightly, but he replied with perfect politeness :

'When I am so highly honoured as to be sighed for by you, Lady Flora, I shall certainly be willing to apologise most amply.'

Lady Flora shrugged her shoulders and was silenced, while Gerty wondered to herself, 'How should I feel if he ever spoke to *me* like that, with that freezing look and manner!'

'I thought you hated the "Row," Stanley,' said Lady Flora's brother, a dissipated, shallow-pated youth —'thought you had a great contempt for the whole affair, horses and people and everything,' he drawled out, evidently enjoying the idea of being able to attack Stanley on any subject.'

'You are right; I do not particularly care for the "Row," Edmund,' replied Stanley, the haughty lip curling unmistakably now as he spoke the few curt words.

'Perhaps,' said Lady Flora, willing to be revenged on Stanley for his speech to herself, 'Mr. Graham has turned Papist in Italy, and comes here to practise mortification.'

'Don't give me credit for any such self-denying motive, Lady Flora. I certainly did *not* come to practise mortification;' and the tone implied so plainly that the presence of herself and her brother *was* a mortification to him, that even the dull-witted youth understood the hint and hurried away, his sister urging her horse after him, without a bow to Stanley Graham, though she pointedly bestowed one on Gerty and Sir Robert.

At once Stanley went up to Gerty's side, the cold look and manner gone, and the look and voice she knew so well already stirring her heart once more, and dispelling like a mist what remained of the last night's anguish.

'I hope Amina did not keep you awake last night, Miss Mannering; and that you did not get up and walk broken bridges, or do anything of the sort?' and he laughed kindly, as he rode on by Gerty's side, his friends following with Sir Robert.

Gertrude blushed slightly.

'Well, I did dream that I was Amina; but I woke suddenly by the bridge seeming to break; so I don't know how I might have ended but for that.'

How little he knew, as the sweet voice spoke so gaily, and as he met the bright smile raised to his face, —how little he knew of that last night's pain, of its bitter tears and home yearnings; how still less he knew of the 'still small voice' which was whispering to the girlish heart even now, but from which she turned shrinkingly, trying not to hear it in her new absorbing joy! For nearly an hour they rode on together, up and down, Gerty hearing nothing but Stanley Graham's voice, seeing nothing but his face, as she raised hers to meet his gaze, while they talked on as earnestly as was consistent with their horse exercise, Gerty knowing and caring nothing about the remarks which were being passed upon her, and Stanley Graham supremely indifferent to them, if he guessed at their existence.

'Is Stanley Graham bewitched by that little Miss Mannering?' exclaimed one lady to the gentleman with whom she was riding.

'It looks like it,' was the reply; 'for I never saw him do such a thing before as ride for a whole hour in the "Row," much less devoting himself to a young lady all the time.'

'Who *is* that girl who is managing to fascinate Stanley Graham into making a fool of himself?' asked another, who did not know Gerty, a young officer, a friend of Stanley's. 'She is pretty enough for anything, to be sure, and there seems nothing fast about her; but still it is so unlike Stanley.'

'Don't you know who she is?' laughed his brother officer. 'She is a cousin of Lady Hunter's, a little girl from the country; wonderfully pretty and wonderfully natural and unaffected too; quite refreshing, as I discovered the other night at the Duchess of N———'s ball; being a *protégée* of the Hunters may account for some of haughty Stanley's attention to her, but hardly for so much of it as he is bestowing just now.'

All unconscious of the talk she excited, Gerty rode on in her elysium, until Sir Robert again drew close up to her, asking her if she would not like to return home now to luncheon, as they were going to a morning concert immediately afterwards.

'O, yes, certainly, Sir Robert; I am ready any time,' she replied quickly; and they turned their horses' heads homewards, Gerty wondering vaguely how long they had been out, and whether she ought to have proposed of herself to go in sooner.

Stanley Graham bade good-morning to his two friends and rode home with Sir Robert and Gerty, though he could not remain to luncheon, as he had an appointment elsewhere. But he was coming to-night to a literary *soirée* which Lady Hunter always gave towards the close of every season, and the thought made Gerty's heart bound as he bade her a temporary adieu.

'It is only for a few hours—only for a few hours,' it seemed to repeat with an inner joyous song.

'Whatever have you been doing!' exclaimed her ladyship as she came into the hall to meet her husband and Gerty. 'You will have to lunch very quickly, so I hope you are not very hungry, you two dusty tired creatures;' and she made Gerty sit down just as she was, in her habit, as she would have to dress directly for the concert.

'Well, we are rather late, I believe,' said Sir Robert; 'but we all seemed to be enjoying ourselves so much, that we evidently forgot the time—eh, Gerty?' and he spoke so kindly, and so unmistakably without any *arrière pensée*, that Gerty could not feel uncomfortable, though she might have done could she have known that her cousin, seeing deeper and more quickly than Sir Robert, was wondering what had so bewitched Stanley Graham as to make him remain thus long in a place for which he cared but little, and that the wondering led her on to further reflections.

'Surely it cannot be that.—But no, she is too young and girlish; he would never think of her in that way. And if even it were so, there could be no objection to it, rather the contrary, even from a doting father like hers. Except indeed—' and some thought seemed to strike her, from which she turned away as painful or useless, smiling brightly again as she rid herself of it.

As Gerty dressed for the concert, she was hardly thinking of her toilette, but of the last hour or two; of her ride in the 'Row' with Mr. Graham; of their conversation, even of their intervals of silence, which had seemed only another stage of her elysium, with those piercing gray eyes bent upon her so kindly—the eyes which but that morning she had seen *could* look so coldly and scornfully if they chose.

'How strange,' she began to think, 'that we have never yet named religion, hardly anything approaching to it! He did name monasteries and convents, to be sure, in a general way, when he was telling me so much about Italy, but never as if he thought for a minute I could be particularly interested in them or in what he thought of them. Will he be surprised, I wonder, when he finds I am a Catholic? Would he be so very kind if he knew it? Would it make any difference, I wonder? Didn't Julia say that he despised and disliked *all* religion?' Then suddenly a deep blush rose to her face as the delicate conscience suggested the next thought. 'Have I been at all afraid of the subject? have I kept from letting him know my religion as long as possible, not directly perhaps, but indirectly? preferring to talk of other things, because I was so weak, because I was afraid he might not like to hear I was a Catholic, that it might make him not so kind?' For as yet Gerty used no more tender term to describe Stanley Graham's manner to her, even in her own thoughts. 'Ah, I *wish* I knew if I *have* done, if I have been wrong like that! O, what would papa and Father Walmsley say, what would the nuns say, if they thought such a thing of me!' and she longed to be free of the presence of the maid who was dressing her, so that she might kneel down and bury her face in her hands while she asked God's pardon for the cowardice of which she fancied she had been guilty,—she, the daughter of such an old Catholic house, which in its time had suffered so joyfully for the faith, —descendant of glorious confessors who would have shamed to own one who was afraid of a little coldness, a little inward pain, endured for the cause for which they would have freely given their lives!

'And so would I too—so would I too—O, yes!' and

as the 'martyr spirit,' of which her father had spoken on the eve of their separation, rose within her young enthusiastic heart, Gerty resolved that another day should not pass without Stanley Graham hearing from her own lips that she was a Catholic, even if she should have to go out of her way to tell him so.

And the resolution seemed to bring back some of its holy peace and calmness to her heart, tempering the restless joy which had taken possession of it, though a kind of weary chilly desolation tried to enter too now, at the thought of what she might bring upon herself by her avowal, of the changed cold tones of the voice which was becoming like delicious music in her ears, of the haughty though polite contempt which might come over the face whose image had so engraven itself on her heart, though as yet she never dreamed or dared to hope for a return of the feeling which was making her, as it were, into a new creature,—into a woman all at once, with a woman's cares and trials.

Perhaps the maid thought, somehow, that her taste and artistic skill in hairdressing were wasted to-day on her young mistress; for the bright face looked so troubled and perplexed, that it was easy to see that even when the eyes did glance towards the mirror, their owner's thoughts were but little occupied with what they saw there.

And for the first time in Gerty's life she felt glad she could not write to her father again just yet, as he was still in retreat, and would be for the next few days. How could she bear to write unless she could say from her heart that she longed to return home, to be alone with him again, in spite of all her present enjoyment? and how *could* she say it with this new joy, this new yearning, this other self which had arisen for her, driving out her own old free girlish life, and making her live but in another's presence?

'Is this what the world is doing for me?' she sighed to herself, as she sat with her cousin at the concert, listening dreamily to the music, but hardly following it. 'Is it making me forget papa and home and everything I have loved and treasured all my life till now?'

And up from the midst of that brilliant concert-room there rose from one young overburdened heart a prayer for strength to be guided to do right, that she might not lose herself amongst the snares which were surrounding her in this earthly paradise, this new existence which had begun for her.

CHAPTER X.

THE opportunity Gerty wished for came to her more easily than she had hoped, without any seeking on her part, that very evening. Her cousin's drawing-rooms were filled with a select company, comprising many well-known authors and authoresses, poets, and men of letters of various grades and descriptions, together with a number of Lady Hunter's own private friends. It was the first reception of the kind which Gerty had been present at, and it was a real delight to her, little hero-worshipper as she was, to see and listen to so many celebrated persons, of whom before she had only heard or read. But her pleasure was marred—rudely so sometimes—during the evening, as on all sides around her she heard open infidelity talked and discussed, in a refined intellectual manner, it is true, but none the less making her blood run cold as she listened, longing the while that she were able to speak out, as powerfully as could these unbelievers, what was in her heart—the faith so strong and deep, the indignation and horror which burned in it—as the cold sceptical words struck on her ears.

'If I were only older and more clever, and could speak to them!' she sighed.

But who of that intellectual company thought of courting discussion with the young girl, their hostess' cousin, little more than a child as she seemed, and who, they thought, doubtless shared her cousin's irreligious opinions, if she were troubled as yet with any ideas on such subjects? How little they knew or could have understood of the spirit which animated that girlish frame, making the warm heart beat as now and then she made upon it her quiet secret sign of the cross! And foremost in many an argument of this kind was Stanley Graham, with poor Gerty's wistful eyes watching him unobserved, her ears listening, when he was within hearing, with a pain keener a thousand times than when they heard the like sentiments from any one else. And yet all the while her throbbing heart could not but allow that to-night he showed to still greater advantage than in mere brilliant assemblies of pleasure, here, where his splendid intellect had full play and was in its congenial element, heightening in its animation even the outward beauty which of itself alone was such an all-powerful attraction.

But in the midst even of such sympathetic spirits Stanley Graham never forgot the corner where Gerty sat so quietly and shyly. He kept turning to it as to a haven of rest and delicious refreshment, coming to the young girl's side with that smile which already she was learning to see was hers only, which never greeted his other friends as it greeted her, talking to her with that gentle respectful tenderness which riveted still more strongly that poor little heart's growing idolatry. It seemed as though he could not keep long away from her side, as though he must come to see if she were attended to and amused; if she wanted to know anything about any of the guests, who they were and their different histories; to inquire if she would like to move to a different part of the room, or to be introduced to any one; until Lady Hunter at last said laughingly that Stanley quite took the care of Gerty out of her hands.

Sir Robert chanced to be standing near to Gerty on one of these occasions when Stanley Graham came up to her; and when he had stood with her a minute or two he turned to Sir Robert with a changed tone, and with a look of scorn and annoyance:

'I was very sorry to hear just now from old Mr. Beddowes, Sir Robert, that his son, who became a Romanist two years ago, you remember, is about to join those detested Jesuits.'

'O Mr. Graham!' burst from Gerty almost unconsciously, as the colour rose quickly to her face.

Her tone was so painful, and as Stanley Graham turned to her with surprise there was such a look of reproach in her soft eyes, that he said very quietly, with a smile:

'What have I done, Miss Mannering? Surely you don't want me to believe *you* are an advocate of the Jesuits?' Then another thought struck him, and he continued quickly, 'Perhaps you knew Mr. Beddowes, and are shocked to hear my news of him, Miss Mannering?'

'No, no, Mr. Graham, I never heard of him before. But—I have a brother—a Jesuit. I am a Catholic myself, Mr. Graham.'

And, with the colour deepening on her face, Gerty looked out straight before her, dreading, perhaps, the change she might see in his expression if she met his gaze.

'Ah, to be sure! Didn't you know, Stanley?' asked Sir Robert with his courteous smile. 'I suppose it never happened to come out before that Gerty was a Catholic (she does not like us to say Roman Catholic, Stanley), and of course you must have thought that could be the very last thing she could be, being our relative. So that must be his apology,' he added, turning to Gerty.

'I have hardly seen Mr. Beddowes myself yet, Stanley, so I will go and try to find him;' and he left them alone again together.

Instead of the scorn and coldness which Gerty had pictured would come over Stanley Graham's face at her avowal, there was a look of intense perplexed pain, and a tenderness in the gray eyes which would have startled Gerty had she been looking up at him. But she still looked out before her, and Stanley's face was calm again as he sat down by her side.

'I am *very* sorry to have offended you, Miss Mannering;' and the gentle tone made Gerty's heart leap as she looked up now, meeting a smile instead of the polite coldness she had expected. 'I had no idea you were a—Catholic. You have not been so long, I suppose?'

The idea of being taken for a convert made Gerty laugh almost, and she looked up straight into her questioner's face with a bright smile.

'All my life, Mr. Graham. I was born a Catholic.' And even to his sceptical ears her tone said so plainly, ' and I glory in it,' that the painful expression came again for an instant to Stanley Graham's face; but he forced it away as he spoke again:

'Ah, then, you belong to a family which has always been—Catholic, of course? Will you think me impertinent, I wonder, if I ask if you are related to the Mannerings of Whitewell Grange in B——shire, your own county, I believe?'

Gerty laughed outright now, while the blushes rose again to her face:

'Whitewell Grange is my home. I am Mr. Mannering's only daughter. Why, have you heard of us, Mr. Graham?' she asked with a frank smile.

He laughed too as he answered:

'It is rather strange I should not have found it out before, isn't it, that you belong to the family I have often heard spoken of by some friends of mine in B——shire? I visited them last year for a few days, and I several times heard them mention Whitewell Grange. Once we passed it in a drive, but could not see the house from the road, of course.'

Gerty's eyes sparkled now.

'Ah, how strange! Then you have actually been so near my home. I wish you could have seen it, Mr. Graham: it is such a dear old place. Not very grand, perhaps, though *I* think it the grandest place on earth, and I know papa does too in his heart. Did they—your friends—tell you we were a Catholic family, Mr. Graham?'

He smiled at her eagerness.

'O yes, Miss Mannering; and they told me that your family lost a good deal at the time of the Reformation. But I should have listened with much more interest could I have known I was going to make your acquaintance, of course.' And the gray eyes looked down so tenderly that Gerty averted hers for a minute.

'That is what we are so proud of, Mr. Graham,' she said warmly, 'knowing how much our family suffered—for the faith.' And she spoke the last words bravely, scorning the word 'Reformation,' which to her sensitive conscience would have seemed a cowardly one in this case, when she was so determined to make amends for her previous shyness on the subject. 'We are quite proud of not being very rich, you know, because it was for *that* we were impoverished.'

Stanley Graham turned away a moment, as though the sight of her bright face pained him; but he continued directly:

'And your brother, Miss Mannering, is he in England or abroad?'

'O, in England, Mr. Graham, at N—— College, in the seminary there. He is only young—not twenty yet—and he has only just finished his novitiate, you know. O Mr. Graham, if you only knew the Jesuits properly you would never think them so dreadful; you would admire them as much as any one must who knows them *really*.'

Her very earnestness seemed to trouble him; but he strove to hide the feeling, as he said gently but somewhat uneasily:

'You are determined, then, not to forget my offence? What shall I do to repair it fully?'

'Indeed I did not refer to that at all—really I did not, Mr. Graham. O, do not think so, please.' And the sweet eyes smiled with a gentle pleading. 'Of course, if you have been brought up to think of the Jesuits and Catholics altogether as bad, or at least worthless, how can you help it, Mr. Graham? I was not blaming you, but I *wish* it were not so; that you could know how different it is in reality, the same as I wish for Lady Hunter and Sir Robert.'

And as she sighed there came such an earnest yearning look over Gerty's face as showed her companion what a deep true nature and sympathetic woman's heart lay hidden beneath the girlish exterior.

'You are very good, Miss Mannering,' he said earnestly. 'I assure you I appreciate your kindness in thinking of me as a friend like this, and I must thank you for your wish very sincerely, though I—cannot echo it.'

And before Gerty could speak again, a gentleman came up, and putting his arm in Stanley's, drew him away into the centre of a group some yards off, where Gerty soon lost sight of him.

But a great load seemed lifted from her heart, which was singing inwardly, as it were, as she sat there alone again, absorbed in her own thoughts. How she had been mistaken in Stanley Graham; how different had been his behaviour from the coldness which she had expected; how kind he had been, more so than ever almost, in manner if not in words; until the sacrifice she had been prepared to make had completely slipped away, quite uncalled for now! Perhaps there might even be a hope that some day he himself might receive the grace of conversion. More unlikely things had come to pass; and why should she not pray and hope for the grace for his soul as well as for any other? Perhaps he was not so bitterly irreligious after all, as her cousin had told her. Lady Hunter might be mistaken, or was it— and as another thought half rose in Gerty's mind the colour mounted again to her face and her heart beat tremblingly. Could it be that her own hidden feeling was not so wholly unreturned? did Stanley Graham perhaps care for her just a little, as surely his manner implied? and was his hatred or contempt of religion softened on finding that *she* was a Catholic, that she was so proud of being one?

'O, if I could be the means of his conversion!' was her enthusiastic thought. 'If through poor little me such a one as he is, so noble and gifted, should become a Catholic some day, how grand it would be! But if any one could know I was even dreaming of such a thing, wouldn't I die nearly! How could he ever care really for *me*, a bit of a thing like me; and he so run after, so superior to any one I ever knew!' and the fond adoring heart sighed wearily. 'Well, I can pray for him all the same, as I do for Julia and Sir Robert; he will never know how I could have—loved him. I shall go back to papa, and be an old maid all my life:

"Miss Mannering of Whitewell Grange," people will call me. I shall have plenty to do, taking care of the poor, and helping Rupert's poor too, when he is on the mission, out of what is his own, after all. Nobody need ever know that there is something in my heart which will prevent me from ever marrying, as *I* know there is and always will be; and if they *could* know, they would only laugh—even Father Walmsley would, perhaps, to think that my heart could have gone so entirely to any one I have known only a few days. I'm not afraid of ever betraying it to any one, even to papa, because it would make *him* unhappy if he thought *I* was.' But though Gerty tried to smile and look cheerfully at the dreary prospect she had conjured up, hope would whisper to her heart, trying to drive away the gloomy picture.

When the evening was over, when she had received Stanley Graham's earnest tender adieux, with his voice still ringing in her ears, Gerty stood a few minutes with her cousin before going up-stairs, and told her of her conversation with him during the evening.

'It seemed so natural to be talking to him like that, Julia; and I wonder how it never all came out before. But he did seem surprised to hear I was a Catholic, Julia.'

'I told you he would be, love. He would be the very last one to think that any one in whom he felt interested should turn out to be a Catholic—indeed he would purposely avoid talking of religion at all, I know, for fear of clashing with any prejudices; and this will be how the fact has been so long in coming out, dear. For however quiet and unconcerned he may have seemed to you on the subject, Gerty, he *is* very bitter in his heart, and so scornfully and impatiently so, that, unlikely as I am to become a Roman

Catholic, I am a thousand times more likely than Stanley Graham is ever to have any faith at all.'

But even these last cheerless words could not drive away the new hope that had arisen in her heart.

'Julia does not know what prayer can do; she knows nothing of God's grace and the changes it can work if He chooses. She does not know how powerful our Blessed Lady is in interceding for us with God, when our own prayers are not worthy to be granted.'

And Gerty slept that night with a greater peace and calmness in her heart than had dwelt in it since the night before, when she had wept so bitterly as the discovery forced itself upon her of the change that was coming over her so quickly, the discovery that the old girlish life was ebbing away and the woman's life beginning for her; that her idolised father was losing the first place in her heart and thoughts, giving it up to a mere stranger; that the prospect of returning to the dear old home no longer filled her with unmixed delight.

CHAPTER XI.

'Poor papa!' and Gertrude's tears fell, as she sat alone in her bedroom with a letter from her father in her hand.

Nearly a fortnight had elapsed since the evening recorded in the last chapter. The month in London was coming to an end; it was the day before the one settled for her return home, and Gerty had just received a letter from Mr. Mannering, telling her how he longed to see her again, to welcome his darling back once more to the old sweet life together. He was sending the housekeeper to fetch her home, as he himself wished to be there before her to see that all was nice and comfortable to receive her, as he said.

'I am like a child almost, Gerty,' he wrote, 'in impatience for the arrival of the day after to-morrow. Father Walmsley must think so too, I fancy, for he broke through his rule of never dining out on Sunday, and actually came home with me after Mass, to help me to behave rationally, I suppose. How will my little girl look when I kiss her again, I wonder. A little paler, perhaps (but that can soon be remedied), but not changed at all in reality; not grown very stately or fashionable, I hope—indeed, I am *sure*. One thing I know: she will look happy, and feel so too, to be with her lonely old father—not a bit sorry to leave all the grandeur of London. Have I not guessed rightly, Sunbeam? I wonder now how I lived all those years you were at the convent, Gerty. I have so much to tell you, about Rupert and the College, and about my retreat; and I shall have so much to listen to also, I know, though you have written such nice long letters. I have just been up again to look at your room, to see how they have put up the new picture of the College I have brought home for you. You will be delighted with it, I expect; and I have had it hung opposite the bed, as I thought you would like. I am writing to Lady Hunter to-day too, for the least I can do is to thank her myself for all her kindness to my little girl; but you must also say everything that is nice to her for me;' and with a few more loving words the letter concluded. And Gerty sat there like one in a dream, with the letter in her hand, gazing out before her with tearful eyes and pale fixed face, as the past month rose in retrospect before her. It was all over now, with its pleasures and bewildering delights; the end was at hand of her brief elysium, and she was going back to the old life, the life which seemed so long past now, with its sweet simple duties and joys.

And why was she so pale and tearful? why was there none of that delight in her face which she had so fondly pictured would be hers when this day should come, which but three short weeks ago she had felt so sure she would feel? Was she regretting the pleasures and amusements, the elegant society and admiration, she was about to leave? No, O, no! If it had been *only* these, how easily, nay gladly, would she have turned her back on them to go once more to the father who yearned so for her presence! But there was another life, apart from the outward one of gaiety, which would not be cast off or left behind—a new existence of restless joy and hope and care, which had become part of herself, changing the happy careless girl into a thoughtful woman, which must go with her wherever she went, its very presence making any other life seem cold and dark. And for this it was that the tears were falling—the knowledge that she could not, as she had so merrily promised, take back with her to her father her happy free girlish heart; that it was hers no longer, but given up wholly to another, given with all the depth and fervour of the nature which until now even she herself had scarce known was hers, and this with yet no assurance that such a love as she gave was bestowed in return, no assurance yet, but only a trembling though almost certain hope.

Every day for the last fortnight Gerty had met Stanley Graham. Riding, driving, at the opera or elsewhere, he had been ever at her side, until society was now growing accustomed to the fact that haughty Stanley Graham had at last been fairly conquered, and that sooner or later Lady Hunter's pretty little cousin would win the position so long coveted in vain by many an older, prouder beauty.

Lady Hunter herself viewed the course of events with a mixed feeling of delight and vague uneasiness, which latter she more than once expressed to Sir Robert, who, however, failed to share it.

'I hope it will all turn out happily,' she said to him. 'To us of course there seems no reason why it should not; for I can hardly believe sometimes that our little Gerty has made such a conquest, and so quickly too. But you see, Robert dear, her father is such a very stanch Romanist, and I know more than you do of the faith and practice of strict Catholics like they are, especially since Gerty has been with me; and I can't help wondering how it will please him to see her marry one who is not only not of their religion, but of no

H

religion at all. And another thing, Robert: how will Stanley, with his ideas, like a Catholic wife? how will he reconcile himself to see her constantly practising all those observances which he holds in such contempt? Perhaps his love for her might soften his dislike to her religion, but I can't help thinking otherwise. I ought to know Stanley well enough by this time; and it seems to me that much as he might love his wife, he would never allow her to act in opposition to his wishes in that respect. He will make a fond adoring husband, one to be *proud* of too, so long as his wife makes his will hers; but in the other case, if she should want her *own* too much now and then in anything important, why, I shouldn't like to change places with her, that's all. He won't spoil his wife, Robert, like you do;' and Lady Hunter kissed her husband with a fond affection.

He smiled kindly and cheerily.

'I hope you are wrong, Julia. I hope so; and though I do not like to contradict, I think you are, my dear. You are too anxious about Gerty, because, of course, you feel a certain responsibility now attaching to you on her account. Of course I don't know so much as you do of Catholics, but it seems to me that a young girl like Gerty would soon give in to the superior judgment of one like Stanley, especially if she loved him as any girl must love such a husband as he would be, more than all a sensitive enthusiastic little thing like she is. She would die, Julia, depend on it, sooner than go against his wishes. And as to Mr. Mannering, it may be a blow at first, but it would be a blow to give her to any one at all just yet, whether of their own religion or not, and if he sees her happy he must soon grow reconciled.' And he smiled again cheerily in his kindly ignorance of even the meaning of the words faith and religion, which he spoke so lightly, as though they were things to be worn or cast aside at pleasure or convenience; as though there were no heaven or hell at stake, no God to be pleased or offended; as though truth and error were alike in His sight.

'Well,' sighed her ladyship, 'I hope you are right, dear, I'm sure; for if Gerty ever came to any sorrow through my fault, I should wish to have cut my hand off sooner than have written the letter inviting her here. And it is too late now to remedy matters. Stanley evidently means to ask her to be his wife, though I should not be surprised if he did not do it just yet; and poor Gerty, much as she tries to hide it, cannot conceal from me where her heart is; for I know, Robert, as plainly as if she told me, that the love which comes only once in a lifetime in all its full strength and fervour, has come to her now at eighteen.'

And Gertrude herself, the object of all this solicitude, occupying just now no small share of the attention of society, the society which a month before had been ignorant of her very existence, how did she view the change that had come over her? What had been her inner life during this outwardly brilliant one, which was now on the eve of its close, as she sat with such pale tear-stained face alone in her room, with her father's letter on her knee? She knew now—she had known for a certainty very soon after the first few days—that it was no passing romantic fancy she felt for Stanley Graham, but the deep true love of a woman, strong and sweet at the same time, like her own nature. She knew too that she must have felt it even had it met with no encouragement or sign of return—she must have felt it still, though then she must have striven to conquer it, to bury it away unseen in her heart, bearing the pain with a smile bravely. But shy and modest as she was, with her schoolgirl bashfulness still upon her, Gerty could not but see that this self-suppression was uncalled for; she could not but see it a hundred times a day when she was in Stanley Graham's presence, if only by the very sound of his voice when addressing her, so much more tender than she heard it when he spoke to others; by the very glance of his gray eyes, which never looked coldly or haughtily at *her*, never otherwise than with the eloquent yet respectful gaze which somehow would have made Gerty, with the heart's true instinct, trust herself with him to the world's end, even had she not known beforehand what a refined noble nature was his. And she grew to live only in his presence, as it were—to yearn for it as a daily necessity which never failed her; she fed, as it were, upon the sweet attentions which were so doubly precious, coming from one so haughty and exclusive, until her love became in this short time a species of idolatry—a pure unselfish one indeed, but still idolatry, too great and too absorbing to be given to any human creature, however perfect, however great —a love which should be given only to God, which can only bring rest and peace to the heart when rendered to Him. And she knew this, poor Gerty, she felt it, in the midst of her bewildering joy and hope; she knew she 'loved not wisely, but too well.' She prayed on her knees every night that if it were wrong she might not grow to love too strongly; that she might not forget God for His creature. But though the spirit was willing, the flesh was weak, and the poor heart, which felt so strong after its refreshment of prayer, fell again into its fond idolatry with the daylight, when its idol was present once more.

'After all, it can be no harm to love him so, if—he

loves me,' she would tell herself. 'If I am ever his wife, it will only be right, it will be my duty, to think more of him than all the world. And if I help to lead him to God, if through me he should learn to love instead of hating religion, if he should become a Catholic, I shall not have loved him for myself only, but for God's glory, and to gain another soul for heaven.'

But there was one care, one hidden trouble, which she dared hardly acknowledge to her own heart, but which was there nevertheless, amounting to agony at times. Suppose her hope should be vain; suppose Stanley Graham, instead of growing reconciled to the thought of religion, should persist in his contempt for it; suppose, even if he ever should really ask her to become his wife, he should object to seeing her practise her religion; suppose, as would be but natural in one so proud, he should demur to submitting to a marriage before a priest only, without the Protestant ceremony. But Gerty would throw off these fears—she could not entertain them and live, it seemed to her, during these halcyon yet restless days. The thoughts were suggested to her partly by Lady Hunter's words concerning Stanley Graham, and partly by the fact that since the evening on which she herself had told him she was a Catholic he had never referred directly to the subject, never questioned her about her religion at all, or seemed to care to speak of it when she tried to bring the conversation round to it, as she sometimes did in her generous repentance for what seemed to her her previous cowardice. In a word, he seemed to ignore her religion altogether—to wish to keep the fact of it out of his own mind, if possible. And it troubled Gerty, because she could not divine the cause, whether her religion was really indifferent to him or whether it was that he did not wish to pain her by speaking of his own bitter prejudice against it. The terrible fear, already spoken of, that it might be *because* of his very hatred that he was so silent on the subject, *because* he would never endure that his wife should continue a Catholic, much less ever hope for him to become one,—this terrible fear she dare not entertain, it dwelt in her heart, hidden down deep, never consciously acknowledged.

'If he really loved me, so as to wish to make me his wife, he would not ask me to choose between him and my religion; he would take me *with* my religion, caring for none himself. He cannot think there is any harm in faith, so he could not have any objection to seeing it in his wife; there is nothing dishonourable in it, surely, even in his eyes, and honour is his religion.'

But in spite of her self-consolation, there were times when Gerty longed for counsel and advice—for some one to whom she could open her heart, even while she felt that had such a one been at hand, she could not have done it, she could not have spoken to any one of the love which was yet unasked.

'Even Father Walmsley I could not tell yet, O, no; more especially as Mr. Graham is what he is: if he were a Catholic, it would be easier. But if he were here, I should long to tell him, I know, though I should never be able to do it yet.'

Gerty had written to Father Walmsley once since her arrival in London, before she had met Stanley Graham—an innocent, lively letter, such as he had looked for from her; but after that it seemed to become impossible to write freely, and so his kindly, fatherly reply had brought no further letter from Gerty, much as she longed to write to her best friend. It was almost a bitter task now to write even to her darling father, a task to do what so long had been her delight, for every line seemed almost like a lie to her sensitive, truthful nature; every time she wrote the name 'Mr. Graham,' in telling of where she had been and what she had been doing, she felt like a traitor, because she could not tell that dear father that this stranger, of whom she wrote apparently so carelessly, had stolen her heart from himself, who had loved and cared for her so long and untiringly, stolen it from the dear old home in so short a time. Because, too, every time she sat down to write to him there came to her mind's eye the prospect of the day when she might have to tell him all, that she wanted to leave him, to give herself to another one—and this would be the bitter part, she knew —who was not a Catholic, one who despised religion, who at best would only be submitting to it in her because of his love for her. How would her father bear it, he who was so proud of his Catholic ancestry, of their stainless devotion to the faith, of the very obscurity into which his family had fallen through that steadfast devotion? How would Rupert, her idolised brother, the young follower of the glorious St. Ignatius—how would he bear to hear that his dear little sister, the loved companion of his childhood, was going to give herself to this proud scornful heretic, nay, infidel? The thought was so hard, so bitter at times to Gerty, that she yearned wearily to be able to throw herself on her knees before Jesus in His Sacramental Presence on the altar, as she could so easily have done at home, there to beg grace and guidance in the trials which were coming upon her with the mighty human love which was absorbing her heart. Here in London she seldom had the opportunity she yearned for, except on the Sundays; but more than once the wish grew so strong upon her that when out driving with Lady Hunter, anywhere in the region of one of the Catholic churches, she had asked her to let the carriage stop for a few minutes while she tried to enter, and had been rejoiced on finding she was able to do so. Lady Hunter had gone in with her, partly through curiosity, partly through kindliness; but Gerty had soon almost forgotten her presence as she knelt in that Veiled Presence in the tabernacle, making the most of the precious minutes to pour out her pent-up heart in earnest trembling prayer, while her cousin gazed at the bowed figure, envious of its absorption, envious of the faith she could not share.

But it was only at intervals that these shadows as of coming trouble darkened Gerty's present halcyon existence, only at times that the thought of her father and home was so bitter as not to be chased away by the new joy in her heart, the sweet almost certain hope of Stanley Graham's love, and of the changes it must work in his haughty nature, with its scorn and contempt of religion. Generally she revelled only in the sweet present, shutting her eyes to any thought but that of continued happiness in the future. All her awe of Stanley had vanished now, driven away by the strong love which had come to her so quickly. She could talk to him now freely on every subject but the one he so carefully avoided, and almost insensibly she grew to defer to his opinion in everything, making his likes and dislikes her own, with just enough of merry artless opposition to charm haughty Stanley the more, because of the graceful confiding way in which she almost always eventually yielded.

In short, Gerty had set up an idol in her heart—a noble one, it is true, but still only a faulty human creature—whom she worshipped with a fond idolatry, unconscious that to observant eyes she betrayed her secret, even by the soft love-light that shone so often now in the sweet eyes, spite of her earnest efforts to hide her feeling, spite of the maiden bashfulness which recoiled from the thought that she might have been seeking before she first was sought.

And now it was all over, at least for a time; she must leave her earthly paradise behind and go back to the old home with its quiet routine, to the dear father who awaited her with such longing love, but who, alas, could never be first in her heart again!

Stanley Graham was coming this evening to escort Lady Hunter and Gerty to the opera, and afterwards to a farewell entertainment at the house of a common friend; and as Gerty sat now in her room with her tear-stained face bent over her father's letter, the thought kept coming to her, not to be driven away—

'*When* shall I see him again? After to-night, when we say good-bye, *when* shall we meet again? When we do, will he be the same, still unchanged, as I shall be?'

She knew that her cousin wished her to pay them a visit at their country seat in L——shire, and she had promised to do so sometime about Christmas, if her father could spare her.

Was there not a secret hope in her heart that Stanley Graham might be there too, though Lady Hunter had not as yet exactly spoken of inviting him? At the same time, was it not this hope that was helping Gerty to bear the thought of the separation that was so near, of the farewell that must be said this very evening, this last night, which was coming all too quickly?

CHAPTER XII.

THE evening came, and Gertrude and Stanley Graham sat at the opera together. Rather curiously, the representation was once more the *Sonnambula*, as it had been on that first night three weeks since; but Gerty knew beforehand that it would not affect her now as it had done then—that the joys and sorrows of the heroine would move her only to a still keener realisation of the hopes and fears in her own preoccupied heart. She sat very quiet, enjoying the music in a dreamy kind of way, and trying to look interested in the performance, trying to drive away the knowledge that it was Stanley Graham's presence which made her sole enjoyment, and not to wish that the opera was over, so that she could hear him talk to her again freely, as he could hardly do here, so that she might drink-in the rich sweet voice, which was better to her than any music—which, after to-night, would be silent for her, for how long she knew not.

A less keen observer than Stanley Graham must have noticed her abstraction from the stage, and the efforts she made against it. Lady Hunter saw it too, and perhaps guessed rightly at the cause; but she only said smilingly, as the curtain fell finally, and they rose from their seats:

'You are getting quite hardened now, you see, Gerty; isn't she, Stanley? You can look at poor Amina now without a tear, eh, love?'

Gerty blushed, as she always did at anything that

seemed to indicate that she was betraying what she thought her secret; but Stanley Graham came to her rescue with a kind frank smile, as he said:

'I fancy Miss Mannering would be more likely to shed tears to-night at the sight of you, Lady Hunter, at the thought of having to leave you so soon. You have none to spare for Amina's imaginary troubles, have you?' And he spoke so very freely and kindly that Gerty could not feel embarrassed any longer, but could only thank him with an eloquent smile.

'No, indeed, I don't think I can, Mr. Graham; I must keep them all for Julia. But still I think I must be getting very hardened too, as she says, and all in three weeks!' And the idea made Gerty laugh genuinely now, as they made their way to the carriage.

'Besides,' said Lady Hunter, as they drove off, 'you know, Gerty, I am going to claim you again very soon. It is quite a promise, Stanley, that she comes to us at Christmas at Nethercotes for at least a fortnight.'

'Then we shall meet again, Miss Mannering,' said Stanley; 'for I, too, have promised to visit Nethercotes about then.'

'Of course you have, Stanley. It would not be Christmas there without you. We should miss him almost as much as the mince-pies, Gerty, if they failed to appear,' laughed her ladyship.

How thankful Gerty felt that it was a dark starless night, and that the light of the street-lamps was hardly sufficient to let her companions see the deep blush which she felt had risen to her face as she heard the confirmation of her hope! She strove to hide it still more by joining in her cousin's laughter, and then, trying to speak calmly, she said:

'Well, I have promised to come if I *can*, you know, Julia, if papa can spare me so soon again.'

Stanley Graham turned towards her with a quick anxious look, which deepened the blush on her face; but Lady Hunter only laughed kindly and carelessly.

'Spare you, Gerty! of course he will. Why, if he refuses, he will only have me coming down upon him to carry you off myself; so he might as well let you be with us by less violent means. Besides, I don't feel as if you knew us properly, or fully belonged to us, until you have been with us at Nethercotes; so remember.' And she tapped Gerty's hand playfully with her fan.

They only remained an hour or two at the reception to which they went after the opera, because Lady Hunter wanted Gerty to rest well for her journey home in the morning. And short as the time was, it seemed still shorter to Gerty—the precious moments fleeing all too swiftly on towards the hour which would bring darkness and weary longing to the adoring heart, at least for a time.

More than once, as Stanley Graham sat by her side to-night, talking to her as usual, but with even more tenderness and earnestness, Gerty could not but perceive that he became agitated, and seemed on the point of saying something from which he quickly checked himself; and the conviction made her tremble with a joyful hope and wonder.

'How happy you are,' he said in his own calm tone again, after one of these occasions, ' to be returning to a home like yours, with your father all impatience to welcome you, and loving the very walls of your old home as you do! The word "home" is but a strange sound to a wanderer like myself, and as yet perhaps I hardly care for it to be anything else. I have a nominal home, of course, and I cannot complain of it for want of beauty or comfort; but since my poor mother's death it has been desolate for me, and I cannot rest there. Perhaps some day I may settle down in it—I may grow to love it again, and not care any longer to be an aimless wanderer, as I am at present.' And he sighed slightly, almost imperceptibly.

'I hope so, Mr. Graham,' Gerty said gently; for to have hesitated would have betrayed embarrassment. 'It seems so sad not to care for home, not to be able to love it, doesn't it? But though I am so fortunate, though I have so dear a home to go to, and though I am longing to see papa again, still I am sorry to go away from London. I always seem doomed never to be *all* glad or *all* sorry about anything, but to have a mixture of both always. You see my cousin and Sir Robert have been so very kind that I cannot help being sorry to leave them; and—and everybody,' she added, blushing now for fear she was saying too much.

But Stanley looked at her more earnestly than ever as he said, with his own attractive smile:

'Miss Mannering, when we meet at Nethercotes (for you have *promised* to be there, you know), will you promise to be glad to see me just a little—not to have forgotten me quite?'

Did he really feel so uncertain yet of her sentiments towards him, or was he only making assurance doubly sure before he separated from her? Gerty could not tell: she felt, with a dismal sinking of the heart, that it *might* be only friendship he was showing her after all; and the temporary chill enabled her to look up with a frank smile, though the blush was still upon her face.

'I shall be very glad indeed to see you, Mr. Graham,' she said; and Stanley could not know how the brave little heart was beating and yearning as she spoke the conventional words so quietly.

Another minute, and Lady Hunter came up to them:

'Well, love, are you ready? Are you prepared to

make your bow to society, and tear yourself away?' she asked laughingly. 'I think we must go now, if I want you not to go home to-morrow looking so pale and tired as to draw down a scolding letter upon me from your papa.'

'I am quite ready, Julia;' and Gerty laughed too, as though there were no terrible pain just then in her heart—as though she were not wondering what life would be like when the next few minutes should be over.

Another gentleman escorted Lady Hunter to the carriage, and Stanley gave his arm to Gerty, lingering behind with her a minute on the staircase.

'Miss Mannering,' he said, almost in a whisper, '*promise* me I shall see you at Nethercotes; promise me to be glad to see me when we meet there.'

He was so agitated that Gerty strove to force back her own perturbation, and to say, gently and soothingly:

'Indeed I shall be there, if I can, Mr. Graham; and I shall be very pleased to see you again.'

She saw his firm lips quiver ere he spoke again, as they went on towards the carriage.

'God bless you, Miss Mannering, and keep you safe and well!' he whispered, with the faith of his boyhood unconsciously returning to him in the moment of agitation. 'I may not tell you yet how I thank you for that promise.' And the next minute Gerty was seated by her cousin's side in the carriage, and her hand was in Stanley's farewell grasp.

'Good-bye, Miss Mannering.'

'Good-bye, Mr. Graham.' And the carriage rolled away, bearing Gerty each moment farther from the sight and presence of her earthly idol.

She sat very quiet and silent during the drive home,

her heart beating with a wondrous joy, and yet a joy that must be patient and untold through the weary time of waiting, which was beginning for her to-night. Lady Hunter saw her abstraction, and kindly closed her eyes, feigning to be tired, so that Gerty might not feel called upon to talk. When they reached home, Gerty stayed a few minutes down-stairs with her cousin and Sir Robert; and as she said good-night at last, she added, somewhat hesitatingly:

'Julia, you won't mind, will you, if I ask to be called very early in the morning? I should like to go out to —to Mass—at Farm-street, if you would not think it strange. I shall only be out about an hour.'

Gerty had often longed to ask this before, to be able to go out sometimes to Mass in the morning; but the fatigue caused by the constant late hours, and the fear of perhaps annoying her cousin or Sir Robert by doing what to them must have seemed a strange unnecessary proceeding, perhaps calling down even the remarks of their servants, had always prevented her. But on this last night something made her feel that she must hear Mass before her return home—that she must be present at the Holy Sacrifice, and beg for grace and strength in the future, amid whatever trials it might bring forth; for already trouble seemed vaguely looming in the distance much as she strove to shut her eyes to its vision, and listen only to the joyful whisperings of hope in her heart. She felt somehow that before she left London she must kneel in Jesus' Sacramental Presence, and pray for, O, so many things—for light and grace to be sent to more than one soul which now knew not Him or His truth—most especially to *one* dearer to her than life, dearer to her than all the world beside—dearer, alas, than father, brother, and home!

Lady Hunter smiled at Gerty's request.

'Of course you shall go if you like, love; but I am only afraid you will tire yourself by getting up so early. They will think you are going to elope, or something of the sort, Gerty, seeing you go out alone so early.'

Gerty laughed. 'You see it doesn't seem anything to me, Julia: I am so accustomed to it at home. I want to go on the last morning, you know, to pray for my safe journey.'

'How good you Catholics are, to be sure!' and her ladyship sighed among her smiles. 'I go here and there without ever thinking of praying for safety, taking it all for granted. By-the-bye, love, I wish we could have persuaded Mrs. Leeson to come to London to-night, and have stayed here. It will be all coming and going for her to-morrow.'

'O, thank you, Julia; but I don't think any consideration would make Mrs. Leeson sleep a night away from the Grange. She will not mind the journey at all in the morning, if only because she is coming to fetch *me*; and she will only have about an hour to wait at the station, you know.'

'Well, whatever shall we do without you, Gerty, when you are gone! We shall miss you so dreadfully, love, shall we not, Robert?'

'So much, Gerty,' said the baronet, with his kind smile, 'that it is a good thing we are going away ourselves next week. I wish, but for your father's sake, we were taking you with us back to Nethercotes.'

'You are very kind, Sir Robert;' and the tears came to Gerty's eyes, springing from the warm heart, so sensitive to kindness.

'And we are going to lose Stanley Graham again,' said Lady Hunter, as she took Gerty's hand caressingly. 'I suppose he told you, love, that he is going abroad for three months?'

Gerty could not hide the tell-tale blush that rose to her face, but she replied quietly:

'He said he was going abroad, and would only return in time to go to you at Nethercotes for Christmas, Julia.'

'Yes, he is going to Nice, to stay with his uncle, his mother's brother, a bachelor, and his only relative that I know of. He is an infirm old man, and it can be no great pleasure to Stanley to visit him; but it was a promise that he would spend this autumn with him, and Stanley would never break a promise, however disagreeable it may be to keep. Besides, the old man is very much attached to him for his mother's sake, and for the same reason Stanley pays him great respect always, for Mrs. Graham was very, very fond of her brother, I believe. But he is an ailing old man now, with only a slender income; and but for the society Stanley makes for himself in Nice, his visits there cannot be very enjoyable. It is two years since he stayed there so long before. Well, I wish these partings were over, and we were all at Nethercotes together;' and she gave Gerty a hearty lingering kiss, and the latter went up-stairs to try and grow accustomed to the thought of the next three weary months, to the patient waiting for the brightness to come back to her life.

As the door closed on Gerty, Lady Hunter turned to her husband as she said earnestly:

'Do you know, Robert, I feel relieved that things have got no further yet between Stanley and Gerty. Not that I expected anything would be settled yet, more especially as he has this tiresome visit to Nice to take him away for so long; and besides, Stanley is not one to ask a girl for her heart before she has had time to be sure she can really and truly give it to him. He is too honourable to draw any girl into a hasty engagement, though I fancy it must have been a struggle to part with her in this unsettled way; for *I* feel sure where the child's heart is, if *he* does not. But I should not have liked it all to come about just yet, somehow; for I have the feeling still that all may not be as smooth and easy as it seems to *us* it should be, Robert.'

'You are thinking of her father, Julia, of course, and the religious question, I know; but I think, dear, you exaggerate its importance. If she loves Stanley, as you think, she will yield to him in that as in other things; and Mr. Mannering would not destroy her happiness by withholding his consent to the marriage. Besides, Stanley may himself be more pliable than you think in the matter, and there may be no cause for any unpleasantness at all.'

Lady Hunter smiled.

'You're always a cheery prophet, my dear old Robert, and I hope from my heart you will be a true one in this case; for, as I said before, I should never be happy again if sorrow ever came to Gerty through what has, after all, been my doing.'

CHAPTER XIII.

THE journey was over; Gerty was safe at home again. Once more Mr. Mannering had got his darling back with him—his little 'Sunbeam,' who would gladden his heart and brighten up the old house as had ever been her wont, so he told himself. She looked a little pale, and was thinner than she had been, he thought, with a kind of elegant air about her, due perhaps to her fashionable attire, he fancied; but that was all. She was his little girl still, his own Gerty, all unchanged, as she stepped quickly from the train and rushed into his arms, forgetting everything else for the minute but that she was safe back with him again, her own dear, dear father. How could he know, while she kissed him so often and smiled her own old smile up into his face—how could he see yet that she could never be all his own again; that she brought back a secret he must not share; that her heart was gone, whether for joy or for sorrow, into the keeping of a stranger whom he knew not? After those first few moments, the terrible consciousness of the change in herself came over Gerty with redoubled force; and, as though to hide it as long as possible even from suspicion, she laughed and chatted gaily all the way home, as they drove along the familiar roads and through the friendly village, so gaily and happily apparently, as quite to deceive and satisfy Mr. Mannering, though more than once she herself scarcely knew what she was saying, because of the painful self-reproach in her heart, and the ever-recurring thought:

'Everything is just the same but myself; nothing else is changed in the least since I left it all only a month since. How careless and free I was then—how little I knew what was coming! And yet, would I go back to the old peaceful life if I could—the time before I knew Stanley Graham? O no, no! Whatever is to come of it, I would bear it rather than wake and find the past month all a dream.' And even as she sat there by her father's side, with her hand in his caressingly, trying to laugh and answer him merrily, the vision of that noble face rose up before her, making her yearn wearily for the sound of the one voice which was music now in her ears.

'Father Walmsley is coming to see you this evening, Gerty,' said her father, after a minute's pause. 'He would not promise to come to dinner, because he knew "Sunbeam" would want to brighten me up a bit first of all by herself, and would have so much to tell me that even he would feel *de trop* until later on in the evening.'

Gerty had roused herself almost with a start to listen as her father began to speak; but as he paused the pain was too great to bear quietly any longer—the pain of the thought of the deception she would have to keep up all through these weary coming months, and of the shock that might come at the end to this dear, dear father when his darling should want to leave him so soon, to give herself—as, alas, she hoped to do—to one whom she *felt* he could so little approve. The tears sprang to her eyes, and she stole her arm round her father's neck with a half-sob.

'O papa, why did I ever leave you at all? Why didn't we stay here always together?'

For a moment Mr. Mannering was startled with a kind of vague fear, but he drove it away, thinking Gerty fancied he had been feeling lonely, and blamed herself for it. No doubt her emotion was to be attributed to her joy at being again at home, safe with him once more in the old familiar place; and perhaps too she was thoroughly tired out now with the past month's gaieties, and a little thing would soon upset her until she was quite strong again.

'Gerty darling, don't you know I *wanted* you to go? Why, even if I have felt a little lonely sometimes, it is all the more treat to have you now back again, eh, Sunbeam? Besides, we are going to be together now till we get quite tired of each other, you know, with not even Rupert able to come and rouse us up again this side of Christmas.'

She could not grieve that kindly unselfish heart, whose love she never failed to appreciate, even now in her new absorbing idolatry; so she dashed the tears away, with a strong resolve that for as long as possible she would be outwardly the same, bright and cheerful always, for his sake.

'I'm all right again now, papa. I was only silly a minute, just to show you that I *am* silly yet, not grown wise and solemn with my experience of the grand world;' and she laughed as brightly as though no such things as love and sorrow and separation existed on this earth. 'Julia was quite afraid you would be dreadfully cross with her, papa, if you thought me looking pale or thin or anything; but you don't think so, do you, papa? At least, I only want a little of my native air to set me to rights again, don't I?'

'That's all, I think, Gerty. A little country air to blow back the roses to your face, and a little piety to clear away the worldliness, and we'll do, sha'n't we? So you did not manage to convert Lady Hunter, eh, Gerty?'

'O dear no, papa; it would take more than me to do that, nice and delightful as she is. But she is so good, really—I mean in listening to explanations about religion. She never scoffs openly, like some of them do.'

'That may be partly, love, because she would not hurt your feelings. However, it *may* be something more than that; so we must go on praying for her, Gerty.'

'Yes, indeed, papa, and for dear old Sir Robert too.'

'Well, I hardly hope so much for him even as Lady Hunter; but we can never tell where God may send His grace, can we, Gerty?'

Gerty sighed, thinking of that other one she could not name—at least not yet—specially like this; later, she must bring herself to speak of him calmly, as of any other friend of her cousin's.

'Well, here we are, and there is Mrs. Leeson, home before us with the luggage. Now run up-stairs first thing and see your room, Gerty, because I want to know how you like the position of the picture of the College that Rupert sent, you know.'

'Yes, papa;' and having first exchanged hearty greetings with the servants who flocked forward to see her, Gerty ran up-stairs to her own little sanctuary, which she had left a happy careless girl, and to which in a few short weeks she returned a woman, with a woman's weary restless heart—with its longing love and hope and care.

She took off her things, and began to help the maid to unpack her trunks, putting away the pretty dresses, for so few of which she would have need again just yet, lingering over the occupation with a kind of blissful pain, not because she was regretting the gay scenes in which she had worn them, but because they seemed to speak to her of the one image in her heart. She sighed as she handled the costume she had worn that night at the Duchess of N——'s ball, the night she had first met Stanley Graham, the night she had found herself admiring his noble face and figure, when she had likened him to some chivalrous crusader or knight of old romance. She sighed even while her heart beat with its hidden love and trembling hope; and then, turning aside from the occupation for the present, quickly began to dress for the *tête-à-tête* dinner with her father, simply but brightly and prettily, as she thought he would like to see her.

Mr. Mannering caught her in his arms as she came into the old dining-room, which looked more old-fashioned still when the graceful sylph-like figure in the pretty dress crossed its threshold.

'Does it all look very quiet and solemn, Sunbeam, after Lady Hunter's bright modern rooms?'

'Not *too* quiet and solemn, papa, don't be afraid,' she replied, with the old fond smile. 'It *does* seem more old-fashioned than it used to do, of course; but I like it better than those grand new-looking places, papa, and I'm *so* glad to be back in it again.' And Gerty only spoke the truth; for it was not with the fashion and splendour of the past month that she had left her heart—not *them* that she sighed for one instant —but for the one presence which for her would have made paradise of a desert.

She was so bright and happy outwardly during dinner that Mr. Mannering not only forgot his vague fear entirely, but congratulated himself on having parted with his darling for the past month, because she was all the sweeter and more precious to him now on her return, and she was improved too, he thought, if there had been any room at all for improvement in his loving eyes.

'There is something about her which reminds me more than ever of her mother,' he said to himself, seeing not yet that it was the softened light in the sweet eyes, the more earnest, less childish ring in her very voice, the unconscious changes imparted by the woman's true deep love, never to leave her more.

As he had promised, Father Walmsley came in during the evening, unconscious of the pain the first sight of him gave to Gerty, as she met her old friend for the first time in her life with a secret in her heart she could not tell even him—not yet, while her love was not openly asked for. He drew back at the sight of her with a kindly laugh.

'Mr. Mannering, is this really Gerty, our little country girl, or some fashionable young lady she has sent in her place?'

Gerty laughed too as she shook hands.

'Now, Father Walmsley, you're too bad. If you are going to quarrel with this pretty dress that I put on just to show you and papa a bit of a glimpse of the latest fashions, I shall be sorry I didn't alarm you outright by putting on something really gorgeous—the last dinner-dress my cousin gave me. Indeed, if you don't believe at once that it is really *me*, I'll go up and put it on directly, to show that I am the same wicked individual as ever.'

'Don't trouble, Gerty, for I am quite convinced now,' the priest replied, with his kind smile. Then, more seriously, he added: 'If the change is only outward like this—if it can be put aside with the dress—we shall not quarrel with it, shall we, Mr. Mannering?'

Did he see the quick conscious colour that rose to Gerty's face, though she turned aside with a merry laugh to hide it? Perhaps it did not entirely escape his fatherly experienced eye, though he may have thought but little of it just then and forbore from noticing it.

'I hardly know whether Gerty or I have talked the most yet, Father Walmsley,' said Mr. Mannering. 'About equally, I think, with my questions and her answers, eh, Sunbeam?'

'No, *I* talked the most, papa, I think. And I shall have nearly as much to say to Father Walmsley, for I only wrote once to him, didn't I, father?' and she turned towards him. 'It was a great shame of me, after the nice letter I had from you, and I'm so very, very sorry; but you see I was so given up to idleness and gaiety that I knew you'd forgive me, won't you?' She had guessed he must have thought her negligent in the matter, and with a vague dread of being questioned about it, even in joke, she had entered on the subject herself to disarm suspicion, as it were. O, how unlike the old, guileless, childlike Gerty already to have to resort to these wiles, innocent though they were, to guard her precious secret from her dearest friends!

'I must forgive you, my child, I suppose, on condition that you make amends by growing very good and pious again very quickly. What do you say, Gerty?'

'O, I mean to do, don't I, papa? You'll see me at Mass again in the morning as if nothing had happened, and I'll begin to-morrow to go and see as many poor people as you like, though just yet you must not give me any *very* cross old women; and, O, Father Walmsley, you must promise not to preach very hard sermons again just yet either, or you'll frighten me away again, you know.'

The good priest laughed heartily now.

'I shall be afraid to preach at all, I think, Gerty, after so many injunctions.'

'Well, perhaps it *would* be better to wait until we come back from the seaside, Father Walmsley,' laughed Mr. Mannering. 'I think we had better try to get off next week, and then, after a fortnight of bracing air, Gerty will be quite ready for harness again.'

Something made Gerty sigh, but she laughed it away, and began again to talk brightly, to tell Father Walmsley about her life of the past month, of its pleasures and gaieties, of her cousin and Sir Robert, even naming Stanley Graham once or twice when it could not be avoided, quietly and with apparent unconcern, as she did any other of her cousin's friends. He had been so much a part of her life in London, so frequent a companion, that to have avoided speaking of him altogether would have been an impossibility; and, after all, was it not better that her father should at least grow accustomed to his name before the time when he might be called upon to welcome him as the one to whom she, Gerty, had given her whole heart?

'Is this Mr. Graham a relative of the Hunters, Gerty?' asked Mr. Mannering, as the name was mentioned again.

'O, no, papa, only a very great friend, almost like a brother to Julia. She knew his mother very well, and since her death Mr. Graham has always been a good deal with the Hunters, at least when he is at home, for he is abroad a great deal.'

'He is not a Catholic, Gerty, of course; there is no need to ask.'

'O, dear no, papa! He cares for no religion; indeed,

I think he—he despises the very idea of it,' replied Gerty, forcing herself by a desperate effort to speak calmly, and scorning to keep back the truth when it could be told—the truth which they might be *obliged* to hear some day.

How she longed to add the praises of Stanley which welled up in her heart, of his nobility of character, of his fine intellect and manly beauty, and of his constant kindness to herself! But she repressed the yearning so bravely and with so little outward sign, that not even Father Walmsley yet suspected that this Mr. Graham was anything to her but an acquaintance, much less that he was the idol of her heart, worshipped with a love almost too absorbing to be given to any creature.

'Another subject for your prayers, poor fellow, eh, Gerty?' said her father with a smile, guessing little what secret ardent prayers hers were for him every day.

Then, as though the strain were too great to keep calm and cheerful on this subject, Gerty began to ask again about Rupert, and made her father tell her still more about his retreat at the College; and so the evening passed, until Father Walmsley rose to go, saying Gerty would be tired and must not be kept up late this first night of her return home. When he was gone and she had bade the old loving good-night to her father and was safe alone in her own room, Gerty could bear up no longer, but wept out on her knees the pent-up emotion—wept out, not only her weary yearning for the one loved presence, but the bitter self-reproach in her heart, the pain of finding that home was the old home no longer to her, never could be again.

'Only three weeks since how I longed for this time, and now! Don't I seem years older, don't I know I can never be the same again, and I must go on letting them think I am unchanged, until I am *quite* sure that he loves me! Will it seem unkind, even when I tell papa I have promised to go to Nethercotes so soon? And yet I *must* go; have I not promised *him* he shall meet me there when he comes back to England?'

CHAPTER XIV.

Mr. Mannering and Gerty were at home again after their fortnight at the sea-side, and there was a cloud often now on Mr. Mannering's face, a sad perplexed look at times which it had never worn in the old days before Gerty went to London. Perhaps he himself could hardly have told what it was that was troubling him, making him feel again that vague anxiety about his darling which had come to him first for one brief space on the evening of her return home. But, acknowledged or not, the anxiety was there in his heart, the sad conviction that a change of some sort, indefinable as yet, perhaps, had come over his little Gerty, though at times she was able to shake it off and be again the bright happy girl she once had always been. He had not noticed it so much during the first few days at home, because if she seemed at all thoughtful or preoccupied then, he had put it down to fatigue and the reaction after the past month's gaieties, and told himself she would be quite restored after the stay at the sea-side. Besides, the preparations for going away and the return to all her old duties and occupations had kept Gerty outwardly so busy that she was able generally to appear bright and cheerful, keeping back her tears and sighs until she could be alone and under no necessity for restraint.

But when they were fairly established in the quiet little hotel they chose at Beachdown—the small retired watering-place Mr. Mannering in his unconsciousness had thought best for Gerty, with only the moaning ever-restless sea before them and the quiet walks behind, quite alone together, with not even kind Father Walmsley to come between them,—then it was that in a very few days Mr. Mannering became conscious of the change in his bright little 'Sunbeam.'

It was not that Gerty was less affectionate than of old, less attentive to his every wish; on the contrary, there was something more loving and tender about her than ever, a kind of clinging softness in her manner, a quicker anticipation even than before of his every little want or wish, born of the self-reproach in her heart, and the knowledge of how soon he might have to lose her, to be left solitary and alone again, —born of the very love and idolatry which had driven him, her dear father, from the first place in her heart. But try as she would, Gerty could not be *always* her old bright self, she broke down at times in the effort, making the contrast appear then all the greater. There was an unconscious sadness and care even on her face at times when she did not know her father was watching her; there was a growing reserve about speaking any more closely of her London life, which she herself feared more than once must be apparent.

But it was all a change which was somehow more felt than seen, and Mr. Mannering never for an instant let Gerty see that he noticed it or had any anxiety on her account. He tried to quiet himself with the hope that time and rest would set all to rights again, and strove to make himself happy meanwhile with having his darling safe back at least once more. Their life outwardly was just such as Gerty would have revelled in once, in the past peaceful happy days. They took long delicious strolls together on the quiet shore, they sat for hours under the shadow of the rocks, watching the tide ebb and flow, or gazing admiringly at the beautiful sunsets, those balmy September evenings. Then sometimes when it grew chilly they would sit indoors in the twilight, looking at the shadows gathering over the sea, until Gerty often fell into one of her fits of musing and abstraction, knowing not how her father as he watched her yearned to ask her to come to his arms and whisper in his ear whatever of care or trouble had come to her, if such it was that ailed her. But he was always silent, waiting patiently until Gerty roused herself with a start and kissed him with a lingering tenderness, often going then to the piano and forcing herself to sing as brightly as ever for him some favourite little song.

She had chosen one of these evenings, as they sat together in the twilight, to tell her father of her promise to visit Nethercotes at Christmas. She had put it off from day to day, dreading in the consciousness of her secret even having to tell him that she should want to leave him again so soon, though it would be for so short a time, and though she knew he would be pleased at the prospect of further enjoyment for her.

'Papa,' she began quietly, but glad somehow too of the friendly twilight, ' Julia wants me so much to visit them at Nethercotes after Christmas—indeed they insisted on it, both she and Sir Robert. So I promised I would, papa, just for a fortnight, if—if you could spare me, of course.'

'Well, I must try, Gerty, mustn't I?' and he stroked her bright dark hair as she sat there close beside him. 'Of course you must go, love; I have been thinking they ought to invite you to Nethercotes. I should like you to see it, for it is a beautiful place. I was there once for a week with your mother, shortly before you were born, Gerty,—soon after Sir Robert had brought home your cousin a bride, and—and I have never been since.'

Gerty came closer and kissed away the sigh that escaped her father's lips at the recollections he had conjured up. Had she ever loved him sufficiently, this dear kind father? Was she worthy of his untiring devotion now, when she was hoping soon to leave him for a comparative stranger, whose love, even when she should be assured of it, must of its very nature be jealous and exacting, unlike the quiet unselfish affection which had guarded her from childhood? Was she worthy of it, when she wished to leave its sweet shelter now, when she was just beginning to supply her dead mother's place?

'Papa,' she continued after a pause, 'if I am to go to Nethercotes I will not pay my promised visit to the Convent before Christmas, you know. I would rather put it off until later, when Rupert has been—sometime before Lent. I want to stay with you *quite* until I go to Nethercotes, papa; not to go anywhere without you, even for a day.' And the almost sad kind of clinging tenderness was in Gerty's manner again just then, making her father's heart fill with its new vague uneasiness.

But he laughed as he said cheerily:

'Well, we must settle that with the nuns, Gerty. If they will wait, I shall be all the better off, you know, Sunbeam; so you must write in good time to Sister Teresa to announce the disappointment.'

So it was settled, *quite* settled now, that she was to go to Nethercotes, the dear unselfish father being even wishful that she should go. Gerty sat up late that night by the window in her little sea-side bedroom, listening to the moan of the waves, picturing to herself what the meeting would be like at Nethercotes, the meeting again with Stanley Graham. 'Would papa be so wishful for me to go if he knew what it may lead to? He would, I know, if he felt it was for my happiness, dear, dear papa, even if he had to give me up at once; but would he wish it if he knew what Stanley Graham is like, that he is a despiser of religion, though he has never openly scoffed at it since he knew I was a Catholic. Will he welcome an infidel as my husband, if it comes to that, though he may be a kind indulgent one, letting me be unmolested in my religion, consenting to all I should have to ask, as he would do, of course, caring so little about it himself?' But then suddenly there came up out of its hiding-place in her heart the old fear, the terrible scarcely-acknowledged fear that it *might* be otherwise—that haughty Stanley Graham, despising faith himself, understanding its existence so little, might not tolerate its practice in his wife—might refuse to grant the concessions without which she could not take him for her husband. The fear came so sharp and strong this time that Gerty fell on her knees almost in bodily pain.

'O God, anything but that; do not ask that sarifice from me! I cannot give him up if he loves me, my life, my *whole* happiness. If it be Thy will, keep that trial from me; or let me die if I should be too weak to bear it!'

Then with a vigorous effort she drove away the terrible vision, and prayed on more quietly that she might never be led into sin by any temptation, however strong; that the future might be made easy for her; that even the light of faith, whether through her poor means or not, might be vouchsafed to Stanley Graham.

'He was baptised in his infancy—I know that much—

K

Julia told me,' she said to herself, as she rose and began to undress. 'If it was rightly done, he is a Christian, without knowing or caring about it; he has at least the grace of baptism, which may work some good for him some day.' And cheered and consoled, she succeeded entirely in hiding that terrible fear away again out of sight and acknowledgment.

A few days before they left Beachdown, Gerty had received a letter from Nethercotes from Lady Hunter, a chatty, affectionate letter, full of kind inquiries for herself, and telling her that she and Sir Robert were looking forward to her promised visit.

'We are always talking about you, Gerty,' she wrote, 'and saying that when you are here we will do so and so, or go such and such a ride or drive. Your papa is quite used to the idea by this time, of course, that I am going to steal you again for a fortnight so soon? By the bye, I must tell you that I heard from Stanley Graham yesterday morning. He has arrived in Nice, and found his uncle very much aged even since he last saw him, so that he will not be able to get away at all under the promised three months. He asks after you, and desires to be very kindly remembered, and says I must tell you he is looking forward with great pleasure to meeting you at Nethercotes. So, dear, with so many looking out for you, you must not on any account dream of disappointing us;' and with a few more affectionate words her ladyship concluded.

Gerty stood reading her letter close to the window, with her back to her father, so that he could not see the colour that rose to her face, while her heart beat with the rapture called up by even that slight message from her heart's idol. She was very much relieved that her cousin said nothing more pointed or particular about Stanley Graham—nothing more, after all, than might have been said of any gentleman of whom Gerty had seen a good deal in London—because it would have looked strange and unkind to her father not to have read her cousin's letter to him. So turning round, as soon as she felt calm enough, she said with a smile, 'Shall I read it to you, papa? It is from Julia.' And at once she read it through aloud, controlling herself with a strong effort when she came to the message from Stanley Graham, so as to read it, if possible, in as ordinary a tone as the rest. Perhaps she did not wholly succeed; perhaps the mention of herself and the message, slight as they were, aroused a vague far-off idea of the truth in Mr. Mannering's mind for the first time; for though he listened quietly, without remark, the cloud settled oftener on his brow from that hour, the anxiety was more constant and definite in his heart.

He concealed it from Gerty, wishing to spare her any additional pain to that she was perhaps already enduring; but one day, now that they were at home again, he opened his mind to Father Walmsley and told him the fear that was troubling him.

'I don't know why I connect the change I fancy I see in her with this Mr. Graham, Father Walmsley,' he said. 'I did not do so until that last letter from Lady Hunter, but something or other has made me do so ever since; perhaps because she speaks of him so little, though we know she saw him constantly in London. I would not for worlds she guessed that I suspect anything of the kind; and if she has given you her confidence, Father Walmsley, I am content to know nothing until she chooses.'

'She has told me nothing, Mr. Mannering; given me no confidence,' replied the priest rather sadly. 'I may even tell you now that I have noticed she avoids me as much as possible, and has done so since her return.

God grant she may not be in any trouble, poor child, and that we may prove to be mistaken! Mind, I do not fear for an instant that there can be anything *wrong* or even anything *settled* of any kind; I trust I know Gerty too well to suspect her of having been led into any decided engagement that she would conceal from you; but if it will be any satisfaction to you, Mr. Mannering, I will try to gain her confidence, or at least find that we are mistaken altogether.'

Father Walmsley was right: even Gerty herself was conscious he must see that she almost avoided him, that she was no longer child-like and open with him, as of old. She had gone to confession a day or two after her return home, devoutly and sincerely, though scarcely so easily as ever, but that was all; she had spoken only of what was necessary, and had evidently shrunk from any further questioning from Father Walmsley, kind and friendly as it was meant to be. It had been the same when she went again, when she and her father returned home together from Beachdown; so that the good priest had resolved to leave her to herself for a time and to make no further efforts to gain her confidence; but only to pray more earnestly than ever to our Lady to take care herself of her child and preserve her from harm.

But now that Mr. Mannering had so spoken to him, he brought himself to try once more to speak to Gerty, a day or two later, as he came into the church vestry and found her there arranging flowers for the evening's Benediction. When they had talked a few minutes, he added very earnestly:

'Gerty, there is nothing ails you, is there, my child? You are paler and quieter ever since you came home, and I am afraid sometimes there may be something, some little care or trouble, you have not liked to tell me—something you would like to ask me about, if you could once begin? Am I mistaken, Gerty? is it all my fancy?' and he smiled very, very kindly.

Gerty bent for a minute or two over her flowers, but not so as to hide her deep blush from her old friend, and during that brief minute a painful struggle went on in her heart. *Could* she tell all to Father Walmsley; ought she to do so, perhaps; would it not be easy after this kind invitation? O, no, no, not yet; she could not speak of her love while still it was unasked, while yet no open promise existed between her and its object. Was there, too, a fear in her mind as to what Father Walmsley might say if he heard what manner of man it was to whom she had given her heart (and she must tell *all* or nothing)? was there a vague fear that he might even advise her not to go to Nethercotes, as she had promised—not yet at least? And this she knew she could not consent to—to break her promise, given almost solemnly to Stanley Graham in that parting minute—given to him whose affianced wife she *might* have been now but for that journey abroad which he could not escape.

'Would it not look like coqueting with him to stay away without some good reason? No, no, I cannot tell even Father Walmsley yet; even poor papa will have to wonder on a little longer, if he *does* wonder.' And stifling a sigh, she said aloud, but still bending over her flowers:

'There is nothing, indeed, Father Walmsley, that—I want to tell you, at least—that—that I can tell you yet. You don't think I would keep anything *wrong* from you, Father Walmsley?' and the painful colour rose again.

'No, no, my child, nothing *wrong;* how could I? Don't I know you better than that, Gerty? Wel if there is nothing you wish to say to me, I ask no more, of course; but you know where you have a friend if ever you want one, my child. May God bless you and take care of you always!' and he was leaving her, convinced now that Gerty had a secret from him and her father, something they must not seek yet for her to tell them.

'O Father Walmsley, don't think me ungrateful,— *don't*, whatever you do, whatever I may seem just now!' and she went after him with the tears in her eyes.

'I never shall, Gerty; I promise always to trust you, the descendant of martyrs and confessors, you know, my child.' And with a world of kind counsel hidden under the smiling words, he left her; and when he next saw her father, he told him that he was afraid there *was* some hidden care, some secret in Gerty's heart, but that they must not seek yet to know it; that they must trust her to God and her disposition to respond to His helping grace; that they must grow accustomed to the painful knowledge, if need be, that the bright careless child who had left them had come back a woman.

And a day or two after that interview with Father Walmsley, Gerty wrote to the Convent, to her dear Sister Teresa, to announce the postponement of her promised visit.

'I shall be *sure* to come to you sometime, sister, when I come back from Nethercotes, and when Rupert has been to see us, even if I have to come in Lent. I am *so* sorry I shall have to be so long without seeing you; but you understand how it is, that I don't like to leave papa, even for a day, before I go to my cousin's. Will you promise to pray for me when I am there, sister, very, very hard? I *may* need your prayers very much, though I cannot yet tell you why—though I perhaps hardly know myself; at least they will do no harm to

'Your ever-loving child,
'GERTY MARY MANNERING,
'*Enfant de Marie.*'

CHAPTER XV.

CHRISTMAS had come round at last; the weary, anxious three months were over for Gerty, and she was to go to Nethercotes the day after Christmas-day. That day itself she would not spend away from her father, though Lady Hunter had wished her very much to be with them for it.

'I could not leave papa, you know, Julia, on Christmas-day,' she had written. 'Besides, as you are so far from a Catholic church, I should be out for two or three hours when I went out to Mass, and you would not like that, so it is better to wait, isn't it?'

And so to-day, Christmas-day, Gerty and her father were alone together before their temporary separation. Father Walmsley had gone home with them to dinner after the afternoon's Benediction, and then towards evening left them, guessing they would perhaps prefer to spend the last evening quite alone.

'God bless you, my child,' he had said to Gerty as he bade her good-bye, 'and send you back to us safe and well;' and Gerty responded to his kind smile with a grateful eloquent look, though her heart was too full just then to let her speak.

Since that day on which the good priest had vainly sought her confidence, the subject had never been renewed between them; and there had grown up a kind of barrier, of respectful reserve on her part, and on his a scrupulous avoidance of anything like questioning her beyond what he was strictly obliged to do, but without any change otherwise in the old, kind, fatherly manner, and with a still more earnest recommendation of her every day to God. And even between her and her father there seemed to be a kind of tacit acknowledgment that something existed which could not be spoken of between them; for Gerty could not but see at times her father's anxiety about herself, any more than she could help often breaking down in the effort to be her old bright self, and go about all the old duties and occupations in her once free light-hearted manner as though she had no thought beyond. But outwardly all was unchanged: the old life was still going on, the very feeling that all was *not* the same seeming to have confirmed that still greater tenderness in Gerty's manner to her father and her every little attention to his wishes.

They had been at the midnight Mass together, and then out again to Communion; and on their return Gerty found a letter awaiting her from Lady Hunter, telling her how they were longing to welcome her at Nethercotes.

'The house is quite full now; all our visitors have arrived but yourself,' wrote her ladyship. 'Stanley Graham got here two days since, straight from the Continent, having only been home to Briardale for an hour or two on the way. He is looking very well, and I have made him promise to stay with us at least a fortnight or three weeks.' And Gerty had read the letter to her father as usual, confirming afresh the suspicion now settled in his heart.

She played and sang for him and talked to him by turns, as they sat together all the evening after Father Walmsley had gone, the sadness in their manner growing more evident to each other as the hour drew near for saying good-night.

When it came, Mr. Mannering held Gerty long and closely in his embrace with a silent eloquence.

'You won't be *too* lonely without me, papa?' she said. 'It is only for a fortnight;' but she nearly broke down as she spoke.

'That's all, Gerty; only a fortnight,' he said, smiling cheerily. 'And now it is really time for you to be in bed, little girl, with a journey before you in the morning, and all the gaieties of Nethercotes;' and he let her go, but she turned back for a minute to whisper, as if with an irresistible impulse:

'Papa, nothing would ever make you think—make you afraid, I mean,—that I could ever love you any less, could it, papa?'

'Afraid that my child could ever care any less for her old father! Never, Sunbeam. But why do you think of such a thing?'

'I don't know, papa; I can't tell; but going away, leaving you again so soon, makes me—sad, somehow.'

'Never be sad for me, Gerty. Don't you think it makes me happy to see you going away when it is to enjoy yourself, as it is now?' And he smiled again, hiding the aching fear of coming sorrow and separation in his heart—hiding it until Gerty was safe out of sight, until she had gone up-stairs, not to sleep just yet, but to lie awake in trembling but delicious joy at the thought of the morrow—joy which still was mixed with a vague foreboding of pain and sorrow.

Nethercotes was but little more than an hour's journey from Whitewell, so Gerty travelled alone, sitting quietly in a corner of the railway carriage, trying to hide from her fellow-passengers the tears which fell for some minutes after the parting with her father. 'When

I see him again, when I come back, how will it be with me?' she kept asking herself, her heart beating painfully and wonderingly as each minute bore her on nearer to the crisis in her life. She felt in a kind of dream when she got out at the station nearest Nethercotes and found Lady Hunter's carriage waiting for her, with her ladyship's own maid to meet her and look after her luggage.

'Lady Hunter would have come herself, Miss Mannering,' the young woman said to Gerty, 'but she took a little cold last night, and thought it best to stay indoors all to-day, as it is so cold.'

'Of course, Roberts; I am glad she has not come.' And Gerty was glad for other reasons too, for she was thankful to be alone during the three miles' drive to Nethercotes; thankful to be able to be silent and try to realise where she was, *whom* she was about to meet again after the long waiting and yearning; to try and realise all that meeting might bring forth—that she was, perhaps, about to be called on to take the step which must decide her fate for life.

'And only a year ago I was just leaving the Convent, thinking of nothing but being so sorry to leave them all, and so very, very happy to be going home at last to be always with papa. Am I going to leave him already? shall I want to do so if—I am asked?' And though the girlish heart almost shrank with a kind of fear from what might be coming—the new untried existence—it yet answered quickly, 'Ah, yes, yes, if *he* asks me; wouldn't I go to the world's end, content to lose *all* else, all I love so dearly, if only *he* asked me?'

She roused herself with a start as they reached Nethercotes and entered the park, whose extent and beauty Gerty could see even on this gloomy wintry day.

'I should like to see it in summer,' she said to herself, trying to throw off her deep preoccupation, and to bring a smile to her face ere they reached the house, which now appeared in sight—a splendid, quite modern edifice, which Gerty knew had been built by the present baronet, Sir Robert, before his marriage.

'How different from our old Grange!' was her thought as she ran up the steps and through the pillared entrance into the warm luxurious-looking hall, where her cousin met her with a hearty kiss and a close embrace.

'Welcome, love, at last, to Nethercotes,' she said, with her sweet smile; 'I was getting quite impatient listening for the carriage. Why, you're as cold as an icicle, and trembling like a leaf; but no wonder, on such a day. So we'll go up at once to my little sanctum, and as soon as you have thrown off your wraps, we will have some tea sent up, and you shall thaw before the fire for a good hour before we need begin to dress for dinner. Nearly everybody is out but myself. Sir Robert and all the men are gone to the Haverstock Meet, and most of the ladies too; so we shall be quite unmolested until we have had a good chat and a long look again at each other.'

The very sound of her cousin's voice was like the first return to the life of bewildering joy which had been hers for that brief space in London, lifting away, as it were with a magic power, the restraint and pain of the past three months, making the pent-up heart expand again under its influence. She laughed gaily in reply to the hearty welcome, and putting her arm affectionately in her cousin's, let her lead her up-stairs.

'I'm a perfect bundle of furs and things, Julia,' she laughed; 'but poor papa would not be satisfied till I promised to keep them all on.'

'Of course he wouldn't, you little goose; but I'll

release you now.' And Lady Hunter led Gerty into a perfect little gem of a room, her own special sanctum, furnished with every imaginable comfort and elegance.

This is better than London, love, isn't it?' And when Gerty was freed from her hat and wraps, she made her sit closer to the fire on a low stool, and then rang for some tea.

'Now,' she said, when it came, 'for a regular good gossip over it like two old maids. Now begin to tell me everything—how your papa is; and Rupert, poor boy (don't be vexed, Gerty); and what you've been doing ever since, buried away at Whitewell; and why you are not looking so rosy as you ought to do after such a long rest in the country, away from my worldly society.'

Gerty was beginning laughingly to reply to the shower of questions, when Lady Hunter interrupted her:

'But I forgot love; I must tell you that some one is decidedly impatient to see my little country girl again, and was quite inclined to be dreadfully disappointed at not finding her here on his arrival, until I mollified his imperial highness by assuring him she would be here to-day—that he would only have to wait until dinner-time this evening. I believe he only went to the Meet to-day to make the time pass more quickly, for he does not care about hunting, though he is such a splendid rider.' And though her ladyship spoke laughingly, and apparently in jest, as she had often done latterly in London, the tell-tale colour rose to Gerty's face, while her heart beat so fast as almost to suffocate her.

But she tried to laugh carelessly, and began at once to talk of other things, unconscious that Lady Hunter had not spoken merely for the love of idle teasing, but to satisfy herself whether her young cousin's heart was unchanged, as she suspected,—whether the event which she hoped, and yet somehow dreaded, might be looked for soon to take place here at Nethercotes; and also, too, with the kindly wish to reassure Gerty herself about Stanley Graham's own evident sentiments before she should meet him again that evening.

CHAPTER XVI.

Two hours later Gerty was dressed for dinner, ready to go down-stairs, but lingering yet a few minutes, as though dreading what was coming, trying in vain to subdue her heart's beating and to look calm and unperturbed. Then, almost unconsciously, she took one look at the glass, which she had nearly forgotten to do at all during her dressing, one look at the bright sweet face, and then, becoming aware of *why* she did so, turned quickly away, and without delaying further went downstairs.

Stanley Graham was not yet in the drawing-room. Gerty saw that at once, or felt it rather, almost before her quick eager glance went round the room, and she sighed, almost in relief, that the meeting was deferred yet a few minutes longer. She sat down next to a lady to whom her cousin introduced her, and who at once began to talk pleasantly to her, though Gerty somehow could not always listen or answer so attentively, perhaps, as politeness might have demanded.

The door opened again at last, and looking up, Gerty saw that it was Stanley Graham who entered. Again her eyes rested on the noble face which had haunted her ever, even in her dreams, since she had last beheld it; she looked once more, after her weary longing, on him who was all her world now, the object of her fresh young heart's passionate idolatry, for whose sake she had been content for the past three months to be, as it were, alienated, at least in part, from her dear tender father. Her heart beat so fast now that she clasped her hands together upon it for a minute, quickly and convulsively, and then sat quite still, watching the one figure—from whose sight she was hidden as she sat. Was *he* feeling it all as she was? was it of her he was thinking now as he entered the room, or was it a blissful dream which the next few minutes might dispel? He stood for a while near the door, detained in talk by two or three gentlemen; but Gerty saw his gaze wander restlessly about the room until at last it reached her corner and their eyes met. Then the pale proud face softened, as if by magic, into the attractive smile Gerty knew so well—the smile which had stolen its way to her heart almost before she had exchanged a sentence with him on the first night of their acquaintance. She saw him speak some excuse to his companions, and then at once he crossed the room straight to where she sat, caring not who saw or remarked the pointed action.

'I am *very* glad to see you, Miss Mannering. You are quite well, I hope?' And the darkness and shadowy doubt were lifted away from Gerty's heart as her hand rested in Stanley Graham's fervent grasp, as the music of his voice sounded in her ears again with an eloquence which depended not on the outward polite conventional words.

'I am quite well, Mr. Graham, thank you; I hope you are so too.' And though she tried to speak calmly, the rosy colour overspread her face as she raised her eyes to his—the sweet eyes for whose gaze proud Stanley Graham had been yearning every day and hour, though she knew it not.

'Quite *well*, thank you, but very tired and weary at last of being abroad—very thankful and rejoicing to be back again in England.' And again the earnest tender gaze rested upon Gerty, charming her back wholly into the paradise from which she had been excluded during the past weary months.

Stanley was about to take a seat again by her side, which her lady companion had kindly vacated, seeing that they appeared old acquaintances, when the dinner-bell sounded, and he was obliged to leave her to escort the lady allotted to him, while Gerty fell to the share of a nephew of Sir Robert's, whom Lady Hunter brought to introduce to her.

'I am very sorry, love, to interrupt you,' she managed to whisper quietly to Gerty; 'but you understand; it cannot be helped.' And Gerty was borne away by her new companion. She could hardly have told how she got through the dinner, or what she talked about to her companion, who was a pleasant amiable young man, bent on making himself agreeable; for he had been admiring Gerty ever since she had entered the drawing-room, and was perhaps disappointed to find that she was hardly so sweet and bewitching as he had told himself the owner of that bright face must prove on acquaintance. Poor Gerty, all unconscious of his thoughts, was but exerting herself not to appear unkind or stupid, wondering the while how long it would be before the dinner was over, and Stanley Graham free to come to her side once more, free to let her worshipping heart once more rejoice in the close presence of its idol.

Lady Hunter rose at last, and as Gerty followed her with the rest of the ladies, she caught Stanley Graham's smile fixed on her for a moment as she passed out of the room.

'Now, Gerty, I want to introduce you to everybody, at least to all the ladies,' said Lady Hunter as they re-

L

entered the drawing-room; 'there was hardly time before dinner.' And taking Gerty's arm affectionately, she introduced her to the company with evident pride and pleasure — two or three among them claiming Gerty's acquaintance already, having known her during her stay in London.

'Stanley Graham found a minute before dinner to speak to you, didn't he, love?' her ladyship asked in a low tone as she and Gerty stood apart before the fire, when they had spoken to every one.

'Yes, we spoke just for a minute or two, Julia,' replied Gerty, looking into the fire, away from her cousin's face.

'That's right. I was afraid you had done no more than shake hands when I was obliged to come and interrupt you. But talk of a person and he appears,' she added as the door opened and Stanley Graham entered alone.

'That's a good fellow!' she said as she went to meet him. 'I wish you could manage to indoctrinate a few more gentlemen with your dislike to the barbarous English custom of sending away the ladies, to stay behind deliberately to drink far too much wine;' and her ladyship laughed gaily, knowing the while in her heart that it was not Stanley's dislike to the custom that had alone brought him so soon into their company this evening.

Until some more of the gentlemen came in he stood on the hearthrug with Lady Hunter, talking to her; but his attention was really given to Gerty, who had taken a seat on a sofa near, where she sat silently, meeting his smile whenever she looked up.

'Well, and how do you think Gerty is looking, Stanley?' her ladyship asked now, turning round to her as she spoke. 'You see she has turned up safe and sound, as I promised you, but hardly looking so well, *I* think, as she should do after such a long rest at home.'

Perhaps Stanley, with his quick observation, saw that the last remark, laughing and kindly as it was, embarrassed Gerty; for he said at once, going nearer to her:

'She *says* she is quite well, Lady Hunter; mustn't we believe her?'

'O, if you are going to elect yourself her champion against me, I'll leave you, I think, Stanley;' and she moved away with a smile, seeing that the rest of the gentlemen were coming in, and that it would no longer excite remark if Stanley were left to devote himself as exclusively as he liked to Gerty.

'Miss Mannering,' he said as he took a seat by her side, 'you made me a promise, when we parted in London, to be glad to see me when we should meet again here. You have not told me yet whether your promise is kept—whether you *are* glad to see me. Let me hear you say so, Miss Mannering;' and the proud lips parted in that sweet smile as the piercing gray eyes looked at her with the tender pleading which for the time took away every trace of sternness from his face.

Gerty looked up with a smile too, her heart beating now with such an exquisite bliss, such a certainty of hope, that to have gone on in it for ever would have seemed enough—to have gone on through eternity with no greater joy would have seemed heaven just then to the poor little heart in its idolatry.

'I *am* glad to see you, Mr. Graham; very glad, if you like that better,' she said, with a shy trembling in her voice, but with the old confidence coming back to her as she grew accustomed once more to his presence.

'Thank you; now I am satisfied,' he replied in a tone that again spoke volumes to the happy listener. 'I wonder if the last three months have passed as slowly with you, Miss Mannering, as they have with me. Hardly, with a home and father loved like yours. If you knew how long the time has been to me!'

Gerty could not tell him what those past months had been like for her—of their weary yearnings, their doubt and care; of the tacit alienation they had wrought between her and those so dear to her; she could not tell him that the beloved home of which he spoke could never be the same to her again. She could only smile and turn aside to try to hide her deep blush from her companion, who saw it, however, and began to talk to her freely on all subjects, as he had been wont to do in London, drawing her on to do the same, until every vestige of timidity vanished, and she was charming him again with the merry artlessness to which she abandoned herself in her joy, with no effort in it now, as there had been in it so often, nay always, latterly at home. She asked Stanley all about his stay in Nice, listening to every little detail, even about his old invalid uncle, with an interest which would have amused him had it not been so very sweet and precious to his proud heart.

'After all, you must have been very quiet and lonely sometimes too, Mr. Graham. No wonder the time seemed so long,' she said simply, and then blushing again at her own last remark.

But Stanley only laughed kindly.

'Yes, I was very lonely sometimes, quite home-sick, I assure you; and I feel yet like a schoolboy home for the holidays after it. You should have been with us yesterday, Miss Mannering. Lady Hunter was lamenting your absence nearly all day. But you scarcely liked to be away from home on Christmas-day, I suppose?'

'O, no, I could not have left papa alone, you know, for anything. I feel cruel enough at having left him at all, though he will never let me say so;' and Stanley thought he saw her lips quiver slightly as a sad shadow passed over the bright face. 'We always go together to midnight Mass, you know, and two or three times to church again afterwards during the day;' and she spoke with gentle instinctive hesitation now. 'It would not seem like Christmas-day to papa if we were not together for all that, all those—duties, you know, Mr. Graham.'

Gerty did not look up quickly enough to see the shade that crossed her companion's face—the frown, half painful, half perplexed, that contracted the perfect features, marring their beauty for an instant, but which was changed for a smile, tender though somewhat sad, Gerty thought, when she raised her eyes to meet it, and which was all the reply he made to her last observation. Perhaps for a brief space there arose within her a wish that he *had* replied more freely and sympathetically, as he did to her every other slightest remark; perhaps that deep buried fear, forgotten for the last happy hour or two, strove to assert its existence, but only for an instant; both wonder and fear were quickly driven away again, drowned by the inner joyous song that seemed sounding in her heart.

They had talked for some time, heedless of observation, when Stanley was forced to tear himself away by some of the gentlemen who evidently thought he had devoted himself already too long to 'Lady Hunter's cousin, pretty and fascinating as she was; so that for the rest of the evening Gerty was fain to be content with watching him when she could do so unnoticed; regarding the noble graceful figure as it moved about the room, every other looking so inferior—even that of dear old Sir Robert himself—to that of her 'knight,' her beau ideal of some chivalrous crusader of old; content to watch him as he talked to others with his own forcible eloquence, he who had been happy in talking so long and so absorbingly to her simple little self.

But when the evening came to an end, then Stanley Graham made his way again to Gerty, for an earnest 'good-night,' a tender pressure of the hand, more tender still than she had yet known.

'Miss Mannering,' he said, as he lingered a minute by her side, 'Lady Hunter tells me she wants to take us all a very favourite walk of hers in the morning, if this clear weather continues,—to a celebrated cavern which it is orthodox always to visit when staying at Nethercotes;' and he smiled as he paused a minute. 'Will you let me be your companion during the walk? I have been so often that I am a safe guide, you see. May I look on it as an engagement that you take me for your escort, Miss Mannering?' and though he smiled again, there was an earnestness in his eyes and in his tone that made Gerty's heart beat strangely.

'Certainly, Mr. Graham; you are very kind; I shall be very glad,' she found voice to reply.

'Thank you, Miss Mannering; you will not forget. Good-night;' and he released her hand at last from his lingering grasp and was gone.

CHAPTER XVII.

It was late when Gerty awoke next morning, for she had lain awake for hours during the night, unable to calm her trembling yet delicious joy; and as she rose quickly, she saw that the day was bright and frosty, just what was wanted for the intended walk. Then, as she knelt at her prayers, ere she rose from her knees, she murmured almost aloud, from the very depths of her heart:

'My God, if it is to be as I hope, make me worthy of so much happiness; let me be the means, if it is Thy will, of his coming to know and love Thee and Thy holy Church!'

During breakfast she was not near Stanley Graham, but he found a minute to shake hands and wish her good-morning, with an earnest look which she felt was a tacit reminder of her promise. Then she was borne off by her cousin and two or three of the other ladies to Lady Hunter's boudoir, where they stayed chatting until it was time to dress for the walk, for those who wished to go.

'Come down to the hall when you're ready, Gerty; we will wait for you there,' her cousin said to her. 'I fancy most of the gentlemen are gone on already, and we shall pick them up on the way and make them escort us.'

Gerty dressed quickly, wondering where Stanley Graham was; whether he had gone on too, or whether she should find him down-stairs waiting for her. She went down to the hall, which she found empty; but in another minute Lady Hunter came down with her friends to claim Gerty as she had promised.

'What, Gerty, all alone, after all! I almost expected to find you carried off; but as no one has taken possession of you yet, you shall honour us, love, at least till we join the rest.'

What could Gerty do? She could not for worlds say to her cousin, especially before these friends, whom she knew but slightly, 'I have promised Stanley Graham to go with him.' She could not for worlds, since he had not appeared to claim her promise; so with a smile she went out with Lady Hunter and the rest, trying to laugh and join in the conversation as well as she could. They soon overtook another party, amongst whom was the young man who had been her companion during the previous night's dinner, and who now at once joined her for another attempt to make her respond to his efforts to be agreeable. They had not gone much further when Gerty heard footsteps approaching quickly behind them, and in another minute Stanley Graham was at her side. She looked up and met his gaze fixed on her with that expression she had seen on his face before, but never there for *her* until now—the cold stern look she had more than once asked herself how she could bear, if it should ever greet her. Her talkative companion's attention was for the minute engaged with one of the party a step or two in advance, so that he did not hear Stanley's curt question:

'Have you forgotten your promise, Miss Mannering, or repented it, perhaps?' And as the polite freezing tone echoed in poor Gerty's ears, somehow, she knew not why, that terrible hidden fear rose again in her heart—the fear that the future might not be all so smooth and easy as she prayed for—the dread that this haughty scorner of religion, to whom she had given up her heart so entirely, might not grant all she must ask without a struggle.

'I have not forgotten it, Mr. Graham, and I am very sorry to seem rude,' she said gently, but with pain ringing in every word; 'but I did not see you anywhere, so that I thought you might have gone on; and when my cousin asked me to come with her and the rest, I—I did not like to refuse.'

Before he could reply, Lady Hunter turned round.

'O, you're here, Stanley; but whatever are you looking so savage at Gerty for?' and she lingered behind with them a minute, speaking half in jest, half in earnest. 'She looks scared to death, the child!'

'I promised Mr. Graham—to go with him, Julia;' and Gerty tried to smile.

At once Lady Hunter saw the state of affairs.

'Ah, I see; and while he was searching for you, we carried you off; so now his highness is quarrelling with you for not waiting for him like patience on a monument. Well, Stanley, please to be reasonable and blame the real culprit, which is myself; and don't quite frighten Gerty away from us altogether, back to Whitewell; but apologise to her as well as you can. His favourite route to the cavern, Gerty, is by that other road turning off there; so if you are not afraid of him after his savage behaviour, I daresay he will guide you safely, and we shall meet you there;' and with her kindly laugh, she left them and hastened after her companions.

'Miss Mannering, will you forgive me?' and at the tender tone, and the still more tender gaze of repentance which greeted her, the tears sprang to Gerty's eyes.

'If there *is* anything to forgive, Mr. Graham,' she faltered; 'but there is not. I *must* have appeared rude and forgetful.'

'Please do not say so, Miss Mannering. *I* was the one to blame, in expecting you to know that I was looking for you—in expecting you to tell your cousin of our engagement. I was a brute to speak to you like that.' And as the bitter tone of self-reproach sounded in her ears, even while it distressed her, it sent back all the sweet joy and hope into her heart.

'O, *do* not think so much of it, Mr. Graham; indeed *I* do not.'

'You see, I have been a restless untamed wanderer so long that I have grown irritable and morose, I am afraid, and want some kindly angel to calm and refine me. There have not been wanting those who would have made the attempt, but until now I never wished or asked for any one to do so, Miss Mannering. I wonder if I have frightened you from listening to me any further—from listening to what I have been wanting to say to you ever since we parted—longing with an impatience which would perhaps make you think even still more indulgently of the cruel way in which I spoke my disappointment just now;' and his voice obviously trembled. Gerty was trembling so that she could not even turn to look towards him, and no one being in sight, Stanley stopped short in his walk and stood before her.

'Will you hear me, Gerty—if I may call you so, if you do not forbid me?' And though she did not speak, she let him take her hand, and did not draw it away from the fervent grasp as they stood there for a minute on the quiet lonely road. Then as they went slowly on, with no human creature to see them, and no sound to break the clear frosty air but the sighing of the wind now and then through the bare leafless trees, Gerty listened to the old sweet story—the story of which no one is ever tired, though men and women have been telling it and listening to it ever since the world began. As one in a blissful dream, she listened to the tale of love from Stanley Graham's lips; she heard how he had loved her from that first night of their acquaintance, though just for a brief space he had himself almost refused to believe it—he who had thought himself so calm and cold, so insensible to love's sweet charm.

'If you knew, Gerty, what it was to me to have to part as we did, without any definite word or sign of what was burning in my heart, because, going away as I was, I did not wish to draw you into a hasty engagement —even should you prove to be willing—for which your friends might have blamed me. And then too, Gerty, though I *hoped* my feeling was returned, though I thought I was not unacceptable to you, still I was not sure. You were very young, I knew, and fresh to the world; you might be mistaking regard for me, for one who had shown you attention, for real love; and after a struggle with myself I resolved to spare you the risk of such a painful discovery as in that case would have awaited you. I resolved to go away with my love untold, knowing that if it were returned at all by a heart like yours, Gerty, I should find it unchanged and confirmed when I asked for it on my return; that at least you could make no mistake now, that time would have saved you from that. Forgive me if I have been cruel, Gerty; if I misjudged you, if I have seemed neglectful, if I might have gone away with the sweet assurance of one day calling you my wife.' And he stopped again and once more took her unresisting hand; and read his answer in the beautiful eyes raised to his face—eyes in which the happy tears were glistening. He took her in his arms, there on the lonely road, and took his first kiss from her lips as he whispered,

'My darling, if you can, tell me that even then you knew you loved me; let me hear my name from your lips as I have longed to do so often.'

'Stanley,' she murmured, lingering on the name she spoke thus familiarly for the first time, ' I—think—I did; nay, I am sure.' And she looked up again with that sweet joyful smile.

'Gerty, if you knew what it is to me to hear you tell me this, how sweet and precious—if you knew how I have longed for you all these weary months!'

'And if you knew, Stanley, how like a dream it all seems to me, a delicious dream, and how afraid I am of waking from it!' And the love-light sparkled in her eyes, the inward bliss rang out in every word, so sweet to the world-weary listener.

'You never shall wake then, Gerty; never, while you love me, while you trust your happiness to me, my darling!'

Ah, how sweet the endearing word was from his lips! how delicious to the fond little idolatress, the tender term which, in all his life before, haughty Stanley had never spoken to any other creature! What wonder if Gerty revelled with an entire abandonment in the blissful present, giving herself up to it with a joy which was ample compensation for the past weary doubt and pain! What wonder if she drove away the warning whisper that strove to make itself heard—if she turned away from the 'still small voice' as yet, the voice of conscience, which bade her speak even now, thus early, of the one subject—the religion which he despised—to the proud man of whom she was making a god in her heart, who was to be the master of her life from henceforth!

'Not now, not to-day,' she said to herself. 'Let me be *wholly* happy to-day. To-morrow, before I write to papa, I will speak of it and settle it all—obtain all I must ask. He has been so generous, so thoughtful for *me*, I cannot speak to-day of what may give him a minute's pain or annoyance.'

'How good you have been, Stanley, how thoughtful for me! May I be able to repay you, all through my life!' she said aloud.

'If there was anything to repay, you have more than done it already, Gerty. But I wonder if your dear father will not think I shall be everlastingly in his debt, when I have stolen away his precious little Sunbeam?'

'Ah, Julia has told you that is papa's name for me;' and a bright smile and blush rose to her face. 'How you will love him too, Stanley, when you know him!'

Then he went on to speak still more of her father, to tell her he never meant to steal her from him entirely; how, if she wished, he should be nearly always with them if he would; how he himself would be ready any time to go home with her to her dear old Grange to cheer that dear parent's loneliness; how, though he would wish to take her abroad as soon as they were married, they should only remain as long as she chose, until she grew home-sick; while Gerty wondered if she ever could grow home-sick with Stanley by her side—whether a desert would not seem a happy home with him to take care of her always. And so the time passed unheeded, as they walked on, seeing and hearing nothing but each other, until at a turn in the road Stanley halted suddenly.

'Gerty, I must really beg your pardon!' he exclaimed. 'I am so very sorry, but I have led you a mile or two past the turning to the cavern, and it is almost too late to go there now, unless you very much wish it.'

Gerty laughed merrily, a low joyous laugh,

'Are *you* very much disappointed, Stanley? Because if you are, I'm not a bit tired, and can walk as fast as you like back to the turning; but I don't think *I* care very particularly about the cavern to-day.' And she looked up with a bright merry mischief in her eyes which made Stanley imprison the little hand again as they stood there in their comic dismay, his proud heart throbbing with a strange joy as he gazed at her, the sweet treasure he had won to be his very own through life—the life which had been so weary and void before.

'You little gipsy, it is all your fault! But for this lucky turning, you would have charmed me on for miles further. Well, we must hasten back to Nethercotes now, if we want to be in time for luncheon, and not to have scouts sent out to search for us.'

'How my cousin will scold us for not turning up at the cavern!' And Gerty laughed so heartily at the prospect, that Stanley thought he could willingly endure a hundred scoldings, if he might hear that sweet innocent sound daily as a reward.

The rest of the party had all returned home when they reached Nethercotes, and they had to reply as well as they could to the laughter and playful reproaches which assailed them, by owning they had somehow lost the way; but they were spared a good deal by the fact of luncheon being quite ready, and having to sit down to it almost immediately. Perhaps Lady Hunter too said less than she might have done, seeing doubtless from Gerty's flushed happy face and the smile which softened Stanley's proud features what had happened—guessing, perhaps, what the rest could not yet be expected to do.

As they rose from table, Gerty, unobserved by the others, looked across at Stanley with a smile, and then whispered to her cousin:

'Julia, may I come to your sanctum with you alone for a few minutes? I want to speak to you.'

'Indeed you may, love. Come now at once, before any one else takes possession of us.' And they quietly left the room together.

As soon as they were safely shut in alone in the little boudoir, Gerty half sat, half knelt on the hearth-rug, looking with a sweet blush into Lady Hunter's face as she sat on a low seat by her side.

'Julia, what do you think I am going to tell you?' And the bright sparkling eyes looked away now into the fire. Lady Hunter took both the trembling little hands in her own, as she whispered,

'Is it really that, Gerty, which I have been hoping for,—that my little cousin is to be so very happy, that proud Stanley Graham has asked her to be his wife?' And as Gerty looked up again with another of those sweet blushes, her cousin took her in her arms and nearly smothered her with kisses.

'O Julia, I can hardly believe it yet, you know!' Gerty said at last. 'It seems almost too great happiness that it should be really true—that one like he is should care so much for poor little me.'

'And perhaps *he* is wondering why such a sweet little girl should care so much for a haughty individual like himself, you silly little idolatress.' And then Lady Hunter listened while Gerty whisperingly told her what had passed—how it had come about that, before they had parted from her many minutes that morning, Stanley Graham had told her the story of his deep tender love, and had won the confession of her own in return.

'Well, Gerty, my darling,' her cousin said, as she paused, 'you ought to be very, very happy. I could tell you, if I chose, of many a one who will envy you, almost to bitterness; not that Stanley ever in his life before gave any one any cause to *hope* even, for he is too honourable. *I* saw from the first, love, how it was going to be with him in *your* case, and forgive me if I guessed too where *your* heart was. Well, he will have a little wife who will not only love him with her whole soul, but who will appreciate and be proud of him too.' Then half laughingly, half in earnest, she added: 'I don't prophesy, love, that he will make quite such an easy husband as I possess; I don't think you will always get so much of your own way as I have always done, Gerty; for Stanley is peculiar, you know—terribly proud and stern sometimes—and his little wife will have to give in to him a great deal in exchange for the deep love and happiness he will lavish upon her. But you're not afraid, are you, love, though I am making out my favourite such a terrible tyrant?' And she laughed kindly, while yet she looked earnestly at Gerty, who laughed too now, merrily.

'Not a bit afraid, Julia! How could I ever be afraid of Stanley?' And she lingered fondly on the loved name. 'Shall I ever care for any will or pleasure but his? Sha'n't I always think his wishes the best, and make them mine?' But even as she spoke a strange chill struck at her heart, as again the warning voice whispered that there *might* be times when his will would clash with hers—when she must disobey his wishes if she would not forsake a nearer duty still than she would owe to him. But again it was driven away by the cheering thought: 'No, no; he will never be stern and harsh like that. If once he promises me all, I shall have no fear.'

'What news for your papa, Gerty darling! What ever will he say to losing his one little treasure? Perhaps blame me for it all! You will write to-day, love, of course, to tell him?' And Lady Hunter tried to appear not to notice the shadow which passed over Gerty's face as she replied,

'Not to-day, Julia; I will write to-morrow, such a long letter as it will have to be. You see he will have got my few lines this morning, telling him I am here all safe, so I would rather wait till to-morrow before I write again. I could hardly collect my thoughts so as to be able to tell him all about it to-day fully, as I want to do. Isn't it good of Stanley, Julia, to promise, without being asked, that I shall be so much with papa, or he with us?'

'But only what I could have told you he *would* promise, darling; for with all his pride and sternness, he will be very tender where he loves, Gerty. Well, I may go now and tell the happy news to Sir Robert, may I not, so that he may congratulate his little favourite as soon as possible? And I must find Stanley too at once, and congratulate *him* on having at last found such a dear little mistress for Briardale; for I am tired of waiting to visit there; and I shall get there soon now, Gerty, of course, with you to invite and entertain us.' And letting Gerty run away to her own room for a while, Lady Hunter went off on her errand.

If she could, if it had been possible, Gerty would have prolonged that day for ever—that blissful halcyon day. She would have let an end never come to the long delicious ride with Stanley in the afternoon, her first ride quite alone with him, so much better even in itself than the stately hemmed-in rides in London up and down Rotten Row, halting every now and then to talk, to hear him describe to her his beautiful country seat at Briardale, which he would grow to love again for her sake, because she would be its mistress. She would have let the evening too last for ever—the happy evening, which was so full of kind congratulations from everybody, best of all from dear old Sir Robert, when she overcame her nervousness at her cousin's request, and sang for them her sweet little songs, with Stanley standing close by her side with a fond pride of ownership. But it came to an end; it came to the parting 'good-night' with Stanley; to the hour when she was alone again in her room, free to pause and think, to rise from her dream of bliss and face the thought of the task which awaited her on the morrow— the speaking to her future husband of her religion, and all he must grant concerning it; and the writing to her father, that dear tender father, who must soon now be left lonely and solitary in the old home. And there arose before her the vision of the past happy life, the long years at the convent; there rose the vision of her kindly friend, Father Walmsley, with his pale saintly face, as his words again seemed to sound in her ears,

'I promise to trust you always, Gerty, descendant of martyrs and confessors as you are!'

And falling on her knees she prayed long and fervently for strength not to shrink or swerve an inch from the task awaiting her; not to delay another day without obtaining *all* she must ask from him to whom she was giving such a wealth of adoring love.

CHAPTER XVIII.

'STANLEY, before you go out, I want to speak to you —to say something. Can you come into the library for a few minutes?' And Gerty tried to smile brightly, to hide her agitation, as she made her request to Stanley as soon as breakfast was over next morning.

He was going to ride with Sir Robert into the town, on business upon which he had often accompanied him before in his visits to Nethercotes, and upon which he had promised to accompany him again before Gerty had arrived. The baronet had now wished to excuse him, knowing that they should be detained all day, only to return in time for dinner; but Gerty had insisted that he must not lose Stanley's company and advice just for her sake.

'I am not quite so selfish, Sir Robert,' she had said, 'and I am not going to fly away in Stanley's absence, you know;' and she had so requested Stanley to go that, much as he now grudged every hour not spent in her company, he could not be selfish when she was so generous.

So he and Sir Robert were to start about an hour after breakfast, and Gerty knew that she must get through her task before they left, if she wished her letter to her father to be ready for that day's post.

'*Can* I come to the library with you, Gerty? Do you think anything should prevent me, after that invitation?' and Stanley laughed with that gentle tenderness which so softened the beautiful features, stern as they were.

Gerty led the way to the library, where she knelt in her favourite attitude on the hearthrug, gazing into the fire, while Stanley stood leaning against the mantelpiece, looking down at her, little guessing how the heart was beating in that girlish frame.

'Well, and what is it, Gerty? No very dreadful secret, I hope, my darling?'

She looked up with a merry laugh.

'Are you afraid I am going to tell you I have committed a murder in my life, or done something else very dreadful, like a sensation novel? Do you know, Stanley, it is a good thing you are going out, or I should never get my letter written to papa, such a long one as it will be. I may invent all sorts of messages for you, may I not, Stanley? I may tell papa you will take me home, and get to know him and the dear old Grange?'

'May you? Nay, you *must*, dear; for I mean to take you home, whether you ask me or not; you might be stolen on the way, otherwise, Gerty. And I am impatient to know your father, darling,' he added earnestly.

'And how impatient he will be to know you, Stanley!' And Gerty rose from her lowly position and stood up by Stanley's side, placing one little hand gently on his arm. 'Stanley,' and her voice trembled audibly as her heart beat very fast, 'it won't—annoy you, it will not be a trouble to you—to have—a—Catholic for—your wife, will it?'

She was looking into the fire again now, and so did not see the painful expression which contracted Stanley's features ere he replied gently, taking both the little hands into his strong grasp:

'Why should I let it trouble me, Gerty? You cannot

help it; you were born a Catholic; you did not become one of yourself.'

The tone was gentle and tender, but something in the words chilled the beating heart strangely.

'Because, Stanley, I have—so much—to—to ask you about it before—I write, you know, to papa; so —much to say to you;' and as the sweet eyes looked up now with a half-frightened pleading, something made proud Stanley draw her still closer and hold the trembling hands still tighter in his own, though he said nothing.

'First of all, Stanley (and it may seem a strange unreasonable thing to you), when—when we are to be married, I cannot go at all to—a Protestant church for —the ceremony; I can—only be married by a priest in our own; and it may seem unreasonable to ask you—to consent.'

But Stanley only smiled.

'Don't look so frightened, my precious Gerty! There is no need. I think you know, my darling,' he added seriously, 'that I have pretty much the same opinion of all forms of religion, though naturally, perhaps, the most exacting—which is *yours*—is the most displeasing to me.' And for the first time Gerty listened to his sentiments openly expressed to herself. 'I will not conceal from you, Gerty, that the less of religious ceremony there is, the better I shall like it; but as merely a civil one would not satisfy you, then I would as soon be married according to *your* rite (it being legal now) as any other.' And though the haughty lips curled slightly, perhaps unconsciously, and though the godless words shocked, without surprising, the religious heart of the trembling little listener, still Stanley's gray eyes smiled kindly, and a sigh of relief escaped Gerty as he paused.

Was the dreaded task going to prove so easy, so much lighter than she had thought?

'And, Stanley,' she continued, looking up again with her own sweet earnest expression, 'afterwards, when I am—your wife, you will always—let me be just as I am now, a strict Catholic? You will not try to prevent me from—practising my religion, though—you —dislike it so, because you do not know and understand what it is, what faith is, Stanley?'

But even ere she paused, the pale face, as she looked at it, contracted with a strange expression, half stern, half painful, while the grasp which held her hands almost hurt them with its tightened pressure, though it helped her to stand firm in her agitation.

'Gerty,' he said, in a low tone, 'by *practising* your religion, tell me what you mean, what you expect.'

An unspoken prayer rose from the poor little heart ere she answered:

'I mean, Stanley, that—before I become your wife, I shall have to ask you to promise me solemnly that you will never prevent me from going to Mass; never ask me to go to service in any church which is not a Catholic church; that you will never prevent me keeping the holy-days and fast-days; that you will always let me go, as I do now, to—Confession and Communion.' And she trembled even still more on that last sweet sacred word, as though it were profaned by being spoken in those infidel ears.

'Gerty, listen to me!' And while the look on the proud features had deepened to one of terrible pain, the tone was of almost passionate remonstrance and entreaty. 'Thinking, feeling as I do, knowing as I *do*, the wretched system of superstition (forgive me, my darling, when I say it to you now at last) which has implanted all these ideas in your heart, which would enslave you still, alienating you from all independence and freedom, could I promise not to try to save you from it, to lead you by the gentlest influence to see it as I do? Gerty, could I see my wife, my one treasure, continue to frequent that—detested Confession, for instance, knowing each time I saw her go that she was seeking guidance and advice from another than her natural protector—from one who would tell her that her husband was a heretic, an infidel, and must be viewed and defied as such? Would our life be a happy one like that, Gerty?'

Gerty was very calm now, calm with the resignation of despair, as from before her eyes she saw fleeing the happy undisturbed future which she had fondly pictured, and rising in its stead the vision of strife and care, of daily, hourly endurance, which might be her lot as a wife. That he, her heart's idol, would *persist* in refusing what she asked, she would not believe; and his word of honour once given, all she would have to fear then would be his occasional estrangement and displeasure; and this she was ready to bear for his love, hoping to win him one day by her patient example, not only to continue grudgingly to allow *her* to practise her religion, but even to love it himself. But she tried to smile, as she looked into his face with that sweet pleading:

'O Stanley, how little you know! How terribly you are mistaken about it all—about God's holy Church altogether—to fancy that going to Confession—our consoling preparation, you know, Stanley, for receiving the still holier, greater Sacrament of—the—Holy Eucharist—to think that Confession could make a wife wish to alienate herself from her husband, or that in it she could be told to defy him! The only thing upon which I should be interrogated, in regard to which I should be *obliged* to disobey you, Stanley, would be in what I am asking you about now beforehand, if you should refuse to allow me to continue to practise my religion. In everything else I should be advised, nay, *bound* to defer to you; and though you might not know it, I should be a better wife to you, Stanley, for going to Confession; better a thousand times than if I gave it up to please you for the time, knowing as I *do* that I should be offending God and risking my soul by doing so. And I need never let it trouble or inconvenience you, my religion; I can practise it quietly, so that outwardly you shall hardly notice it. Why, Stanley,' and she tried to smile playfully, 'I have always been to Confession, all my life since I was seven years old, and it has not made me so very dreadful, you see. Perhaps, but for it, you might never have loved me, Stanley; I might not have been as pleasing to you as I am; I might not have had even as much good about me as I *do* possess, if it had not been for its holy influence, though you may not understand it yet, Stanley.'

Moved to the depths of his proud heart, but unyielding still, nay, more inflexible than ever in his hatred of the religion which shared his darling's heart with him, Stanley, still holding her hands in one of his, with the other drew her to his breast, encircling her with his arm.

'My darling owe anything to—to a practice like *that!* Want me to believe I could *ever* have known her and not loved her! You are what you are, Gerty, in *spite* of it, not *because* of it. Gerty, could you ask me to see you, my wife, the mother of my children, perhaps, practising a form of religion which you would know to be hateful to me, and in which *they* could have no part?'

With a sudden impulse, Gerty drew her hands from his grasp, and tried to free herself from his embrace, as she looked out again before her, with the colour rising painfully now to her otherwise pale despairing face.

'O Stanley, about that too I have to speak to you—even for that too I must ask, that if—there should be children, they may be like I am. I may not see them brought up otherwise than as Catholics.'

Stanley released her now, and stood with folded arms, looking down at her.

'See them brought up to despise and dread their father as a heretic; see them brought up in a superstition, or a religion if you will, which he knows to be degrading!' And the stern bitter look, which she had fondly thought never again to see there for *her*, greeted Gerty as she glanced up at his face.

She clasped her hands together tightly, as if for strength, and then spoke again in a low hoarse tone:

'Stanley, if what you call degrading superstition *I* know to be the holy practice of the one true faith, God's own religion, which He came on earth to teach, what kind of mother should I be (if I ever became one) to see my children grow up in ignorance or hatred of it, the one faith in which I believe souls can be saved? Would even you, Stanley,' she added more gently, 'wish to see them grow up godless, without religion—*you*, who are *naturally* honourable and good, which *they* might not be?'

And he saw her shudder, as he asked himself if this was really Gerty, whom he had thought so soft and yielding, ready to bow to his slightest wish.

But in that minute he loved her more than ever. Less than ever could he bear to lose her, though the struggle would be hard, he knew now, before he should conquer.

'Gerty, my own Gerty,' and his voice trembled now, 'they shall not be godless infidels, as I am; you shall teach them the religion of the *heart*, which is the only one required by God—the God even I believe in and understand, and whom you will learn to see as I do in time. And if at times you wish still for more, you shall go to church, Gerty, to the church at Briardale, the one which contented my mother always;' and he would have taken her hands again, but she gently resisted as she shook her head sadly.

'And that which you call religion of the heart, Stanley, we Catholics know to be *no* religion; for *you* have it even now. And the church at Briardale, which contented your mother, Stanley, because she knew of no better—had never heard, perhaps, anything but falsehood of the one true faith—it could not content *me*, a Catholic. I could not even enter it to join in its service, Stanley.'

He was about to reply, when a knock came to the door, and Lady Hunter entered; Gerty at once forcing her face into a smile, but turning round to the fire to hide her paleness.

'I thought I should find you here,' laughed her ladyship, 'having a farewell chat for the day. Sir Robert is ready, Stanley, and the horses are round; so if Gerty will let you go, it is time to start;' and with another kindly laugh she left them to their temporary adieux.

Then Stanley turned again to Gerty for a minute.

'Gerty, I am almost glad now that I shall be away for the day; for I know that when I return my darling will have seen it all as I do; that she will not force me to seem harsh and stern to her who is dearer to me than life, whose heart and thoughts I will share with no one and nothing, least of all with a cruel exacting religion.' And as Gerty stood motionless, powerless to resist, he pressed a lingering kiss on her lips, and was gone.

Like one in a dream, Gerty went to the window, and stood there until she had seen Sir Robert and Stanley ride away, and then went slowly up-stairs to her own room. But she did not stay there: it was as though she dare not pause to think any more yet, as though she must not be alone with her own thoughts. She could not even pray; she dare not allow to herself that there was any need for prayer, except for strength to be patient in the future, as the wife of the man who could be so stern and unbending yet so tender too, as she had found now with that bitter pain of heart—that worshipping heart, which still did not shrink from its idol, which yet did not fear to give itself into his keeping. That he could still continue to refuse what she asked, she *wholly* refused to believe, or *told* herself she did so.

'When I see him again this evening, when I make him understand that I cannot be his wife at all if he persists, that he must give me up if he will not grant me all, he will not oppose me any longer. He did not understand fully, I see now; and knowing so little of religion, of faith at all, as he does, of course I seemed unreasonable, and it made him speak sternly sometimes. But I can bear that, O, yes, even in the future, so long as he loves me, as I shall have to do, perhaps, even while he lets me do as I wish. But how *can* any one hate religion so, as he does?'

She took up some needlework and went down-stairs to the morning-room, where Lady Hunter and the rest of the ladies were sitting, and the sound of their voices was pleasant and cheerful in her half-numbed suspended state of feeling.

'How pale you are, Gerty love!' exclaimed her cousin.

'I have a headache, Julia, that's all.' And Gerty

tried to smile. 'But it makes it worse to think of writing; so I have put off my letter to papa till to-morrow, and come down to you here.'

'Of course, love; you had better do nothing but rest for a while.' And Lady Hunter made her lie on the sofa, as she added in a whisper, 'I know what it is, love, of course; you will be all right when Stanley comes back. It is a long time to lose him for—a whole day—so soon after all has been settled; but you must not always take it so to heart, or you will spoil him, love. We shall not tire you with our talking, shall we, dear?'

'O, no, Julia; I shall like it,' she replied, trying to laugh, afraid she must appear somewhat whimsical. 'My headache is not much; it will be better soon.'

And while the rest of the ladies talked on for an hour or two Gerty lay quite still on the sofa, listening dreamily to the cheerful sound, sometimes with closed eyes, trying not to think at all, but failing all the more because of the very effort, nerving herself for the evening and its coming renewal of the struggle with the thought, 'It will be all over by this time to-morrow, and I shall be writing to tell papa.'

Gerty could never tell afterwards how she got through that day: how she managed to make a pretence of eating at luncheon, and of enjoying the walking and driving in the afternoon, trying to laugh and talk with the rest all the time, and not to betray herself when her cousin rallied her affectionately as the hour drew near for Stanley's return. She hardly knew how she got through the dressing for dinner, or how she looked as she went down to the drawing-room and met Stanley again as he rose and came forwards to her, though she knew *his* gaze was very, very tender, and full of an anxiety which she noticed, though the rest, perhaps, did not.

'She has been looking like a ghost all day, Stanley,' laughed Lady Hunter; 'but you will soon bring back the roses.'

And she was right; for the deep colour came quickly to Gerty's face—not all for joy, alas, now, as her cousin fancied.

Dinner was announced directly, and Gerty let Stanley lead her in and attend to her during it, as he did with a gentle tenderness which made the trembling little heart ask itself how he could be so stern, so jealous and exacting. She was very pale again and quiet now, but she smiled and talked to him as well as she could, so as to avoid remark, so as to show no resentment or wounded feeling; so that haughty Stanley began to tell himself he had already conquered, that the precious treasure he coveted would be *wholly* his.

It all got over at last, and when Stanley had been back in the drawing-room a few minutes, just as Gerty was nerving her throbbing heart for a renewal of her task, he forestalled her by whispering as he stood by her:

'May I speak to you, Gerty, again for a few minutes in the library ?'

And she rose at once and followed him, no one wondering at them for going away for a quiet hour together after the day's separation.

'My darling,' Stanley began, as soon as they were shut in together alone, 'I spoke very harshly this morning, more than once. Will you forgive me for having to seem so stern and cruel? You will never let me need to appear so again, Gerty, will you? I *know* you will trust me now—that you will believe I know it to be all for the best, for your happiness, my darling.'

O, how the poor heart thrilled at the tender voice, the tender glance, to which it must steel itself with its yearning love!

'I feel no resentment, Stanley, for anything you said,' she faltered. 'How could I feel any against *you*? I only long and pray all the more that—that one day God may send you His grace to make you love what you hate so now. But I may not change one word I said this morning; I cannot—become your wife *at all*, if you refuse to grant me anything of what I asked, Stanley.' And her heart beat nearly to suffocation while she continued, going closer to him as she clasped her hands in her agitation, 'If even there were no other higher reason to make *it* appear scarcely of weight at all, how could I write to papa and tell him I was going to leave him to give myself to one who would oblige me to give up my religion; that I had consented to do so rather than not become his wife,—I, the daughter too of an old Catholic house like ours! Even if I *could* consent to lose my own soul for you, Stanley, could I break papa's heart, as I should if—I did as you ask? And when you think of it, Stanley, could *you* respect your wife if she gave in so weakly to what you would know her to believe to be sin, deadly sin? if she gave up God for His creature, would you not be afraid she might not always be true to *you* in turn?'

But he turned from her with a gesture of impatience, and then folded his arms and leaned against the mantelpiece again as he looked at her.

'May God (if there be one),' he said bitterly, 'forgive those who have taught you all this, who would rejoice to rob me of the one treasure I covet! Gerty, you ask me if I should respect you for yielding to me, for submitting to my judgment. How could I do otherwise than respect my wife for obeying me, for having shown her trust in me now, even before I became her husband, by promising what she knows I believe to be for *her* happiness as well as my own? And your father, Gerty, who is a good man, I know, would he bid you defy your husband? Would he even now bid you give up the one to whom you have given your heart and promise? Would he tell you, even for the sake of the religion in which he has been brought up to believe, to give up your life's happiness, to try to tear the love out of your heart—its sweet natural love?'

'If he would not have me risk my soul, Stanley, if he would not have me offend God, he would, he *must* bid me do so if necessary. But his whole life would be a prayer for me afterwards, Stanley, that I might have strength never to shrink from the cross laid upon me; that I might embrace it for the sake of Him who died for us all, who bade us take up the cross daily and follow Him.'

And the sweet tearful eyes looked out with a far-off gaze, as though seeing—dimly as yet, perhaps—the heavenly consolation which awaited the throbbing heart that each moment felt the *earthly* joy departing from its grasp.

Stanley unfolded his arms, and took the clasped hands into his own so firmly that they could not resist.

'O Gerty, do not drive me mad. Do not make me wish I had been base and dishonourable, and had promised what I never meant to perform, and then by gentle influence won you entirely to my wishes, as I *know* I could if you were once my wife, Gerty. O my darling, if you knew the love and happiness which should surround you, shielding you from the very breath of heaven if it blew upon you too roughly; how I would cherish you as never wife was before; how I would be your slave, Gerty, in all else, if in this one thing *you* would yield to *me!*'

She looked up a moment at the pale proud face in its beauty, contracted and convulsed now with its terrible entreaty, and then struggled vainly in his grasp.

'O Stanley, do not tempt me!' she cried out in her agony. 'I am only a weak girl; do not tempt me like that. You do not know what it is to see God on one side and earthly love and joy on the other, and to have to choose between; to know, as I *do*, without a *doubt*, that if I choose the last I shall lose God and my own soul. Ask me to give up everything else, ask me even to go to the world's end with you, and never see my father again, and I would do it, if you *could* ask me such a thing, Stanley; but not to give up my religion, to lose God for you. Ask me anything but that, Stanley.'

'And that is the one only thing I do ask you, not to persist in your mad superstition, and you refuse me. Gerty, you do not love me; I have been mistaken.'

And releasing her now, he turned away with a bitter compression of the haughty lips.

O, how hard he was, how stern! It was too much now for the half-breaking heart, but she did not reproach him; she did not tell him that, having no faith himself, caring for none, he could not love her truly if he refused to allow her to practise hers, which he must see was dearer than life to her; she only turned to him with a sob, almost a wail.

'O Stanley, don't say that—that I do not love you, when my heart is breaking because, if you persist, I may not become your wife, because my dream of joy has been so short. Don't I love you now more than ever, when you have been so honourable and true, scorning to do as many might have done, won me by false promises, justifying the falsehood for the sake of the end in view? Whatever comes, never say that, Stanley,—that I did not love you.'

The first tear he had shed since his mother's death fell from Stanley's eye, but he would not yield; the terrible demon of jealousy and pride held him still, strong as ever, even as he took the girlish form in his arms for a last appeal.

'Prove it then, my darling; yield to me and become my wife, and do not drive me to despair. Yield to me, and I will defy the world for your sake, shield you from every reproach. Even your father, dear as he is, shall be as nothing beside the love with which your husband shall surround you, Gerty.'

But she tore herself from his arms and stood before him with clasped hands, deadly pale now and very calm.

'Is this all you have to say, Stanley? Tell me plainly, for the last time, if you refuse what I ask; tell me quickly, I *entreat* you, Stanley.'

Once more the cold stern look rose to his face as he gazed down at the quiet resolute little figure, and slowly and bitterly answered:

'I cannot deceive you, you whom I have loved so dearly. As my wife, I repeat plainly, as you ask, you should never, with my knowledge, practise your religion as—a Catholic. I had hoped it would not come to this— that you might not have spoken of it at all, and so saved me telling you the truth; or that, when named between us, you would trust me to make you see it all one day as I do, and to make you *entirely* happy, as even yet, if you yield, I know I could do.'

Then he paused, and Gerty spoke with a firm voice, but looking out before her, not at him, as the room seemed to reel and go round about her:

N

'Then, Stanley, I must bid you farewell; I can *never* be your wife!'

And turning quickly, she left the room—left him there looking after her, with his arms still folded.

CHAPTER XIX.

QUICKLY but noiselessly Gerty went up-stairs at once to her bedroom, and having locked the door, fearing to be disturbed, even by her cousin, unawares, threw herself just as she was, in her pretty evening dress, face downwards on the bed. For a few minutes she seemed to feel nothing but the stony rigidity into which she had forced herself while she had spoken those final words to Stanley; but then, as she seemed slowly to realise all that she had done, to face the full meaning of the change that had suddenly come in her life,—then there began for her such a struggle as God grant may not often have to take place in any heart, least of all in the tender sensitive heart of a young girl like Gertrude Mannering!

'It is too much,' whispered the tempter, 'too much for human nature—for a young girl to bear! You *cannot* give him up. Marry him, become his wife; he has promised to be content with the Catholic ceremony, and trust to his love afterwards to grant what you ask. He could not be cruel to his wife; he could not see her sad and conscience stricken without relenting, perhaps even himself in the end being won to her religion.' And the vision of the life he had promised her—the powerful sheltering love which would have encircled her upon his breast, shielding her from all pain and reproach if she would but have yielded—rose before Gerty, making her writhe even bodily under the torture. She thought of the stern beautiful face as she had last seen it just now looking down at her, as she rejected that mighty love, and tore herself from that tender strong embrace.

'Let him make you his wife,' repeated the evil spirit; 'tell him you relent—there is yet time—and trust to the rest.'

But with one terrible wrench, as it were, she turned from the tempter.

'O my God, help me! Can I commit a deadly sin *now* by yielding—by promising to do as he asks, in the hope of good coming of it after, in the hope which would prove false, perhaps, to punish me?'

And as she drove away the vision of the love she had, with God's help, renounced, as she shut her eyes to the image of that one face, and closed her ears to the echo still ringing in them of those terrible yearning entreaties, other visions came to soothe that distracted heart in its hour of temptation, the 'temptation' against which she had prayed so simply and earnestly in her sweet ignorance of its strength and meaning as she knelt before the convent altar on that day of leaving school, little more than a year ago. The temptation had come now, stronger and more terrible than she could then have realised or dreamed of; but that prayer stood her in good need in this bitter hour, the simple prayer which she had poured out then before Jesus in His sacramental presence. And the prayers she had offered up so often since, more earnest still lately, because of the terrible need which had come to her for them; those, too, which had been breathed for her so fervently by those to whom she was so dear,—were they not answered now? But for them, if they had been neglected, would the powerful grace have been given to her at once to renounce so resolutely and unflinchingly, young tender girl though she was, the great love without which life would be so dreary and desolate? Without a doubt they were answered now, with all the sweet compassionate grace of Jesus' Sacred Heart, whose love that poor child seemed to feel consoling her already for her sacrifice, as—the evil tempter driven away—she turned to the kindly vision of her father welcoming her back with outstretched arms, welcoming her, dearer and more precious than ever, to the old home so nearly forsaken, to the old peaceful life by his side, sheltered by his unselfish unexacting affection. There need be no secrets from him now—never again! Safe in his arms, she would weep out the story, sad and yet joyful too, of the past few months, with their care and pain; the story of her love and its ending, of her brief delicious dream of earthly happiness. And Father Walmsley too, that kind holy friend of so many happy years, she would never need to avoid and shrink from him again; he might know all now: how, when he had asked for her confidence, she had been unable to tell him of the idolatry she was cherishing in her heart for a haughty unbeliever while yet her love was not openly asked for; how she had not dared to speak of it because of that hidden fear concerning it which she scarce dare *consciously* avow even to herself.

Gradually the trembling heart grew calmer, the aching temples throbbed less painfully, and Gerty uncovered her face and rose from the bed, throwing herself on her knees by its side in an abandonment of thanksgiving and prayer for continued help and strength in the future.

'O my Jesus, I thank Thee!' she murmured repeatedly. 'Mary, sweet Mother, help me to thank Him sufficiently now and through life! O God, if I had let myself be conquered; if I had yielded to Stanley's love and entreaties, and promised to do his will; if he had carried it out, as he *would* have done, however gently, and I had come to die, soon perhaps, within a year, as others have done!' and she shuddered even while she continued her prayer of thanksgiving.

She knelt so long that, when roused at last with a start by some coals falling heavily from the fire-grate, she rose to find herself almost numb, trembling with cold, which she had not seemed to feel before. She threw a warm shawl about her and made up the fire, which had fallen low since she had come up to the room, and was just sitting close over it, when a knock at the door startled her again. She lowered the gas, so that her face might not be distinctly seen, and then opened the door, to find Lady Hunter's maid outside.

'If you please, Miss Mannering, Lady Hunter wishes to know if you are unwell, and if she may come up to you, or if you would like anything. She said I was to tell you that Mr. Graham told her you were not well, and had gone up-stairs; and as you did not come down, they did not like to go to bed without hearing how you are, miss.'

'Thank you, Roberts. Will you say I am better now—quite well, indeed; but that I prefer going to bed at once instead of coming down again, as I have still a slight headache, and it is getting late? Perhaps Lady Hunter will come to me in the morning if I lie a little longer than usual, as I think I must ask her to let me; but if she does not mind, Roberts, tell her I would rather she did not trouble to come now, as I am all right, and shall be in bed directly.'

'And you won't have anything brought up to you, miss?'

'O, no, thank you, Roberts; I don't want anything. Good-night!' And with the sweet courteous smile which made her a favourite with every one, Gerty shut the door, and was alone again.

'He has betrayed nothing, then, yet. But he is too proud ever to do that, whatever he suffers. Is he suffering much, or is his anger too great against me?'

But she dare not think of *his* suffering, the thought of which was more terrible than her own—harder, O, so much harder to bear; the thought that, as he said, he might really bring himself to believe she did not love him, in his inability to appreciate or understand the motives which had obliged her to renounce him.

'I *must* not let myself think of it. It is all over now; I must never see him again unless—unless—but why do I deceive myself *again* with hope?'

Then she stood before the fire, with her hands clasped and a perplexed look on her face.

'No, I must not see him again; I *dare* not trust myself. I *think* I could be strong; I do not *feel* afraid now, but we can never tell; we may not even put ourselves in the *way* of temptation if it can be avoided. I must go away to-morrow—home again to papa. My cousin, when I tell her all, will help me. If he goes out for any length of time I can easily manage it; and he will, I think. But in any case I *must* not see him. God will help me, and will not let me be put in his way, I *know*. My cousin shall give him a note from me when I am gone; and she will excuse me to the rest. She will know best how; she is always so kind, though it will grieve her so terribly—her and dear old Sir Robert. I can telegraph from the station to papa that I am coming home, and then he will not be so startled to see me.' And she thought it all out methodically, as though she were planning, not for herself, but for some one else, with that numbed state of feeling coming over her again.

Then, instead of undressing, she began to make preparations for departure: mechanically she gathered together all her things, her clothes, and all her little possessions which she had brought to Nethercotes, and laid them in readiness to be repacked by the maid in the morning, pursuing her occupation quickly, never pausing until it was finished. Then she drew from her finger the ring which somehow in her agitation she had forgotten until now—the pretty ring which Stanley had given her the evening before, intending, as he told her, to replace it later by a handsomer one which he meant to purchase specially for herself, and which he would like her to choose. She took it off quickly, as though not daring to linger over it or look at it, and put it away to be returned to the giver; then, as she stood by the dressing-table, she glanced at the mirror, almost starting at the sight of the face reflected there —so white and ghastly, years older, she thought, since yesterday. Her task over, she lingered still by the fire, as though reluctant to seek the sleep from which the awakening would be so terrible.

'I could do better, I think, to stay up all night and face it—the life that is before me—for I have now begun to realise it a little. But to have to let myself forget it for a few hours—to go to sleep and *dream* perhaps, and then to wake again to it all! But I *must*, or I should, perhaps, be ill in the morning, and they would not let me go. And I *shall* have to grow used to it at home; the forgetting it in sleep and dreams, and then the awaking, in all the weary days that are only beginning!'

And when once undressed and in bed, with her little convent crucifix clasped tightly in her hand,

Gerty soon fell into the heavy kindly sleep, almost stupor, of exhaustion and utter weariness which often comes when all is over, after a cruel mental struggle such as she had experienced, after a day of such agitation as hers had been.

CHAPTER XX.

THE shock was over, the shock of awakening and remembering everything, which was so much worse even than she had pictured; and Gerty lay still a while longer, with her eyes closed, as though wishing to defer as long as possible at least the bodily facing of the duty which lay before her. She had glanced at her watch, and found it late for an early riser like herself; but she knew Lady Hunter would not expect her down early, and she must keep her room, if she could, until Stanley should go out, as she hoped and felt sure, somehow, he would do.

In a few minutes there was a gentle knock, and the maid entered, bringing a cup of tea, which Lady Hunter had sent up in case Gerty should be awake.

'Lady Hunter will come up directly, miss,' she said.

Gerty drank the tea, and when the maid had left the room she remained sitting up in the bed waiting for her cousin, nerving herself for her task. A few minutes more brought Lady Hunter, who sat down at once by the bedside and took both Gerty's hands as she kissed her.

'My love, how white and ill you look; and I expected to find you all right and blooming again! But you did not look well all day yesterday, and I thought at the time something more must ail you than merely Stanley's day's absence.'

The colour rose now deeply enough to Gerty's face.

'Indeed I am not ill, Julia—not as you think. Nothing ails me—bodily, except I am—a little tired. Julia,' she added, forcing herself to the effort, 'has Stanley gone out, or—is he going?'

Her cousin looked at her anxiously and earnestly.

'Yes, love, he has gone out with the hounds, with Sir Robert and the rest, for the day; but he will be back before the others, an hour or two, he said, love.'

A strange look contracted Gerty's face for an instant, and her lips quivered.

'Julia,' she whispered, 'before he comes back, before he returns this evening, I must be gone away, back home to Whitewell, to papa.'

For a moment Lady Hunter genuinely feared she had gone suddenly demented, or was going to have brain fever or something of the kind; but, seeing her alarm, Gerty smiled so quietly and naturally, though sadly, that the fear of that kind vanished, and she only asked very gently and anxiously:

'O, surely not, Gerty! It cannot be anything so bad as that. Tell me, if you can, love, what is wrong. You and Stanley have not quarrelled; or, if there has been anything, it will be all right again? You take it too much to heart, love, whatever it is; for though Stanley is stern and hasty, no one is more just or tender in reality; no one could be more sorry if he has said anything to hurt you, Gerty.'

Without answering her yet, Gerty questioned her in turn:

'Did he—say anything, Julia, to—to make you think anything was wrong?'

'He *said* nothing, love, not a word, last night. He merely told me he thought you were not very well, and had gone up-stairs, when I wondered why you did not come back to the drawing-room. But his look and manner were so gloomy and abstracted that I could not but suspect something, and that was why I did not come to you last night; because I knew in troubles of that kind one likes to be alone, at first at least. Then you did not come down to breakfast, as I felt you would not, love; and as soon as I saw Stanley this morning he told me he was going out with the rest; at which I was surprised, if only because, you know, he cares so little about hunting. He was very quiet and silent then, until, as they were preparing to go out, he came to me and said that he should be back an hour or so before the rest, if possible; and though he did not say your name, Gerty, I felt, from his look and manner, that it was a kind of message for you, love.'

'And I must not be here when he comes back, Julia; you must let me go this afternoon.' Then, putting her hand again in her cousin's, she continued, her heart beating once more after its unnatural calm: 'You remember, don't you, Julia, saying to me yesterday, when I was telling you the news'—and her lips quivered—'that I should not always get my own way like you do, that I should have to give in a good deal to Stanley when I became his wife; and I laughed and said I was not afraid; that I should never want my own way, because I should always think his wishes the best for me. Even as I said that, Julia, the fear came up in my heart, though I dare not listen to it then, that there might be one thing which he would ask me to do in which I could not obey him, and about which I must make sure before I became his wife. I think you guess, Julia, what I mean: my—religion—whether he would always let me practise it; whether—if—there should be children, I might have them too brought up Catholics. Well, I have asked him,

Julia, spoken to him about it, pleaded with him as well as I could, telling him I could *never* be his wife unless I won from him that promise; and—and he—refused to give it, Julia. He pleaded, on his side, that I would yield, as hard as I did on mine to him; for his hatred of religion —*our* religion—is something terrible, Julia. Even *you* would be startled at it, I think, if you heard how stern it made him, when he saw that I *could* not yield; for, O Julia, he *did* love me so!' And as the pent-up heart poured out some of its agony in words, a terrible sob broke from it too, and Gerty paused a minute, while her cousin made her rest her head on her shoulder. 'He told me what a love he would give me if I would only yield; that never wife had been so cherished before as I should be; and then when I had to break from him and the temptation (you understand me, don't you, Julia, though you do not care for our holy faith?), and when I had to ask him finally if he would grant what I asked, he told me plainly and honourably that he could not—that as his wife I should never practise my religion with his knowledge. Then—then I just said a word of farewell and —left him. You will help me to get away, Julia, won't you, not to pain him again uselessly? for *I* cannot yield, *cannot* lose God for him, Julia, though I would give up *all* else; and *he will not* yield, never will, as he told me so—so sternly.'

There was a minute's silence, for Gerty could say no more, and Lady Hunter's tears were flowing fast.

'Gerty,' she whispered at last, 'is there no other way? Is it not too cruel? God is so good and merciful: does He, even in your idea of Him, ask a sacrifice like this?'

'He has the first claim on us, has He not, Julia? If to please a creature we must give *Him* up, give up what He has revealed as His one holy religion, then He does ask such a sacrifice, even like this; but promising, O, such a reward, Julia—heaven and *His* love for all eternity!' And she paused a minute ere she continued: 'You would not have me give up God, Julia, would you, believing as I do that I should lose my soul by so doing—lose it for ever in *hell*, unless time were given me to repent *truly?* and I could not expect or be sure of that.'

'Gerty, do you remember, when you first came to me in London'—and Lady Hunter spoke slowly and solemnly now—' one day that you were explaining the doctrine of hell to me—at least, why it should be easy to believe, even to those who are not Catholics, who take it of *course* with the rest—and I told you, you only fancied you believed it, but that you could not really do so? Well, I shall *never* say that again, Gerty—never say you do not believe that or any other doctrine. You have proved your faith to me, love, better than a hundred sermons could have done.'

Gerty tried to smile, while a silent thanksgiving rose from her heart for even this slight beginning of her consolation.

'And so you will not grieve about it, Julia, more than you can help; or I shall have to blame myself for having come here only to disturb all your pleasure like this by running away, as if you had not always been so very, very kind, you and Sir Robert.'

'Nay, Gerty, it is *I* who will have to reproach myself all my life, love.' And her voice trembled with agitation. 'But for me you would never have met Stanley Graham; or if even your father can hardly blame me for that, Gerty, which I could not help, unless he blames me for inviting his darling to London at all, still, I shall always feel as if I should have warned you when I saw how it was going to be; for even I, irreligious as I am, felt uneasy, somehow, when I thought of your earnest practical faith, knowing so well as I did Stanley's haughty jealous temper and bitterness against all religion—knowing that while I am only *careless* of it, he *hates* it. But I could not bring myself to spoil your happiness, love; for I never thought even he, when it really came to the question, could be so hard and stern.'

'And if I myself could not have believed it, Julia, why should you be to blame? How could papa blame you, who are not a Catholic, for not warning me? *I* was mistaken in not listening sooner to the fear in my heart, which I hid almost from myself, of how it might be, so as to have learned his sentiments sooner, if possible; for I see now so plainly why he always avoided the subject of religion or any mention of it. O Julia, if the hatred he has now for religion were once turned to love of it, what a grand noble Catholic he would make!'

And the colour rose again for an instant to the pale face.

'And that is why it seems so cruel, such a terrible pity, love, that there is no other way but separation for you to resolve on.' And Lady Hunter spoke very eagerly and warmly. 'As Stanley's wife, Gerty, you might have won him to your views—have won him in time to become so ardent a Catholic as to satisfy even *you*, love; and all might have been so smooth in the end.'

'Don't try to tempt me, Julia; it is too late now. For I—I have conquered, with God's help, and I cannot look back for an instant with any fear while I have that still with me.' And she smiled a sad but peaceful smile. 'And you are only trying to think it would be as you say, Julia, out of your love and care for me, for both of us. You don't really believe it; you don't think it even possible that—that Stanley could so easily become a Catholic. Have you not told me so, in words which I ought to have taken as a warning, Julia? And even if it were likely, we may not do evil that good may come. *You* believe that, Julia; and I could not commit sin now in the hope of good which might *never* come.'

Lady Hunter sighed.

'But how shall I meet Stanley this evening, love? How shall I tell him you are gone, with my help? I must, of course, if you insist, dear; but I hardly dare, I assure you.'

'Julia, how can he be surprised, when the engagement is broken off between us as certainly as if it had never existed, by my own words and his? Who could ask me to stay where we must meet constantly, and where every minute would be so cruel for both? I know you would be in hopes of—of it all coming right again; but *I* know differently, Julia. *He* would only say the same; and I could not change one word I said —one thing I asked for. But I want to—to leave a few lines for him, Julia, just to say good-bye, and tell him it is all my own doing; and you will give them to him, won't you?'

Lady Hunter acquiesced silently, as though her pain and perplexity would not let her speak.

'And now I must get up, Julia,' continued Gerty, with that sad attempt again at a smile; 'it is dreadfully late for *me*. I shall not be long in dressing, and you will let some one come to finish my packing, won't you? See, I have laid everything ready nearly.'

Lady Hunter started as she looked round and saw it was so, for she had not noticed it before, being so absorbed with Gerty herself.

'O Gerty, what a sad ending to the visit that we

have been looking forward to so long! she said, as she rose to leave the room for a while. 'I may send you some breakfast, though, presently, before you get up, love?'

'No, Julia, please don't; indeed I could not eat it; that tea was enough.'

'Well, I will order an early luncheon, love, in my little room, and we will have it together before you leave.'

'Thank you, Julia; because I must get away by two o'clock, mustn't I, to be in time for the train that starts at a quarter to three? I have looked at my little time-table, and I see there is no other direct to Moston till six o'clock, and—and that, you know, is too late, even if papa would not be uneasy if I travelled by dark alone. I can telegraph to him from the station, you know, to say I am coming.'

'Yes; I was going to advise that, love, so as not to startle him;' and with another fond anxious look Lady Hunter left the room, thankful that her guests were all out so opportunely, with the exception of one or two ladies, so that she was more at leisure to sit quietly alone, and think over all that had happened, and how it would end.

'If I could only do *anything* to help to set it right! If I were only not so powerless in the matter, knowing that of course she cannot stay, that I cannot keep her from her father an hour longer, poor darling! But what a grand thing it is, this faith of hers! How brave and resolute the Catholic religion makes even a tender little girl such as she is!' And she sat alone, pondering long and deeply after she had given directions about Gerty's departure.

In less than an hour Gerty came to her, her face looking still paler and more weary by contrast with her dark travelling-dress. Her cousin took both her hands, which she felt trembled in her grasp.

'I have ordered luncheon for twelve, love, and the carriage at two, to take us to the station. Did Deans come to you, dear?'

'Yes, thank you, Julia, and I just showed her what to do and left her. Julia, how they will all wonder what is the matter!' and her lips quivered.

'They think you are not well, love, and that we have agreed it is best for you to return home, as your papa would be anxious if you stayed. I said that to Miss Monckton and Lady Gowenlock, the only two who have not gone out, Gerty; because you see, love, I was obliged to tell them you were going, on account of having to excuse myself to them for the whole morning. You won't mind saying "Good-bye" to them, love, will you?'

'O, no, Julia, of course not. O, what trouble I am giving!' she sighed.

Lady Hunter kissed her with a tender look of reproof, and made her sit by her, close before the bright fire.

'I am only thankful to be able to manage it so well for you, love, and that they are all out. O Gerty, it is perhaps cruel to say it again, but is it really true that there is *no* other way? Do you know, dear, a few years ago I had a great friend who was a strict Wesleyan—as strict in her way as you are in yours. Well, she married a gentleman who disapproved of all particular *forms* of religion, but who attended service at the church whenever he went anywhere—a very good easy kind of man; and because she saw he disliked her going to the Wesleyan chapel, even when she could get to one easily, she gave it all up gradually, and only goes now when he does to church. But she is one of the best women and wives I know, Gerty; and I believe truly religious at heart still, though I have heard her say she has never once regretted changing its outward form.'

Even in her terrible trouble, her absorbing preoccupation, Gerty actually laughed outright.

'And if I were a Wesleyan, Julia, don't you think I would do exactly the same? If one way is as good as another, why not choose your husband's way, if he wishes it, and you see it would make him happier? Wesleyans are only like all other Protestants, telling us that all may choose for themselves which way they will go to heaven; so why should your friend regret having made herself and her husband happier by pleasing him? But Catholics, Julia, know that our Lord came on earth to show us *one* way to heaven, and that there is *no* other; that He taught *one* truth, unless He meant just the opposite of what He said; unless He could distinctly teach one doctrine, and yet be quite satisfied if we chose to believe a contradictory one.'

'I might have known, love, what you would say,' sighed her ladyship. 'It was a foolish parallel to bring to your case. But it is so sad for me to realise it all, when I think of your mother, my poor dead cousin, Gerty; when I remember her sitting with me in this very room, when she and your papa came to stay with us, when I came home a bride, two or three months before you were born. To think that you are that very babe she was then expecting, and all this sad trouble to have come to you so early! And for him—for Stanley too, it will be so dreadful—though his own fault; he will suffer so terribly!'

Gerty's lips quivered once more as she clasped her hands together on her knee.

'That is the worst of all, Julia, the hardest to bear—that—he may—still think I—did not love him!' she whispered.

The morning had worn on now, and in a few minutes the luncheon came up, and Gerty tried to satisfy her cousin by eating something, though each morsel seemed to choke her as she ate it. Then she whispered a word to her cousin and went back again to the bedroom, where she had left writing materials ready, and sat down to write the note to Stanley—the farewell lines which she wished to leave for him. Her hand trembled terribly as she wrote, but she did not pause nor shrink from her task until it was finished. A courage above her strength had been given to her since she had finally triumphed over that awful temptation, and she must go on bravely with the work before her until it should be done—she must not pause until she was safe again in her father's arms.

'Dear Mr. Graham,' she began, feeling that she could not now address him more familiarly, even for the last time, knowing as she did how completely the engagement was broken between them,—'my cousin will give you this note this evening, when she tells you I am gone away, quite of myself, without her advice or any one's. You will not be surprised to find it so, knowing what useless pain it would be for both of us to meet again, when all is over, and when you would only have the same to say, and I could not alter a word of what I had to ask you. But I could not go without saying good-bye, without asking you to forgive me if I was abrupt or unkind at all needlessly last night, if I said one word uselessly to hurt you; for I know you are sincere, and that you think you *could* not grant what I asked without injuring my happiness as well as your own. If you were not, you would not have told me so plainly and honourably the exact truth of what I must expect if I became your wife; when so many others in your place might have brought themselves to think it almost right to evade my questioning, or even have given a promise, careless of how it was meant to be kept. And for this I want to thank you again, with a gratitude which will be life-long; a gratitude which you will hardly understand, knowing so little of the priceless treasure of our holy faith. I shall never forget you in my prayers, though we may never meet again on earth; for the thought of your suffering, even if it be mixed with anger against me, is harder infinitely than my own; because I have a dear home and father to return to, and as yet you have no one. But that God Himself may console you for my loss, and bring you one day to happiness and contentment even on earth, shall always be the prayer of

'GERTRUDE MARY MANNERING.'

Then taking out the ring from its case, she enclosed it carefully in the letter, and having sealed up the envelope and addressed it, she went back again to her cousin.

'You will give it him as soon as you see him, Julia, won't you?'

Lady Hunter took the letter from her gently, and put it carefully away in her pocket-book.

'At once, love, of course. Gerty, I may tell Sir Robert all, may I not?'

'O, yes, Julia, of *course*. How could I wish to keep the truth from him, running away like this, when he has been so kind? Besides, Stanley'—and she hesitated painfully a minute—' would wish him to know at once, I am sure, as he must do in time in any case

Then they sat together before the fire for a while longer, until it was time to start; and when they were all ready and the carriage waiting, Gerty went to say good-bye to the two ladies who were in the house, who had not gone out with the rest; going as bravely as she could through the ordeal of their well-meant expressions of solicitude for her health, and their kindly raillery as to how quickly Mr. Graham would follow her when he returned and found her gone home unwell.

'Don't you think you might have stayed, Miss Mannering, and let us all help to nurse you, Mr. Graham at the head of us?' asked one of them playfully. 'But of course you know best how your father would feel in the matter, about his only daughter too,' she added, perhaps with an instinctive feeling that there was more in it all than met the eye, more than they knew as yet, something perhaps in Gerty's own unconscious look aiding the impression.

Feeling painfully that it must all seem somewhat strange to them, Gerty made her adieux, and was soon driving away by her cousin's side, away from Nethercotes, to which only three days since she had come in such joyous hope.

She sat quite still and almost silent, trying to realise that it was all over, her brief dream of happiness—all over, after the many months of waiting and hoping! It had come, only to be rudely shattered; and she was going back to the old life, to be apparently, in all things external, as though Stanley Graham had never existed, —he of whom she had made a god in her heart all this time.

She tried to rouse herself as they neared the station.

'I will write to you, you know, Julia, to-morrow,' she said.

'If you knew, love, how I shall be looking for your letter!' sighed her cousin. 'And you shall hear from me in a day or two; you would like to do so, I know, dear.'

'Yes, Julia, thank you;' and Gerty's lips quivered as she thought of what her cousin's letter would contain.

They reached the station, and went to telegraph at once to Mr. Mannering, Gerty dictating the words:

'Do not be alarmed. I am coming home to-day by the train that gets to Moston at four o'clock, and will explain all. Do not come yourself to meet me. Send Mrs. Leeson if you get this in time.'

She felt her father would understand that she had some reason for wishing to meet him first quietly at home, and that he would not come, as she did not wish it.

As the train came up and Gerty took her seat in the corner of a carriage, Lady Hunter insisted in wrapping her up well in her rug and furs.

'Don't let me have the sin of you getting your death of cold, in addition to the self-reproach now, love,' she whispered; and Gerty saw that her tears were falling.

'O Julia, don't say that of yourself—never *think* it even!' she pleaded, struggling hard to keep her own tears from the sight of her one or two fellow-passengers.

'Well, good-bye, my darling girl,' Lady Hunter added in a still lower whisper. 'Pray for me, Gerty, if it is not selfish to ask you to think so much of me at a time like this. You do pray for me, I know; but, if you can, pray more than ever for me from to-day.'

Another clasp of the hand and the door was shut, and then directly the train steamed slowly out of the station; Gerty, with her hands tightly clasped under her rug, trying to say her rosary to herself; praying for a renewal of the help from God which was enabling her thus to flee from the temptation which, though conquered, would have been dangerous and alluring still to the idolising heart by its close proximity and persuasive presence.

CHAPTER XXI.

THE train arrived duly at Moston, the station nearest to Whitewell Grange; and at once, as Gerty looked out, she saw that the old housekeeper was there to meet her. Jumping out of the carriage quickly, she ran up to her.

'Papa wasn't frightened, was he, Mrs. Leeson?' she asked anxiously, as she shook hands.

'Well, Miss Gerty, perhaps just a little at first; but he soon saw, of course, that if you were very ill you could not be coming home by yourself. And there was so little time to think about it, because the telegram only came in time for me to get here in the carriage. There is nothing the matter at Nethercotes, Miss Gerty, I hope; or you are not ill?' she asked, with the respectful familiarity which was the privilege of her long years of faithful service.

Even under the homely, kindly gaze Gerty's colour rose.

'I am not very well,' she said; 'and so I knew it was best to come home and be quiet with papa for a while, as the house there is so full of visitors, you know. But Lady Hunter and Sir Robert have been very, very kind,' she added, not wishing to raise any suspicion of unpleasantness on their part.

Perhaps the shrewd old housekeeper was not wholly

devoid of a vague idea in the right direction as to what *kind* of trouble had driven her young mistress home so suddenly, though she had, of course, never heard even the mention of Stanley Graham's name in her life; but she only said very quietly:

'It was the wisest thing to come home, indeed, miss. To be feeling out of sorts in a strange house, full of visitors, is enough to bring on a downright illness. But you'll be all right now, quiet at home, won't you, Miss Gerty?'

'I hope so;' and Gerty tried to smile her own bright smile, and to assume the old gaiety of manner, to hide her breaking heart. 'Don't make me out a regular invalid, though, or else I shall fly back again, and perhaps make myself into one, you know.' But even as she spoke her eyes wandered out of the carriage-window—out into the familiar road, with its vivid recollections.

Was it only three days since she had seen it before—only three days? and it seemed years—years in experience and suffering, the short, too blissful interval of happiness being but like a delicious dream, but a dream which left with its loss all the pain of reality.

It was quite dark when they reached the Grange, and as Gerty ran up the hall-steps her father was there to meet her.

'Gerty!' was all he said as he clasped her in his arms, his darling treasure, who had come back to him so strangely.

Again Gerty forced herself to smile before Mrs. Leeson and the one or two servants who were taking in her luggage.

'I'm so afraid I frightened you, papa! But I'm not so very well, so I knew it was best to come home, though my cousin was so sorry to part with me;' and the cheery voice quite deceived the servants, if it did not wholly succeed with the anxious tender father.

He led Gerty into the breakfast-room, where he had been sitting in the firelight, listening for the sound of the carriage wheels, and looking out at intervals. They were scarcely shut safe in there alone when the courage and firmness which Gerty had kept up all day broke down completely, deserted her at last for a time now that her task was accomplished.

'O papa, I shall never want to go away again! I have come back to stay with you always;' and with her head on his breast and her arms round his neck, she wept out the pent-up pain in a perfect agony of sobs; wept out the yearning and regret for her lost love, for the idol she had renounced.

'My darling!' was all her father said, as for the first few minutes he let her weep freely, only stroking her hair with the old fond caress; the pretty hair, from which she had thrown aside her hat, and which lay tossed and tumbled now against his shoulder.

'Papa,' she whispered as she grew somewhat calmer, 'you have been praying for me, I know, you and Father Walmsley, or—or—I could not have done it; I should have been too weak. It makes me tremble now to think of—last night, to go over it all again.' And as the sobbing words escaped her, Mr. Mannering knew what kind of trouble had come to his little sunbeam, robbing it for ever of its gay brightness; he knew what manner of story his darling was about to pour into his ears.

'God help me to forgive him!' was his bitter thought, 'the man, whoever he is, who has stolen my darling's heart only to break it, to send her back to me like this. Why are my fears realised so soon?'

Looking up, Gerty saw the terrible expression on

her father's face, half bitterness, half tender sorrow, and grew calm again for his sake, disposing of her tears as she whispered:

'O papa, don't look like that; don't take it to heart so dreadfully! You won't when you hear it all, when I've told you quietly all about it;' and drawing him to the fire she made him sit in his easy-chair, as throwing off her wraps she sat close by his knee on a low stool.

'It was just the first, papa, the first seeing you again after it all, that made me so silly, made me cry so. But I can tell you all about it now quite quietly, papa.'

Then taking his hand caressingly, as though its tender touch gave her strength, Gerty began her story, in a low quiet tone, which yet trembled often—the whole sad story from its very beginning. She told her father, as they sat there together in the flickering firelight, how she had first met Stanley Graham; how he had stolen into her heart and taken it captive before she would avow it to herself even; and how she had been unable, from their earliest acquaintance, to avoid seeing what kind of attention it was he paid her so constantly, what kind of love he meant one day to offer her. She described him to her father, with her heart yearning with that hopeless pain; she spoke of his noble character, of his honour and truth, marred only by that terrible, fatal pride; she told of his splendid intellect, of his perfect manly beauty, which had so fascinated her before he had spoken a word to her, the colour rising to her face again at the vivid recollection of that happy, dream-like evening.

'I had never seen a face—like his before, papa, and I—shall never see another like it now. You would not wonder at me if you could know him, papa, if—it were all different. I had been thinking how well he would look as the model of a knight or crusader, papa, when my cousin brought him to introduce to me, and then—'

She paused a minute, and continued, telling of the winning fascination of manner he could exercise, haughty as he was; and how fond Lady Hunter and Sir Robert too were of him. Then it came to the telling of their parting the night before she left London, and of his earnest request that he might see her at Nethercotes, and of the pain of having to come home with a secret she might not yet reveal, a secret which she *felt* had been partly visible.

'If you knew, papa, what it was like all that time, to be as I was with you, you would forgive me for it.'

'My little Gerty, there is nothing to forgive; nothing except to pity and love you for, more than ever;' and the father's arm clasped her round as she leaned against his knee, as though he could never let her go again from that sweet shelter.

'You see, papa, I *could* not bring myself to speak of —of—my love—for him, until I was *openly* sure of his for me, more than ever because he is like he is, you know, an infidel; I felt how hard it would be for you to give me to him, even if he should grant all I should have to ask about religion. And I know *now* that I had another fear—the fear that has come true, papa—that he might refuse altogether what I would ask, and that I might have to give him up. But I did not dare to think even that I had such a fear; I used to drive it away and tell myself it would never come to that; that I could not bear it, that God would not ask me.'

'And He *has* asked you, Gerty; and my little girl has offered Him the sacrifice He wanted, though she thought she would be too weak, though she told me once she was not a bit of a heroine, and was but a poor descendant of confessors and martyrs. But I knew God would make her strong when the need came; that He would give her grace to show the martyr *spirit* of which I spoke, Gerty.' And Gerty felt a tear fall upon her hand as he paused.

Then she told him of the meeting again with Stanley at Nethercotes, three days before, on her arrival there; of his proposal to her, and of the joyous interval before she brought herself to the task, so long dreaded, of speaking to him of religion. 'During that short delicious time I used to think so often, papa, how proud you would be of him; how he would grow as dear to you nearly as Rupert, for my sake; of how we would all pray that God would in time send him even the grace of conversion, and of what a glorious Catholic he would be!' And the poor heart quivered again with that aching pain at the thought of the short blissful dream dispelled so rudely.

But she forced herself to go on and tell her father as she had told her cousin, but more fully, because he would understand it all as Lady Hunter could not: of the struggle with Stanley, of all she said, as well as she could remember; and of his tender though terrible entreaties, ending at last in that stern truthful explanation of his intentions, and her consequent renunciation of him. 'And it is all over, papa, now, and I am safe back with you; and I shall never want to see him again, only to pray for him.'

'And may God give me grace, my darling, to pray for him too!' exclaimed her father solemnly; 'to be able to forgive him freely, not only for having striven so hard to make me have to mourn and grieve over an apostate child, but for having stolen her heart at all, only to wish to tyrannise over its dearest feelings; to be willing to break it rather than grant what she asked so solemnly, though her requests could not harm *him*, though they could not hurt even his outward welfare, though, caring for no faith himself, and pretending too to love her, he might have allowed her to practise hers in peace, infidel as he is. Thank God, you are saved from him, my darling!'

But Gerty was sobbing again now as, taking her hands from her father's grasp, she clasped them on his knee. 'Papa, O, don't say that; O, don't speak of him like that! If you knew him, you would not; if you knew him as I do and as my cousin does, you would know that, while he *does* love me, O, so much, papa, he yet could not promise to see me, as his wife, practise a religion he hates and which he hoped to win me from. He is so terribly proud, papa, and he was jealous of my love—jealous of sharing it with a religion he despises so. So you'll forgive him, papa, and pray for him too, won't you?'

'My darling, may God forgive me for the harsh judgment which escaped me in my anger against the man who has blighted my little girl's life! I do forgive him, poor ignorant unbeliever; and we will pray for him together, Gerty. And if the day should come when God will show him the truth, and, repenting, he embraces it as he now maligns it, may I be able to give my child back to him, if he comes humbly to ask for her, —give her to him without a fear, because *she* trusts so in his tenderness! Or if that day should never come, but he still repents of his harshness and begs for her, though without himself embracing the truth, may I be able to give you to him, Gerty, if it is for your happiness and he brings himself to promise all!'

'Papa, that he will *never* do—not that last you speak of. I have never hoped that for one instant, since last night. And for the other, papa,' she added in a strange solemn tone, 'I do not know, I dare not hope. It seems somehow as if I *must* not, as if—somehow God would not want him only for that, if He brought him to the truth.' And her father started at the strange tone and the painfully solemn manner. Then quickly, as if to take away the impression of her words, even from herself, she added: 'Think, papa, what it would have been for him, with his ideas, to have allowed—his children to be brought up as Catholics! And, papa, he has never had any one for whom he cared to try and keep *any* kind of religion in his mind; for the only one he had, his mother, died just when he left school, before he went to the university. O papa, poor Lady Hunter is so upset about it all, so afraid you may blame her for it, somehow!'

'Poor Lady Hunter! As if I could, Gerty; at least when I came to think how really kind she has been, meaning nothing but kindness through it all, as I know. How could *she* see how it would be?'

'How glad I shall be to tell her what you say, papa, for she will really believe it then! O papa, do you know I cannot help hoping, and even thinking, she will be a Catholic yet some day! If you had heard how she asked me to pray for her, just as we parted!'

'God grant it, Gerty!' echoed her father solemnly, thinking in his heart of hearts that the example of his little girl might go far to work that for which she prayed. 'And now, my darling, you must be starved and weary,' he added, rising. 'I will ring for the lights while you run up-stairs, for it is just dinner-time. I shall not have to be solitary over it again to-night, Gerty, as I thought;' and the look came into his eyes and the expression to his voice, which must be ever in them henceforth with his darling, the unspeakable, renewed tenderness, greater and more reverent, as it were, than the old one. Then, as she was leaving the room, he detained her yet a minute longer. 'Gerty, you would like to see Father Walmsley, I know, soon, even to-night; and it will be better for you not to be too quiet and alone with me this first evening. It is too cold and you are too tired for me to let you walk; besides, you will like to see him by yourself, love, first; so you must have the carriage as soon as dinner is over.'

'Thank you, papa dear!' and Gerty's eyes filled with tears as the old unselfish love, which she had so nearly forsaken, greeted her again. 'I should like to see him, to tell him all—at once—if I can; because, papa, he must have thought me strange and reserved all that time.'

Then she went up-stairs, to take possession once more of her own little room, which she would never want to exchange now for any other better one. Since last she had seen it, had she not faced the fear and conquered in the struggle which then had only loomed threateningly in the distance?

Throwing off her hat and mantle, she hastily washed her face to hide the tear traces, without lingering to make herself look bright and pretty as she had done on that last return home, when her heart had been so full of its earthly idol, and then ran down again to her father, who awaited her in the dining-room. How pale she looked, his darling! how quiet and womanly was every movement of the girlish figure, lately so full of buoyant liveliness and gaiety! But she was his own little Gerty still, dearer than ever, because of the cruel sorrow which had sent her back to him. The dinner was a quiet one, almost silent, because to speak of any indifferent subject yet seemed impossible; but the silence was not as it had been so often lately, one of painful reserve, but of eloquence more expressive than words, a tacit acknowledgment of full sweet confidence for ever restored.

'I shall not be more than an hour away, papa,' Gerty said as, the carriage being announced, she rose and kissed him with a yearning fondness.

'Don't think of me being lonely, for a minute, my darling. If Father Walmsley can send you back looking and feeling the least bit brighter and happier, I shall not grudge the time spent with him, my poor little Gerty;' and he let her go.

As Gerty drove along, her heart beating again now, she tore a leaf from her pocket-book and wrote upon it—

'Dear Father Walmsley,—I have come home unexpectedly, and would like to see you now if I can. Have you a few minutes to spare for your affectionate child,
'GERTY?'

And she sent the note in to Father Walmsley on ascertaining he was at home when she arrived at the presbytery. As she sat waiting in the little parlour, listening absently to the ticking of the timepiece, it struck eight, and Gerty started tremblingly. 'Just this time last night I was in the library at Nethercotes with Stanley!' she said to herself almost aloud; and in another minute, Father Walmsley entered.

'Gerty, my child!' and as she gave him her trembling hand. his look of surprise changed to one of gentle fatherly solicitude; for it needed no words to tell him that it was a tale of trouble and sorrow he was about to hear from his spiritual child.

He made her sit by the fire, for she trembled as if with outward cold; and in less than half an hour Gerty had told her story to her kind fatherly friend, all as she had told her father, without reserve; and had received from him the precious consolation which God Himself teaches those to impart who have themselves given up this world, with its human joys, to save their souls by doing His own blessed work of saving those who are still tossed to and fro amidst its storms.

He had listened to everything, not with much surprise perhaps, as Gerty felt before he told her so, and had with his kind smile satisfied her by speaking the words of forgiveness for the alienation she had shown towards him, for her rejection of his kindly invitation to confidence.

'I trusted you through it all, Gerty, you know, as I told you,' he said then. 'You have done in the end as well as I could have told you how to do if I preached a whole course of sermons about it, my child; you have done it with God's help, granted to prayer.'

'O, yes, father; without that, what might I have been now?' And she shuddered, and then added: 'Can you go into the church for a few minutes to-night, father? I should like so much, if I may, to go to Communion to-morrow.'

'I was thinking you would, Gerty,' he replied seriously, but very kindly, 'to offer your trouble up to our Lord Himself in His bodily presence, and to ask Him for grace and strength not to complain or grow weary; to pray too, my child, for him whom you have to-day renounced for conscience' sake.'

Gerty's colour rose again; but she said with a smile, 'You will have to let me go very often now to Communion, father, until I grow quite strong, quite used to it all;' but he saw her lips quiver as she turned to go with him to the church.

Her confession over, Gerty did not stay long in the church, not wishing to keep the carriage waiting, but soon followed Father Walmsley back into the house, where he shook hands with her very kindly and earnestly as he bade her 'Good-night.'

'Don't come too early to church in the morning, Gerty,' he said with his sweet smile, 'or I shall be angry, you know. You will be very tired and exhausted to-morrow, my child; so only get up to be just in time for Mass.'

'What bad advice, Father Walmsley! You never gave it me before in your life!' and something of the old playful look flitted for an instant over the pale face.

'And I trust I shall never give it to you again, Gerty. But you must follow it this time, remember;' and with another 'good-night' he opened the door for her; and she left him to go back to her father, to assure him that already in her sad desolation the peace of a good conscience was bringing its own sweet comfort.

And the next morning when she awoke, still tired and weary, as Father Walmsley had predicted, that first waking at home which she had so dreaded was rendered easier and scarcely terrible at all by the thought of the all-powerful Consoler who was coming into her heart this morning, who had Himself given her the sweet grace to turn to Him thus early for strength and solace. 'Come unto Me, all ye who labour and are heavy burdened, and I will refresh you,' were the blessed words which seemed to echo in her very heart all the time she was dressing and as she walked to church in the old way, leaning on her father's arm, neither of them speaking much, with that sweet knowledge ever between them now of confidence restored, never to be broken again.

Gerty received Communion, and with Jesus in her breast she knelt there motionless, bowed down in her absorbing prayer:

'O Jesus, give me strength not to complain; never

to grow weary of my cross; not to *hope* even for it to be taken away, unless it is Thy will! And for him whom I have given up for Thee, whom I have loved until now with too earthly a love perhaps, let him come at last to know and humbly love Thee, though now he may so offend Thee by his hatred and pride. But let no thought of self mingle in my prayer for him—no thought of merely earthly joy! Rather let me die than that any thought of me should tarnish his conversion to Thy faith!'

Meanwhile Mr. Mannering had gone into the vestry, where he and Father Walmsley talked long and earnestly on the one subject, the latter consoling, in his own saintly manner, the anxious father in his suffering for his child:

'God will Himself make it easy to you in time, Mr. Mannering, if she is destined never to be her old bright self again, if even what you hope for is denied, and she is to be always now a saddened woman instead of a happy child,—God, who has given *her* strength to renounce this proud infidel of whom she had made such an idol in her young heart. Did we not feel, Mr. Mannering,' he concluded, 'that when the time came, our bright merry little Gerty would prove worthy of her race?'

A few minutes later Gerty rose from her knees, with a sweet peaceful look upon her face, and was soon walking home again with her father, to begin the old life alone together once more.

CHAPTER XXII.

Two days later, while yet the wound was all fresh and sore in her heart, Gerty received the promised letter from Lady Hunter. It was waiting for her when she and her father got in from Mass, and she ran up-stairs to read it first alone.

'My darling Gerty,' wrote her cousin, 'I daresay this will cross on the way with your letter to me, but I cannot wait for its arrival to write to you, though it would only be useless to tell you in words how we are feeling it all, I and Sir Robert, to whom I have told everything, dear, as you wished. He says it has made me visibly older-looking already, to have had such a thing happening to one who was in my care, especially one so dear as you are.

'Last evening (I am going to tell you all exactly, for I feel you would rather know it, though it may seem cruel at first) Stanley Graham came in early, as he had said he would, an hour after I got back from the station. He came up-stairs to me at once, as I was sitting alone, and had left word for him to do so when he came in. I do not know what he thought or expected, but he asked immediately where you were—if you were better; not feeling sure, I suppose, how much I knew. Then I told him briefly that you were gone away—gone home again; and that as things were, I should hardly have detained you, even if I could have done so, which would have been impossible; but that you had left a note for him, which I then gave him. He took it and put it in his pocket, with a look, Gerty, which I shall never forget—such a look of bitter suffering. "Lady Hunter," he said to me, "she does not love me! It was a mistake." And his tone was so stern, that I am afraid, Gerty, I grew angry as well as sad; and I said to him, "You are a tyrant, Stanley, to wish to make her, for your sake, trample under foot feelings and convictions which you and I cannot understand and are not worthy to share. Not love you! How can *you* love *her*, to make her suffer so?" But I was sorry the minute I had spoken; for if ever I saw a man look the personification of grief and perplexity, *he* did, Gerty, as he turned and left me without answering a word. He gave me no opportunity of speaking to him all the evening, but studiously and politely avoided me. No one named you to him, love; for when you were once gone I told them all that the engagement was broken off, for reasons I could not mention; for I knew, dear, you would wish to spare him any additional pain to what he must have been suffering during all last evening, when he could not have absented himself without appearing remarkable. Well, this morning, after breakfast, he asked to speak to me; and he told me he had resolved to bid us farewell at once, and return to Briardale for a week or two, preparatory to going abroad for another year. I was not surprised, Gerty; and I attempted no useless dissuasion, but apologised to him for my harsh words of the day before. Then he said to me:

"Lady Hunter, I have nothing to forgive; and if I had, could I cherish resentment for a few hasty words spoken in sorrow, as they were? But you were right: perhaps I am a tyrant, fittest to be alone and unloved;

perhaps I ought never to have cherished a dream of love and domestic happiness. When you write to your cousin, Lady Hunter, will you thank her from me for her kindly letter? Tell her I cannot write to her myself after what she said of the cruelty of any needless intercourse; and that anything in her that may have pained me during that last interview I ascribe, not to her, but to those who have taught her. Tell her I ask *her* forgiveness for my sternness, which would not let me hide that where I love, as I love her, I must have all or nothing; that I could not *share* her heart, especially with a religion I hate. I should only have made her miserable, perhaps, with my unspoken jealousy, even if I had consented to everything she asked. Tell her so, Lady Hunter, and say farewell to her for me."

'Then he left me abruptly to prepare for his departure, and I did not see him again for two or three hours, when he came to bid good-bye to Sir Robert and myself. He told us not to expect to hear very often from him from abroad: it will be better, he says, for him not to have much intercourse with even such intimate friends as ourselves, for a time. But, Gerty, as he shook hands with me very, very earnestly, his manner was *so* softened as a tear glistened in his eye—a thing I have never seen before in him; and now that he is gone, I cannot but hope from it, love, though I scarcely know for what.

'I will not trouble you by writing any more to-day, love, except to repeat our closest sympathy, Gerty, and every kindest message to your father—especially one of thanks for his forgiveness for our share in it all. Write soon, darling, to say how you are. I need not tell you that our party here has had quite a gloom cast over it; for I cannot conceal that I am anxious and out of spirits, and they all (though they do not know the truth) feel that something sad has happened. *I* can only go on hoping—I *must*, or it would seem too cruel.

'Ever
'Your most loving cousin,
'JULIA HUNTER.'

It brought the tears again, that letter—the kind relieving tears—up from the very depths of her sore heart; and burying her face in her hands, she wept freely—wept out the yearning which must linger still, though the temptation to yield to it was past and conquered.

'He came home to England, this time hoping to remain and be so happy, and I have sent him away—back again to the old weary unloved life. O my God, help me to bear it!' Then, as soon as she could, she rose and dried her tears, and went down-stairs again.

'See, papa,' she said, as she gave him her cousin's letter, 'it is from Lady Hunter. Will you—read it? I—don't think I can—read it—so well for you, papa;' and her voice faltered.

He read it, with a look of pain on his face as he did so, and then gave it back to Gerty, and drew her to him.

'Was it wise, my darling, was it best to tell you all this, as she says?'

'O, yes, papa, indeed. If she had not, I might have fancied—worse, papa; I might have thought of it—more constantly still. But now that I know for certain —that—that—he is going so far away—' She paused, and then added, 'O, yes, papa, it is better to know all exactly; and now—it is all over.'

That day happened to be Father Walmsley's day for dining at the Grange, and he came more willingly than ever, he told Gerty with a smile, to welcome her home.

To him too she showed her cousin's letter; for she wished to tell him all, owing it to him, she told herself, for her past reserve, which he had so kindly forgiven. Then, as he returned it to her, she bent over the fire and laid it on the flames, as he watched her quietly.

'I know that is what you would tell me to do,' she said, with that sad smile so painful to see on the girlish face, ' so I am doing it of myself at once. If I kept it, Father Walmsley, I feel—I should not be able to keep from—often reading it, and thinking over every word; I *know* I should not. So now, I—can't.' But the quiet tone faltered at last, even while she tried to smile bravely again as her father reëntered the room.

And so the old life went on again—the old quiet life, outwardly unchanged; Stanley Graham's name never being mentioned between Gerty and her father —the name which was graven on *her* heart, and which was so often and so painfully in his mind too, as he watched his darling's quiet altered movements, and the sad patient look deepening every day on the sweet pale face.

It seemed to that tender father that he had never loved his precious child fully until now, when, bowed down with sorrow, and yet victorious over it, she had come back to his arms—back to the old routine of duties which she strove never to shrink from or grow weary of, but to perform *cheerfully* when she could, and *willingly* always. It was very beautiful and touching to see now the loving anxious care her father bestowed upon her; so constant, that she herself asked him one day, with a tender look and tone, but still trying to show some of the old playfulness for his sake, if he were afraid the wind would blow her away, unless he took such care of her.

And the honest country people, who all loved Gerty

so much, had not failed to notice how very long 'Miss Mannering' always knelt in church now after Mass and Benediction; how she stayed bowed down, as though quite forgetful of any presence but that One upon the altar. And from her pale quiet looks some of them fancied that some trouble or other must have come to her, in addition to the slight weakness from which they were told she had never been free since her visit to London. And they were told truly, for Gerty was, even bodily, not so strong as she had been; as though the inner wrench with which she had had to tear herself away from her heart's deep idolatry had affected the outward frame, weakening it for ever. She was so soon tired now—she who once never used to grow tired; so weary in the mornings often after the sleepless nights which visited her at intervals—the nights of quiet secret tears, not of complaining, but of patient irresistible yearning. But never could it be said that Gerty looked *unhappy*, even by those who thought her looking saddest and most changed; for the sweet peace ever in her heart in its sorest desolation was shadowed forth always on her girlish face.

Gerty had been at home about three weeks, when Rupert came to pay his promised visit, which was but a short one of three or four days, because he could not leave the college for longer just then. He was in the seminary still, pursuing his studies, and had thought he would not be able to go home yet for another month or two; but a letter from Mr. Mannering to his superiors, asking that he might come at once, if only for a day or two, for his sister's sake, had procured the desired leave, and he was at home now at Whitewell for three short precious days.

His presence was even more of a delight and consolation to Gerty than her father had hoped. She was almost gay again as she talked to her idolised brother, who was mixed up with none of her trouble; who brought no associations or recollections of it to her mind, except the thought of how entirely he would have been lost to her if she had yielded to that terrible temptation. She told her father on one of the three mornings, when they all went to Mass together, that it was well Rupert was staying no longer with them, for she had been dreadfully distracted several times during Mass, watching the sweet heavenly expression that developed itself so strongly upon his face as he prayed.

'I'm afraid, papa,' she said, 'I got thinking how proud we ought to be of him, even now; and how proud we shall be when he is a priest, and I shall hear people praising my Jesuit brother!' And her father smiled, and thanked God that they had been able to procure this consolation for his little girl.

Then Rupert had so much to tell them about the college and his old companions, whose names they knew so well; and they had so much to talk of, without much mention of Gerty's London visit or her short one to Nethercotes, that the evenings passed all too quickly—the pleasant evenings by the fire in the old dining-room, which reminded Rupert and Gerty so much of the days long ago, when they used to play at their favourite game in the priest's hiding-hole, with their father often looking up from his book to watch them. Rupert carefully avoided any open notice of his sister's pale looks and quiet sad demeanour, even when they were most visible, which was not so often during his stay; but Gerty knew how deeply he felt for her, and his silent sympathy, and the prayers she knew he offered for her, were the best comfort he could have given her.

Only once, on the morning of his departure, when they were taking a farewell walk alone together round the park, did Gerty openly speak of the trouble, and mention Stanley Graham's name to Rupert.

'I don't like you to go away thinking I would not speak to you of it, Rupert dear,' she said; and then she talked openly for a few minutes of all that had happened, in a low trembling tone.

'Gerty,' Rupert said, as she paused, 'if you knew what I felt when I got my father's letter and knew what you had escaped, what this—this Mr. Graham had tried to lead you into! Gerty, you might, perhaps, never have seen home again if he had accomplished his task!'

'No, Rupert, I might not; I do not know. You see, I—I think he would have wanted to marry me at once. I should have had to become his wife while I was at Nethercotes, and—we could not have let papa know until it was over.' And her voice trembled very much now. 'He meant that, I know, because I could not have come back and told papa that I had promised to give up my religion; and Stanley would have been afraid of losing me if I once came home again.'

'Thank God, Gerty, he *has* lost you!' said her brother quickly and fervently. 'You yourself can say that too, can't you, dear, while yet you are praying for him?'

'Yes, Rupert.'

And the deep sigh spoke more than words could have done, as they turned again to go into the house. And as they said good-bye, two or three hours later at the station, Gerty whispered:

'Don't think too hardly of him, Rupert; you would not if you knew him. Don't, if only for my sake. Pray for him, Rupert, as you would if you only knew him,' she repeated.

'Don't be afraid, Gerty,' was the reply. 'I shall never forget to do that, to pray for him, whatever I may think of him; and I will try and not think hardly for your sake, and because it is not for us to judge our fellow-creatures, Gerty.'

CHAPTER XXIII.

It wanted but a week from the beginning of Lent, and Gerty was going to pay her promised visit of a few days to N—— Convent, which could be deferred no longer, after the pressing letters she had received from the nuns and one or two of her old companions, the latter, of course, being in entire ignorance that anything had come to sadden their bright sweet favourite, Gerty Mannering. Her father was going to take her, and intended remaining the few days at the little country inn at which he had always stayed during his visits to Gerty when she was at school.

'It will be like the old times, Gerty,' he said; 'and I shall like to see Rev. Mother again and all of them, and the old place itself too.'

'Besides, papa,' she replied, with something of the old arch look, 'you could not lose sight of *me* for so many days, I know.'

And so one bright cold morning very early in March they found themselves in the train, beginning the journey which had so long been such a familiar one during those past happy peaceful years.

When they reached N——, Mr. Mannering sent Gerty on at once to the convent alone.

'I know you would rather go alone first, Gerty,' he said, 'to get the first meeting over; it will be best. Tell Rev. Mother I will come in the morning to see her.'

And with a lingering kiss Gerty left him, and took her seat in the coach which was to take her to the convent.

Her father was right: it was less painful for her to be alone on her first arrival and during the familiar drive, which was so associated with the careless happy past. It was winter too now, as it had been when she had last looked on the quiet country scene, when she had left it, but fourteen months ago, without a cloud on her brow or a trouble in her heart, except those brought by the pain of parting with her dear kind friends the nuns and the companions who had all so loved her. Then as she drove into the convent grounds her heart contracted with a sharper pain still, as she recalled her own words to her father as she had last driven through these familiar spots: 'I wonder how it will all look when I see it again; I wonder if *I* shall be changed at all, papa. I shall look a little older, I suppose; more of a young lady, that's all.'

The time had come now: she looked again upon the beloved scene, and though *it* was unaltered, was *she* not changed as she could never have dreamed of—changed as fully as though the lapse of years had passed over her head, to be the old laughing careless Gerty never, never more? Her heart beat painfully as she waited in the reception-room; but directly Rev. Mother appeared, bringing with her dear Sister Teresa, Gerty forgot her confusion in their hearty kisses and earnest words of welcome. They forbore, as Rupert had done, from noticing her pale looks and visible thinness, knowing as they did, though not yet fully, the story of the terrible shadow that had come so early to darken the bright life of their beloved pupil; but they were shocked at the change nevertheless, though they had been partly expecting it.

Then for the next few days the old convent life existed again for Gerty; because, though they treated her as a visitor, and gave her a nice little room of her own, she insisted on living as much as possible with the girls, most of whom were her old companions, instead of always being apart 'in state,' as she called it. She sat among them at recreation, to their great delight and her own increased popularity, listening to the innocent simple talk which once had been so interesting to her, of all the little changes that had taken place since she left, laughing while one girl who used always to be in scrapes in Gerty's time told her how she never got into any now, but that another had quite taken her place in that line, one who used to be quite a model a year since; and how Sister So-and-so was not half as strict as she used to be; and what a grand retreat they had had last year, and how sorry they had been for Gerty to miss it —until she could have almost wished, as she sat there, to wake and find herself still at school, and the past year all a dream. And yet no, she could not—O, no, not for worlds, spite of the terrible pain and yearning in her heart.

'I *cannot* wish never to have known him, never to have loved him—O, no! Even if I never see him again on earth, I can pray for him always; and if only he ever comes to God, even at the last, all my pain and sorrow will have been but an easy price for a soul like his.'

But though Gerty did her best to be merry and cheerful, and always to hide that any shadow had crossed her life, even the innocent convent girls were not wholly deceived, and were not without an idea that something more than delicate health was the matter with Gerty.

'I never saw any one so changed in my life,' said one confidentially to another, among a group of the elder girls. 'She is not very well, the dear, I know, of course, and she is just as *nice* as ever; but somehow it seems as if she had seen some trouble or other, or were thinking of something quite different from what we are all talking about.'

'And I should not at all wonder if she were,' said another, who was considered rather a worldly girl, and a great authority on worldly matters, having only come to school rather late. 'You don't suppose she has been all this time at home for nothing, and in London too last season,' she added somewhat contemptuously.

'And then,' put in a sweet pious little girl, 'she does have such long talks with Sister Teresa. And I know she is a great deal in the chapel, when she is not with us. She let it out accidentally; and I am sure it is beautiful to see her pray, when we *do* see her, as if she quite forgot everything and everybody but our Lord.'

And so the week passed, with its quiet sweet routine, varied only by the two or three visits of her father to the convent; and on the last evening Gerty knelt at Benediction in her usual place, the one they had allotted to her on her arrival. She had been feeling even physically tired and weary all day, as she often did now, but she stayed in the chapel after the rest were all gone, bowed down alone and motionless; and as she did so a strange feeling seemed to come over her, a thought almost like inspiration, which made her start joyously, and then look up with a trembling wonder.

'O my Jesus,' she prayed, with her gaze fixed on the tabernacle, 'let it be so, if it be Thy will; I am ready, with Thy grace. Take my life for his soul; give to my prayers the grace of his conversion to Thy holy faith; let me not ask in vain for one who would be so great and noble in Thy service. And that no thought of me and our mutual love may sully his turning to Thee, take me away out of life, so that he may be able to serve Thee *perfectly*. I offer myself to Thee without reserve to die, if it be Thy will, to obtain Thy grace for *him;* and, O sweet Jesus, Thyself comfort my father if Thou takest me; comfort him as Thou canst so well do.'

And as she prayed the solemn prayer she felt no excitement or perturbation, but only a strange sweet calm, as though Jesus Himself, speaking from His tabernacle, had asked this sacrifice from her, and had Himself given her the grace to offer it.

That night, when she bade good-night to her dear Sister Teresa, the latter, knowing nothing of the prayer Gerty had offered up, remarked how calm and happy she looked to-night, and told her of it.

'Well, I *feel* calm and happy to-night, somehow, sister,' Gerty answered; 'more so than I have done—since it all happened, in spite of the sorrow of having to part with you again to-morrow, sister dear.' But she said no more—nothing of the strange feeling that had come to her.

And during the journey home, too, she looked so peaceful and was so cheerful, that her father was full of thankful rejoicing, telling himself that her visit to the convent had done his darling more good than he could have hoped for. Only to Father Walmsley, two or three days after she got home, Gerty spoke of what she had done, quietly and simply, half afraid he would disapprove.

'But it was no harm, was it, Father Walmsley?' she said; 'because God will not grant what I asked unless He wills it, you know. He will only take me if He wishes; so it must be all right, must it not?'

Father Walmsley's voice was very earnest and solemn as he replied:

'And you are not afraid, Gerty, that if such a sacrifice

were really asked of you, you would shrink from it; that you would cling to life with regret when the time came for parting with it—regret perhaps for—his sake ?'

'Father Walmsley, I have thought of all that, of everything—even of papa, and I don't think God would let me feel afraid if the time really came any more than I do now. You see, father, I can't tell you how it is, but I have such a strange kind of feeling that if—Stanley Graham ever became a Catholic, God would want him in some special way for Himself; and how could I want to hinder that? O Father Walmsley, if you knew him—how noble he is, how naturally great—you would think me but a poor little price to gain him for God. And if it should be so, if I am right, our Lord will help me to send entirely out of my heart the earthly love that has been so strong—too strong, I think now—and I should be able to care for him only as some one to be saved and made happy in a spiritual way. I should be able to feel like that before I died.'

Father Walmsley was startled and disturbed as he looked at the young sweet face and listened to her speaking so calmly, so evidently without any thought of anything extraordinary in what she said; but he exerted himself to smile and make light of it, fearing her ideas might be the result of overstrained imagination, induced by her trouble and consequent bodily weakness.

'My child, do you think I can let you talk like this, of dying, as if it were nothing? What would your father say, Gerty, if he thought you were so willing to leave him? Do you suppose I was in earnest when I asked you if you were ready to make such a sacrifice? No; in a year's time you will be asking me whatever I thought of you for telling me such a thing, and will be laughing at yourself for it when you are stronger,

Gerty. Meanwhile no harm has been done: the prayer would be pleasing to God, whether it is granted or not.'

But Gerty did not laugh as he had hoped, or look confused; she only smiled as she said quietly,

'Father Walmsley, it is just because I feel that I never *shall* be stronger, that I think God put the idea into my mind—for, you know, I might as well offer to Him for such an object what I may have to give up soon in any case. I have not told any one but you, Father Walmsley'—and she hesitated now—'but I have never felt myself really well since—since that—night; I feel as if I never should, even if—if I became—his wife. I feel it here, so often'—and she put her hand on her heart—'as if it could never really recover—from that—that struggle; as if I had had—a wrench of some kind, which was too strong for me. But *don't* tell papa, Father Walmsley, because, you know, I *may* be mistaken.'

'And I hope and trust you are, Gerty,' he said cheerily but earnestly. 'No wonder you feel like that as yet; but believe me, my child, you will recover, so do not fancy or think about it;' and with a sincere 'God bless you!' he dismissed her, pondering long after she had gone on what had passed.

'What if it is no weak ailing fancy, what if the conviction I have always had at heart should be a true one, and little Gerty is proved to be no ordinary weak girl, but as true and generous a martyr—made so by trouble and God's grace—as any of her ancestors, who gave up their lives and liberty in the days of persecution?'

CHAPTER XXIV.

THE months had passed on to June; everything looked fresh and green again—Whitewell Park all beautiful and luxuriant once more with foliage; but Gerty grew no stronger, only weaker, even on these long bright days, when she could sit out under her beloved trees, listening to the singing of the birds, and breathing the warm sweet summer air.

The change had come on so gradually, and she had hidden it so carefully as long as she could, only laughing when a doctor was mentioned to her, that her father had more than once flattered himself she was getting stronger, and that the weakness that remained was only the natural consequence which lingered after her trouble, and which, with care, would in time leave her altogether. Not that he ever hoped to see his darling the bright happy girl she had once been—not that his little sunbeam could ever regain her old radiance; and indeed it seemed as if, somehow, he had grown to love his sweet sad patient Gerty with a love which surpassed the old one; as if, except for her sake, he was content to have her at least safe back in his care, to be cherished and jealously guarded, until God in His own good time should, if He willed it, restore her even to earthly happiness.

He had learned to think forgivingly of and pray for Stanley Graham, whose name was never mentioned in the old Grange—never openly—though it never left their hearts; he had grown even to pity the proud man in his restless unhappy exile, so young still and so world-weary, whom the demon of pride and human intellect was holding so fast in his toils.

So that it was not until June approached that Mr. Mannering was at last no longer able to ward off his anxiety—no longer able to shut his eyes to the fact that Gerty, instead of recovering, was growing weaker and thinner day by day—fainting too, once or twice, when she had only been sitting quietly with him under the cool shade of the trees. Though fearing to alarm her, he sent, after one of these occasions, for the doctor who had been their attendant for years, who accordingly came, without, however, rousing any of the signs of alarm in Gerty which her father had feared. She answered all his questions quietly and smilingly, and was so cheerful that he told her she deserved to be very quickly well, she was such a good patient. Then he took Mr. Mannering apart, and told him that he could not as yet see any cause for permanent alarm; that there was no chronic disease, only very great weakness and debility, and that great care would be needed, as well as constant nursing, before she would be anything like her old self again.

'She must go away too,' he said, 'to the seaside somewhere, where she could be perfectly quiet, with nothing to excite her;' hinting delicately that there were symptoms that she *had* been over-excited and over-strained in some way.

'Dr. Baldwin,' replied Mr. Mannering, with perfect truth and still keeping the painful secret, 'she has never seemed quite the same to me since her visit to London last summer, when she stayed, you know, with her cousin Lady Hunter. Perhaps I have been negligent in not sooner insisting on having your advice;

but she has been so much against the idea, and so cheerful about her health all through, that—that—you see, I could not—admit anxiety of this kind;' and the pain of the tone, which told of the inward vague fearful forebodings, struck all too plainly on his listener's ear, much as he tried to speak quietly.

But Dr. Baldwin reassured him, telling him that they could hardly have done anything until now, when Miss Mannering's illness first seemed to assume a definite shape; then, promising to call every day until they should leave home, he took his departure, looking as he left the park considerably graver than on entering it.

That evening, when he had bade good-night to Gerty and left her in bed, with Mrs. Leeson sitting with her, Mr. Mannering walked down to the presbytery, and told Father Walmsley the result of the doctor's visit. The good priest was startled, as we all are by bad news, even news which we have been expecting; but he could not betray how little he was surprised to Mr. Mannering; he could not betray Gerty's confidence by telling her father how anxiously though secretly he had watched her all these months, ever since that strange revelation she had made to him, and which he had with such a solemn feeling seen so likely to be proved to be no mere fancy such as he had hoped.

Since that day on which she had confided it to him, the subject had never been mentioned between him and Gerty. He would not speak of it, through fear of keeping up the impression in her mind, and he felt she shrank from perhaps incurring his displeasure by naming it yet again as if of any moment, though he knew it was ever strengthening in her mind with a calm sweet conviction and resignation; he knew it afresh every time she asked him, in that quiet though sometimes trembling tone, to go on praying for Stanley Graham —*never* to forget him. And knowing what he did, he had lately begun seriously to take the alarm, before her father did or dared to do, when Gerty began frequently to be absent from the morning Mass which had been such a loved constant duty, being too weak to rise always so early; and he had been on the point of advising Mr. Mannering quietly to call in medical advice, when he was relieved by the former coming himself to tell him he had done so.

They were to go away in two or three days now, so Father Walmsley came up on the following morning to hear Gerty's confession and give her Communion, because she was too weak to go down to church fasting; and afterwards, when she had taken her slight breakfast, he went up-stairs to her again, and talked to her for a little while kindly and cheerily.

'But you look quite happy, Gerty—quite as if you intended to come back as strong as ever again. Your father needs consolation most of the two, I think,' he said with a smile.

'Poor papa!' and Gerty clasped her hands as if in pain for a minute; then she added in a low earnest tone, 'Father Walmsley, you have always been his best friend; you will be so—always, still, in the future?' and the sweet brown eyes, so calmly lustrous now, looked at him with a mournful entreaty.

'Do you doubt it, my child?' he said, still cheerily; ' and yours too, I hope, Gerty.'

Then as he rose to leave her, as if with an irresistible impulse she turned to him again, with a strangely sweet smile and low quiet voice :

'Father Walmsley, if—it is coming—what I thought, what I told you of, you know, three months since, do not be uneasy, I—am not afraid; I have been growing so—used to it, until God has made me almost wish for it to be His will, because—I know, if—I were taken, it would be in answer—to my prayer—for him, for Stanley Graham; I *know* he would not be let to shut his heart to grace long after, because—if I die—it will be that—God wants him, and I shall be, O, so happy in that knowledge!'

Almost reverently now, the good priest replied,

'Gerty, thank God, who has enabled you to be resigned, to say from your heart, whatever happens, "God's will be done," even if it should be to die and give up all thought of earthly love.' Then recovering from his emotion, he added, still seriously but cheerily:

'But we must not *throw* away our lives, Gerty—we must not knowingly neglect our health; so, while you are away, do all in your power to recover and grow strong; tell yourself you *must* do, for your father's sake; be very obedient and do *whatever* is ordered for your good, or I shall have to write you a lecture, you know, on self-will and morbid fancies, eh, Gerty?' And with a very kind farewell and 'God bless you!' he left her alone, having had a hard struggle to conceal his admiration and edification, no less than the sorrow, despite his cheery words, which had taken root in his heart.

And so, two days later, Gerty and her father, with an old confidential servant to attend as nurse to Gerty, were established once more at Beachdown, the little watering-place which was good for Gerty now, for the reason which had made it not so good before, because it was quiet and retired. And the change and bracing air made her at first often feel so much better and stronger, that her father told himself his darling was going to recover much more quickly than the doctor had expected, refusing even on her weaker days to admit anything like a real fear into his heart that he might be mistaken—that the apparent rallying might be only delusive. How could he, that poor watchful father—how could he yet bring himself to believe that not only the brightness of his little sunbeam, but that sunbeam itself, pale and shadowy as it was now, might soon be hidden from his loving eyes for ever in this world? How could he, when Gerty was so cheerful always, so peaceful and calm during the long delicious talks they held together sitting on the shore, or gazing out over the sea from their window on days when she was too weak to go out, or when he read the cheerful letters she wrote to Lady Hunter as he sat by her sofa, looking up into his face with a sweet smile whenever she paused in her writing? She never said a word that could alarm her cousin; so that when Lady Hunter wrote in reply, though she was anxious and solicitous concerning Gerty's delicate health, she plainly had no fear as to her ultimate recovery.

Once in a letter, which came during the third week of their stay in Beachdown, Lady Hunter mentioned Stanley Graham, from whom Gerty knew she heard but seldom, as he had said must be the case. He was in Italy just now, she wrote, travelling up and down, now and then staying with his uncle at Nice; and then she told that his last letter had betrayed terrible gloom and restless discontent, with all his old uneasiness increased a hundredfold. 'He does not write your name openly, love,' she wrote, 'but his *thoughts* are visible in every line. I am telling you this, darling, because you would *fancy* it all, and even worse, perhaps, if I did not; and I know the certainty is easier to bear, because it makes you have something definite to ask for when you offer up the prayers in which even I can join, Gerty. But if my doing so has caused one useless pain to your cruelly tried heart, forgive me, love, for you know all I would do, if I could, to save you pain and bring you happiness. Write soon, dear, and tell me you are getting quite strong and hopeful again, and how soon I may come and see you in your dear old Grange after the season is over. I wish it were over already, love, for I seem to have no heart for gaiety this time; I think so constantly of last year, and all that has come since.'

Lady Hunter was right, as even Mr. Mannering admitted; for to hear of Stanley Graham as restless and weary gave Gerty more hope, even while it pained her for his sake, than if she had been told he was haughtily calm and undisturbed, expressing no feeling even to so intimate a friend as Lady Hunter.

'It may not be all for my sake that he is restless and unhappy,' she said to herself almost joyously; 'not all because he cannot bring himself to yield and believe that I love him. May it not be also because he is fighting against God's grace, trying not to hear it whispering to his heart? O my God! if it be so, if Thou art calling him, let him not resist too long; let him not weary Thy mercy; give to my prayers the grace of conversion for him; give it in exchange for my life, poor offering though that may be.'

And the hope brought by the never-tiring prayer brought the colour again to Gerty's face, and the bright light to her eyes as she gazed out at the tossing sea, asking herself if she were really the same girl who but a year since had been so full of life and gaiety, who had sat at the opera with Stanley Graham, feeling as though earth could never have a sweeter hour for her, as though to tear herself away for ever from that dreamlike existence would have been a task so dreary as to be impossible. And now here she was, with life ebbing quietly away, without a wish on her own part, or for her own sake, to recall it; with earth and its joys for ever fading from her view; with the love which had been such idolatry changing and softening into the more pure heavenly feeling, which made the sacrifice of her own life appear as nothing by the side of the beloved one's soul saved and gained for God. And sweetly and humbly unconscious of any merit in the willing sacrifice, conscious only of a deep thankfulness for God's grace which had suggested it, Gerty prayed on, with a strength which rose superior to her bodily weakness, during these last quiet days by the sea at Beachdown.

CHAPTER XXV.

'FATHER WALMSLEY, may God help me still to forgive him—the man who has brought her to this, who will have been her murderer!' And Mr. Mannering grasped his friend's hand for a minute, and then, sitting down, buried his face in his hands in the agony of his grief.

It was only a week since they had returned home from Beachdown, but Gerty had grown so much worse, so weak as to be unable to walk, that the doctor had been obliged to declare his alarm to Mr. Mannering, and had asked that a celebrated physician should be sent for from London to give his opinion and advice on Miss Mannering's case, concerning which he himself said nothing more definite yet than that he was afraid there was immediate cause for apprehension.

Frozen, as it were, with the shock, Mr. Mannering seemed unable to ask any questions or do anything but assent mechanically when the doctor offered to telegraph himself to London to arrange, if possible, the consultation with the physician in question for the next day, and then abruptly wishing him good-morning, returned to his post by Gerty's sofa.

But for the presence of Father Walmsley, who devoted almost the rest of that day to the Grange, Mr. Mannering would hardly have been able to endure the hours of alternate despair and persistent hope which intervened before the physician could be expected to arrive with Dr. Baldwin. The good priest had a more difficult task to console him than in attending Gerty herself; for with her, but for her father's sake, it was all sweet peace and resignation, as though the struggle with earth, and its joys and hopes, were long since over—fought in the past terrible hours which were doing their *bodily* work now upon her. Even her father could scarcely murmur in presence of his darling's sweet peaceful face, or as he listened to her tender words of consolation, by which she strove during all that day of suspense to cheer and strengthen him for whatever might be the verdict concerning her.

'Because you know, papa, whatever happens, even if—I am taken from you, I shall be your own little Gerty always, loving and praying for you, if for a time we shall be outwardly separated,' she had whispered, with her arms round his neck, as at last he bade her 'goodnight,' and was persuaded by Father Walmsley to go to bed himself for a few hours.

And now the physician had been, and after having seen Gerty, and having held a long consultation with Dr. Baldwin, he had taken Mr. Mannering into another room to tell him his opinion, or rather his confident, undoubting judgment. Being requested to conceal nothing, he said, as kindly and delicately as he could, that Miss Mannering's case was hopeless. She was dying slowly of a decline which must have begun some months since, and could not have been cured, though it might perhaps have been arrested for a time if it had been noticed in its very early stage; but independent of that, there was also a heart complaint now very strongly developed, which might, if great care were not taken, carry off the patient within a week or two. He added this last sad information in order that every possible care might be taken to prolong the life which need not necessarily end for weeks or even months yet; and as Miss Mannering herself seemed so calm and undisturbed, and to fear so little, it was most favourable to her complaint to leave her so by telling her as little as possible of her state, as yet at least, until she grew anxious and insisted on the knowledge. And knowing nothing of the pure martyr spirit which animated the dying frame he had examined, nothing of how his young patient would have been shocked to have heard him counsel such careless, tardy preparation for death, the great physician pocketed his fee, and with a few polite words of sympathy took his leave of the grief-stricken father, to whom he had been forced to deliver the terrible tidings which by one stroke felled the brightness of his life for ever.

It was as soon as the two doctors had left the house that Mr. Mannering went into the room where Father Walmsley awaited him, and there told him the sad verdict in that agonised exclamation which seemed to come, not from his lips, but up from the very depths of his heart. Then Father Walmsley sat down by him, and spoke to him of God and His wonderful designs; of how we cannot judge them, even if at first the manner of them seems so hard—too hard, often—to bear without His special grace.

'Mr. Mannering, if He has given you a child to bring up for Him, and if now He wants her for Himself, having, through the means of the very man whom it is so hard to forgive, raised her in a brief space to sanctity to which she might not have attained in a lifetime of years if earthly love and joy had been her portion, do you grudge her to Him, the pure soul He wants thus early for Himself?'

'But she is my one treasure left, my ewe-lamb, who

I thought would be the brightness of my old age, Father Walmsley; must I give her up? I have my boy, I know, though him I have given proudly to God's service; but, dear and precious as Rupert is, he is not like my little girl to me—her mother's parting gift. Can God ask me to see Him take her away and live?'

'Mr. Mannering, if she is weary of earth and longs for heaven; if the cruel blow that rent her heart with its too great human love has shown her how vain and fleeting is all earthly joy, so that she can never wish for it again; if she is one of God's own especial favourites, and He wants to take her safe away from any more care and trouble or temptation,—will you not, after the first hard grief is over, be prouder to have a sweet saint to pray and wait for you in heaven—one who will be for evermore your own, dying thus early in her girlhood—than if you had given her into some human keeping, which must of necessity have been dearer than your own to her—given her to a man instead of to God?'

Then for nearly half an hour the good priest spoke on: of Gerty's own sweet resignation; of her generous forgiveness of, and unselfish constant prayers for, the proud infidel who, in his exacting jealous love, had trampled on her tender heart because she could not for his sake belie its most sacred feelings. 'Will you be less generous and forgiving than the sufferer herself, Mr. Mannering? Will you not say, "God's will be done," and still join Gerty in her prayers for that poor restless soul?'

Then Mr. Mannering lifted up his face, ten years older looking, Father Walmsley thought, in that hour, and said in a broken voice, 'May God forgive me, Father Walmsley, for my rebellion; may He help me to say from my heart what I *must* say in fact, "His will be done!" Go to Gerty, Father Walmsley, and tell her that her father will follow soon to pray by her side for him who is the cause of her death.' Then he told Father Walmsley exactly what the physician had said, how carefully any excitement or needless agitation must be warded off from the invalid.

'Do not fear, Mr. Mannering; I will tell her quietly and gently, and as gradually as possible. If I mistake not, she will be neither startled nor afraid, thank God, who has been preparing her so well all these months, though we knew it not!' Then he left the room and went up-stairs to Gerty's bedroom.

She was still lying upon the sofa by the window, with her eyes closed and her hands crossed gently; but she looked up now as Father Walmsley entered, and the old housekeeper, who was with her, rose to leave the room.

'She has been wondering when you would come, Father Walmsley,' she said as she left the priest alone with her young mistress.

'Father Walmsley, you have come to tell me what the doctors said; I saw them go more than an hour since,' and she pointed gently down the park; then turning quickly to Father Walmsley again, without any sign of agitation, she said earnestly, 'Tell me everything exactly, please, Father Walmsley. Don't be afraid of—shocking me; I know it already, you know; God has been telling it me quietly all these months, even when you could not believe it, Father Walmsley.' And there was such a strange sweet smile on the pale face which looked up at him, that the priest, who had known her as a merry careless child, and then as a bright happy girl full of natural earthly longings, felt awed and hushed, as if in presence of a saint.

But he sat down quietly by her side and began his

task, which she had made so easy for him—the task of telling her that a few weeks, or at most months, must see her in the grave; that without great care she might be called away even sooner and more suddenly; and that for her father's sake she must avoid *anything* that could hasten her death—even too much prayer, which might weary her, at least physically, in her weak state. While he was speaking, with that kind gentle voice and fatherly manner, Gerty listened quietly with downcast eyes; then as he paused at last, she raised them, and he saw the tears glistening in their depths.

'Poor papa,' she whispered; 'only the thought of him makes it hard! Only for him it would be so easy, so sweet, with God's grace; so joyful, Father Walmsley, because now I know my prayer—for—*him*—will be heard.'

'And, my child, apart from the thought of your father, apart from that grief which will be holy even at the last, are you sure there is no other earthly regret to overcome? no human love which was so strong in you, yet to make it hard to give up hope—to be ready, now the time is coming, to die so young? Gerty, if it were possible that—Stanley Graham could stand by your side again now—if he came to ask your forgiveness and spoke to you with the old winning words of love, would not the struggle be hard to be *perfectly* resigned to die—not to wish to live? It would be but natural, my child; but I ask you so that, for the time that is left, we may ask God to take away even that from your heart, to make the sacrifice you have already offered, and which He is accepting, *quite* perfect, Gerty.'

For a minute Gerty was silent, with her face bent over her clasped hands, as the vision of Stanley Graham rose in her mind, clear and distinct; as the proud face in its beauty seemed to look at her with that pleading she had seen upon it on that last terrible night; as the rich low voice seemed to ring again like music in her ears; and for a minute earth tried to bring her back from heaven—back to her idolatry and human longings.

But God, whom she had refused to deny for His creature in the past, to whom she had turned for help in her hour of trial, did not desert her now when the evil spirit tried to whisper to her again: He gave her strength to turn from the very thought of temptation, to resist it with scarce a sigh.

'Father Walmsley,' she said at last in a low solemn tone, 'I know I am very weak; I know that without God's grace I should have been at this moment what I dare not think of, a wretched apostate for the sake of him I loved with a feeling far too great and absorbing, I know now, which will be the thing I shall be most afraid to look back upon when I am dying, because I may have to suffer so long for it before I can see God in heaven, Father Walmsley. But still I do not think there will be any regret in my heart, any yearning for him in a human way, though to see him again before I died would be such joy. I *think* I could bid him farewell calmly, joyfully almost, if he were a Catholic, Father Walmsley. You see, father, everything looks so different from what it did a year since, when I shrank from the very idea of dying. The shock was so—great to find—what a dream it had all been—after I had been waiting and hoping so long for it; a dream so very short and brief, that to give up earth now is not what it would have been then; now, too, when I feel this sweet certain hope that I am not dying in vain, but that such a great soul as—*his*, will be gained for God in His own good time.'

Then Father Walmsley told her gently of her father's terrible grief, and of how difficult it was to him to forgive the man who had broken her heart, as he said.

'But he *will* still forgive him, won't he, Father Walmsley? He does not refuse?' she asked in a low painful whisper.

'No, no, my child; no longer now. He has conquered in the struggle, and is coming now to pray by your side for him, so that the act of resignation you both wish to make will be proved to be perfect indeed.' And as he rose to fetch Mr. Mannering, Gerty strove to keep calm for the meeting with the father who must soon close her eyes in death.

He entered and knelt down silently by her side, and as she put her arms round his neck, they wept there together, his tears mingling with hers.

'Poor papa, poor darling papa!' she whispered at last. 'But you are not really losing me, you know, papa; I shall only be outwardly hidden for a while. And you can always, not only at first, but in years to come, when you can hope that I may be, perhaps, safe with God, when I have satisfied for my sins in Purgatory—well, even then you can think of me as your little girl still, always young, and never having left you for any human creature.' And she tried to smile as she looked up into her father's face, while he himself, with a terrible effort, calmed his outward grief, dreading the continued agitation for his darling. 'And, papa,' she added very gently and sweetly, 'I *know* you still forgive—Stanley Graham; so—let us, before Father Walmsley goes, say the rosary together for him, that our Lady may help him not to resist God's grace.'

And kneeling down by Mr. Mannering's side, Father Walmsley recited the rosary aloud, Gerty and her father answering; she herself the calmest and least disturbed of the three in that solemn hour, with the shadow of death hovering over her; the one who so lately seemed to have a long bright life before her, who might have looked to enjoy it still when the two who prayed with her were laid in their graves.

That night Mr. Mannering wrote to Lady Hunter a short agonised letter, telling her all, feeling as he did so what a terrible shock it would be to her; for his last letter from Beachdown, ten days before, had told her that Gerty, if not decidedly better, was at least no worse, anything like danger never having been mentioned to her. To Rupert he felt unable to write—utterly unable to tell the news that Gerty was certainly dying; so Father Walmsley had promised to do it for him, as gently and kindly as possible, with a request that he might come home for a few days if his sister should grow suddenly worse, and he should be sent for.

The next afternoon, when Mr. Mannering was sitting by Gerty's sofa, her little hand laid in his as he tried to read quietly for her from a book Father Walmsley had brought that morning, he was summoned from the room by a message that he was wanted down-stairs, and having reluctantly consigned Gerty to the care of the servant who was her especial attendant, he went into the drawing-room. As he entered, he drew back with a start, for Lady Hunter stood before him, dressed plainly and darkly, and looking terribly pale.

'Mr. Mannering,' she began at once, as he took her hand, 'don't send me away, though I know the sight of me must be painful at first, being as I am the cause, however innocently, of—it all. Let me stay, at least for a time, and help to nurse her, to relieve you a little, though my presence will be but a poor substitute to the poor darling herself. Is it—really—true, that it—is so hopeless? We were so terribly shocked,

Mr. Mannering, Sir Robert and I, for you as much as for—her almost.'

Controlling his emotion as well as he could, he answered her, still holding her hand:

'It *is* true, Lady Hunter; God help me to bear it—not to repine! Do not call yourself the cause of it all, Lady Hunter, if you do not wish to add to my grief, you who have been so kind to her. It is so very, very good of you to come like this—more than we could ever have asked for or expected. You see, much as I can do for her, much as I seem to grudge every instant away from her'—and his voice faltered—'there are things you will be able to do and think of so much better, for you will have to excuse me if there are times when I seem incapable of anything—seem paralysed, somehow, when I realise—it all.'

She laid her hand kindly on his arm.

'I am *so* glad I have come, Mr. Mannering, and so will Sir Robert be—so grateful to you for letting me stay. May I see her now?' and she looked up with the tears in her eyes.

'I will go up first a minute to prepare her, Lady Hunter. It might perhaps startle her to see you without being told you were here, for we did not even observe your cab drive up, as the blind is down in her room;' and he went up-stairs quickly, already feeling a kind of sustaining comfort in Lady Hunter's presence —the soft yet strengthening comfort which only a woman can really give.

'Gerty darling,' he said, as he entered the bedroom 'there is a lady down-stairs who wants to see you, to stay and help to nurse you.'

Gerty looked up with her old bright smile:

'Not Julia, is it, papa?'

'Yes, my darling.'

'Ah, how good of her, papa! It makes me so happy, because she will help you like no one else could, and *make* you take rest when I could not persuade you, papa darling.'

A minute or two later Lady Hunter was by her side, with her arms round her neck, and her tears flowing freely but quietly, because she controlled herself with a strong effort for fear of agitating the dear little invalid.

'Gerty darling,' she said, as Mr. Mannering left them alone for a short time, 'I *cannot* believe it even now, scarcely. It seems so—so cruel. And I thought to come so soon and find you quite well again. Do they really say it is so—hopeless, darling?'

'Yes, Julia,' was the quiet reply; 'I made them tell me everything. But I knew it before, Julia; *I* knew long since I should never get better; and so—you see, I have grown used to the thought, except—for—papa.'

'But, my darling, I cannot understand it. It is so strange, so painful, somehow, for one so young and lately so bright to be so little afraid—so willing to die; I cannot understand it, even after—all you have suffered, love.'

'Because you don't understand yet what God's grace is, Julia—what it can do, even for one young and weak like I am. Besides, if I did resist, and could not be resigned, would that save me, Julia—make me live one hour longer than God wills?'

'But can nothing be done, Gerty? Is it really God's will, as you say, that your poor father is to lose you? Is there no further remedy to be tried, no change of air and scene that might do good at least for a time?' persisted Lady Hunter, in her inability to arrive at the resignation which yet awed and impressed her so in the dying girl herself.

'Julia, papa asked them that many a time over, Father Walmsley told me; but they say that there is nothing to be done now but to let me be quiet and undisturbed; that, with this other complaint, to take me away again might only do harm, for, you see, I only grew worse at Beachdown. I believe they think that I have inherited mamma's delicacy of constitution, only that it has never shown itself before, because I have always been so well and—happy. They say that even —without this complaint I have now, if a fever or any sharp illness had ever come to me, I might have had no strength to resist it; so you see, Julia'—and she lowered her voice to a solemn whisper—'if even I had become Stanley's wife, I might not have lived so long—I might have died very soon, as others have done—as mamma did.' And then, as if fearing her cousin would think she was agitating herself, she added with a smile: 'But it *is* so good of you, Julia, to come in this way—so good to papa as well as to me. And how kind of Sir Robert to spare you to come to us!' and the little thin white hand was laid caressingly in Lady Hunter's.

'Gerty darling, do you think he would consider himself at a time like this; do you think we could have felt satisfied to have remained inactive? for me to have kept away from you, love, now—after it has been so much—my doing?' and Lady Hunter's voice rang with pain. But Gerty put her hand gently on her cousin's lips.

'*Don't* say that, Julia, *don't;* it grieves me so, and poor papa too, that you should think that for one instant.'

Just then Mr. Mannering came into the room, and Lady Hunter rose to go and take possession of the bedroom which was to be hers during her stay. As soon as the maid left her in it alone, she sat down just as she was, with her bonnet still on, and leaning her head in her hands, stayed there motionless for the next few minutes, as if in deep thought and perplexity. Then she rose quickly and went to a small writing-case which the maid had already taken out of her trunk for her, and sat down before it.

'It must be right to do it; at least it cannot be wrong. It would be cruel not to let him know—not to save him, perhaps, from a life's remorse, and I am the only one who can do it;' and with trembling hand and quickened breath she wrote as follows:

'*Whitewell Grange, August* —*th*, 18—.
'My dear Stanley,
'I do not know whether I am doing right, but I cannot think I am wrong, as, if what I am going to tell you is indifferent to you, no harm will have been done, as no one knows I am writing, and I shall have fulfilled what seems to me only a duty of kindness owed to so close a friend as yourself. Stanley, Gertrude Mannering is dying; I have come here to-day to help to nurse her, if I can. She has been ailing for months; but though she herself says she felt from the first she should never recover, it is only lately that any one else suspected danger, especially her father, who is, I need not tell you, half paralysed with grief. It is a decline, they say, which may last for weeks yet; but she has also a heart complaint, which may end her life at any time, if all agitation is not avoided as much as possible. She is very peaceful and calm, and quite willing to die, except for her father's sake; so peaceful as to be painful to see in one so young—at least it is so to me, though it impresses me strangely. I suggest nothing, Stanley, and recommend nothing; but leave all to yourself.

Neither to her nor her father shall I say I have written until I hear from you; but I *think* I may say that, though you are never mentioned, nothing but forgiveness is felt towards you for what may have been stern in your conduct towards the dear child who is dying. I cannot write more. You will forgive abruptness, I know, in this distress.   Ever

'Your most sincere friend,
            'JULIA HUNTER.'

Then she addressed the letter to the hotel in Paris, where from his last to her she knew Stanley would now be staying; and going down-stairs, quietly put it into the post-bag which they showed her lying in its place in the hall.

CHAPTER XXVI.

ON a bright August afternoon, two days after Lady Hunter had written her letter, the sun was streaming into an apartment in the Hôtel —— at Paris, where a young man sat alone, heeding not and scarcely hearing the gay, busy sounds which were incessantly wafted through the open window, as the closed blind was gently stirred by the summer breeze. His head was bowed down upon his arms as he leaned on the table before him, and an open letter lay there near him.

'My God!' he said at last, almost aloud, as the table on which his head rested shook under his strong agony, 'was this needed to make me yield? without this, should I have gone on still resisting, still fighting against Thy grace granted to her prayer? Grace and prayer—empty words to me so long; but seen now to be true as any physical science—nay, truer; perhaps alone true! Why until now have I resisted these strange impulses which at all times and in all places have seemed to move me, in the little village chapel as in stately duomo, in busy cities as in the wild solitudes of the mountains, calling on me sometimes, as with Thy very voice, my God, bidding me believe and worship—telling me, in my pride, that the kneeling *contadina*, whom I have pitied and despised so often for her simple faith, was yet nearer to truth than I? Were not these all Thy grace calling on me, the grace given in answer to *her* prayers—her whose heart I have broken? Why, only now, am I able to say, "I will arise and go to my

Father, and say to Him, Father, I have sinned against heaven and before Thee, and am no longer worthy to be called Thy son"? Must the blow that lays me prostrate at last before Thee be the one that robs me of the one creature dearer to me than life, spite of the sternness and pride which have made me her murderer? My God! must she die, gaining for me by her very death what her sweet living example was unable to accomplish? Proud, blind sinner that I have been, resisting all these months, trying not to hear the voice which has been calling me ever since that night I saw her leave me, carrying with her the cold words that have done their work on the tender heart I trampled on in my jealous hatred of the religion she could not forswear for my sake—the religion that I must *love* and yield to from this hour, whether she lives or dies! Am I not punished too heavily, that the pride which would not yield to her gentle example and the force of her earnest prayers, must bow down now in the very dust to kiss the rod which has struck me at last, bringing with the force of its blow the light and grace which I *dare* not resist, which I see now as never seen before, which I must embrace with a strength equal to that of my long rejection? And it is through *her* prayers, sweet saint whom I have murdered, that God *forces* me to accept His grace, haughty scoffer that I have been! I, who all this time, in my wretched presumption, have told myself that she should yet be mine on my own terms; that she—not I—should yield; that if she really loved me I should win her whenever I chose to return with my cruel temptation to the heart that would be weakened with its yearnings for the love it so bravely renounced before!'

Then with one last powerful effort the evil spirit strove still for the mastery—the demon of pride, which would not be driven out without a further and a terrible struggle.

'It is impossible!' whispered the tempter; 'how can you do it—you, Stanley Graham, how can you bow your intellect to the dictates of a religion you have so long despised? how can you bear the jeers of a world which until now has courted and flattered you, to be treated by you in turn often with lofty disdain? How can you, who are so haughty, so impatient of contradiction, how can you kneel at the feet of a man like yourself, to own your sins and receive admonition and advice in the confessional you have so abhorred and scoffed at? How can you ever bring yourself to obey and submit to others—you who have so loved to rule always, who wished to tyrannise even over her who was loved as you have never loved another creature; you who would have had her *think* only as you directed, and because she could not yield, broke her tender heart! And for what would you do it? what would it gain for you? Would it give her back to you? would it restore her fading life and win her again for yourself? would it make her your wife? Is she not *dying?* could you not seek her equally well, and implore her forgiveness, without embracing her religion? If you knelt by her death-bed to pray for forgiveness and permission to stay by her to the last, would she refuse her pardon because you had not yet become of the same faith as herself? Would even her father, bitter as he may feel against you, refuse to receive you, if you could bring a minute's greater peace and joy to his dying child? How, without her sweet presence, will you bear scorn and contempt and even slander, through long future years, from those who now court your very name, many of them not only your inferiors in intellect, but in everything?'

But with a terrible effort Stanley strove to drive away the tempter, as he rose from his bowed position and paced the room, at intervals throwing back his dark disordered locks with a quick gesture.

'It is God or—hell; I must choose between them!' and he paused a minute in his agitated walk; 'there is no medium. Against my will or not, due perhaps to *her* prayers, the full light has come to me to-day; and if I reject it, it will be with my eyes open—blind no longer, as I have let myself be so long! The struggle I once occasioned to that tender heart has come to me now in turn; but while with her it was earthly love that strove to tempt her from God, with me it is pride —deadly pride! What she was strong enough to do and die for, shall I weakly turn from, when God is calling me so strangely, showing me by one clear vision, and the force of her example, what years of instruction and persuasion might have failed to do? If I resist to-day, may not God abandon me, proud sinner, who have earned this grace, not of my own merit, but by His pure mercy and her sweet prayers?'

Then, as if to another Xavier, the words seemed to whisper, as the pale image of Death seemed to rise before him—Death, which must come so surely to him in his pride as to the meanest creature:

'What will it profit a man if he gain the whole world and suffer the loss of his own soul?'

And kneeling down by the table, he buried his face again upon it.

'O my God, how have I deserved Thy grace—I, who would have lost, not my own soul merely, but would have tempted Thy young tender creature to her eternal ruin with me!'

Then as he knelt, his soul too as it were lay prostrate before his God, accepting the life, devoid of human joy, which must be its portion on earth—earth from which *she* was going who would have made it all bright, she whom his pride had slowly murdered! And ambition too must go now, at least such ambition as he had often dreamed of—that of winning, after his restless, useless life, a great name in his country's service as statesman and author, the powers of both being felt within himself, and the wealth at his command which makes such ambition easier to fulfil and satisfy. This, too, must be sacrificed—this hope, which might have made his loveless existence less dreary in the future; for as a member of God's One Church must not his ambition be a lowly despised one in this world's eyes—that of repairing for his past hatred and injuries by devoting his time and intellect to defence of the religion vouchsafed to him to-day as if by miracle?

He rose at last, his face pale and fixed, and left the room as with some sudden resolve; and a minute later he had taken his hat and was in the street, walking quickly among the gay throng, heeding nothing, scarcely seeing or hearing anything, utterly absorbed in his own thoughts. On he went, until he came to the street in which is situated the celebrated church of Notre Dame des Victoires—the church which had often and particularly been a mark for his scorn and contempt on account of the especial faith which he had heard animated the prayers offered up therein, and to which he now directed his steps, as the first beginning of his reparation, to offer up to God at this shrine of His Mother the victory just granted him over himself and the devil, and to pray for strength to persevere even amid the pain and bereavement which were rending his heart. He entered the church, and taking a chair in a quiet corner, knelt bowed down motionless for some minutes, feeling at first only an overwhelming sense of the difference between this evening and the last time on which he had entered this holy place, when he had come to scoff politely with an acquaintance at the prayers which were being offered up, to tell himself in his bitterness that Gertrude Mannering *could* not love him if she preferred all this to the pure intellectual religion he would have taught her as his wife. And now, yielding at last to the grace which had so long been whispering to his heart, he knelt here with the rest, with a faith as lively and perhaps more humble, acknowledging himself a sinner, rebelling not against the Hand which was robbing him of the sweet treasure of which he had been unworthy.

It was the eve of the Festival of the Assumption, and seeing that the priests were in their confessionals, Stanley rose and quietly placed himself outside that of one—though as yet he knew it not—renowned for his humble sanctity and learning. And as Stanley knelt there among them, people wondered who he was, this young man, with his pale face of such singular beauty, who looked so stern and troubled, and who yet thanked them with such a winning courtesy as they let him pass, guessing somehow as they did so that he was not French, but an Englishman. He entered the confessional, and as he did so, for a minute pride rose again in his heart and strove to shame him back; but, away in England on her peaceful death-bed, Gertrude Mannering was praying for him with her untiring hope, and pride was driven back as Stanley placed himself on his knees before a man like himself, but whom he at last believed was there taking God's own place, with His power to hear and pardon sinners. And then and there he gave the history of his life to the priest in a kind of general confession; and as the minister of God listened, he marvelled at the singular purity which had been observed by this young attractive man amid the temptations of his age and evident position, for even at Oxford Stanley had been by his companions nicknamed 'Bayard,' from his persistent abhorrence and avoidance of anything approaching to immorality or even coarseness. The one deadly sin of his life, the cause of all the others he had committed, had been the pride which he now was so hard upon in his confession to the holy priest, who was saying inwardly to himself the while,

'God must have great mercies, great designs in store for this young man, who while so long His enemy, has been so specially preserved from all sins of grossness and impurity; his very pride and intellectual refinement having doubtless appeared to the *world* as the means which were his preservation—the world that knows not God nor His ways!'

There was no task of argument or still further persuasion to be gone through in Stanley's case, no remaining doubts to be solved; with him it was the whole faith or none, the Catholic Church or infidelity; for a soul like his there was no middle course or hesitation, from the instant grace had conquered in his heart. He had told his confessor at the outset that the outward work of his conversion could not be finished here where he had begun it by this preparatory confession, as he must start in the morning for England; and then as he rose at last from his knees, the priest, knowing now the outline at least of the circumstances which called him thither, promised many and earnest prayers as he bade a kind fatherly adieu to the stranger who had interested him so wonderfully.

With an entirely new peace in his heart, spite of its terrible pain and abiding self-reproach, Stanley left the church slowly when he had finished the task which his stern will, assisted by God's all-powerful grace, had made him accomplish thus early. At once he went back to his hotel, glad that the dinner-hour was long past, so that he need only partake of some slight refreshment, which he ate quickly and mechanically, and then shut himself in his bedroom to face the further task, painful yet soothing, of writing to her who was dying for his sake, as it were, to tell her, in terms which must as little as possible excite the poor worn-out heart, the news that would cause her such joy and wonder, and to crave permission to come to her bedside, there to hear the words of forgiveness from her own lips.

'Gerty, my darling (let me call you thus once more, unworthy as I am),' he wrote, 'they say you are dying, and I—who must feel as if your death will lie at my door, for whom, if it is only too true, all thought of earthly joy shall be for ever past—I, Stanley Graham, who was unworthy of the love I treated so cruelly, entreat that I may come to your side, there to kneel and ask your forgiveness, and through it, perhaps, dare to look to be received, if but coldly, as I deserve, by your father, whose home I have saddened ever since I won your heart, my darling, to treat it so harshly, telling myself that you did not love me, in my mad pride and jealousy of its every feeling. Gerty, on my knees I wish to retract every word I said to you that day of our last meeting—every bitter, cruel word, to the final one with which I let you leave me, when, unmoved as I looked at the last, my heart and brain seemed on fire, my darling. Every word of temptation (and let me tell you this gently, my sweet injured one) with which I strove to lead you to what I now know would have been eternal ruin, I retract too on my knees, and have to-night confessed with sorrow and remorse to God's minister; for, my darling, what your gentle pleadings and noble example failed at the time at once to accomplish, has been worked within me to-day by the blow that brought me the yet scarcely realised news of your hopeless illness. I am a Catholic, Gerty, from henceforth: whether you receive me to your side or not, my life must be from to-day as devoted to defending, as it has until now been to scorning and maligning, God's holy Church. Ever since that night, Gerty, I know now, I have been fighting against grace, against the ever-present force of your sweet example, well-nigh breaking my own heart too, rather than yield to the mercy which surely is due to your prayers, my darling, for *I* have never deserved it. Without book or sermon or instruction, though in secret I have read much, and have abroad here attended at the churches, all at once God brought me to His feet, I scarcely yet understand how, and I cannot go back; I am a Catholic in heart and faith, soon, if God gives me life, to be one in reality and practice. Am I not punished, my darling, that the divine gift which I rejected, when it could have given you also to me with itself, I must receive with such eternal gratitude now when it can bring me no earthly joy? for even this last sad one I crave—of kneeling by your bedside, of being near you at least sometimes, during the days that are left—would not have been refused, I know, by your gentle heart, if I had asked it in my agony, even had I been still averse to your holy religion, for myself. I must not write too long, my own Gerty, through fear of agitating you, through fear of hastening what they tell me is so imminent, though I *cannot* realise it—the death of her who, in return for my sternness and cruelty, has been my sweet saviour, whose bright example has at last brought me to God, *never*, with His grace, to do aught but serve Him through the future. Gerty, I have this evening made a preparatory confession to a holy priest here at the church of Notre Dame des Victoires, and in the morning, when I have there heard Mass, I start for England, to await in London your answer to my appeal—the permission which even your father surely cannot refuse to one whose life must be such a long, weary repentance—the leave to look at least once more upon the face which is dearer than my own life. The little ring you sent back to me in that sweet forgiving letter, and which has been with me night and day ever since, I shall enclose in this packet, asking that, if I am forgiven and summoned to your side, I may see it on your finger when you receive me, that I may believe you are my own in death at least, if I cannot hope for you in life, my darling. Trusting they will give you this gently, as they will best know how, and again on my knees asking your forgiveness, your own, ever in sorest grief and despairing hope,

'STANLEY GRAHAM.

'*Paris, 14th August* 18—.'

Then he folded up the letter, in which he enclosed the ring, and placed it within a slip to Lady Hunter, on which he wrote as follows:

'Dear Lady Hunter,—I cannot thank you sufficiently until I may do it in person. Will you see that the enclosed is given as gently as possible to your cousin, or read to her, if that would agitate her less?

'Yours gratefully,
'STANLEY.'

He then also enclosed his address in London, giving the name of the hotel to which he would proceed at once on his arrival there; and having made up the small packet and directed it to Lady Hunter, laid it ready to be posted early the following morning and began to make preparations for departure, dreading to seek rest in his agitation, trying not to listen to the fear that *would* whisper to him of the cruel complaint that might end all too quickly, even before he could reach her, that sweet life, to save which he would freely have laid down his own.

CHAPTER XXVII.

Lady Hunter had been four days at Whitewell, and the hushed and grief-stricken household were becoming slowly accustomed to the knowledge that their sweet young mistress would never more move about in their midst—that she was dying, peacefully but surely. Her cousin's presence was a real consolation to Gerty, one for which she was never tired of thanking her; for Lady Hunter had such a sweet way of comforting her father by her unobtrusive sympathy, such a quiet art of persuading him to take rest and refreshment when he would have forgotten both, that Gerty saw he had unconsciously learned to lean upon her and confide to her the terrible grief which was too strong at times to bear quietly, but which must be controlled in his darling's presence, because of the ever-threatening fear of agitation for her.

'Julia dear,' she said one day to her cousin, 'if you were not with us, I don't know what papa would do, if he had not you to talk to sometimes. It might be too hard for him to bear, I—think, sometimes; it might have injured him, in some way; and then—it would have been—O, so much harder for me too! As it is, Julia, you see—he—has—grown into—an old man—so quickly. And he bears it so quietly before me, poor darling papa!' and she wept quietly on her cousin's shoulder.

Gerty was right; Mr. Mannering would never be a

hale, erect man again; he looked fully seventy now as he sat by her side so incessantly, generally holding her hand in his, watching every fancied change, only stirring reluctantly to take a few hours' rest at night, or when, on the excuse of leaving Gerty alone with Father Walmsley for a little while, Lady Hunter persuaded him to try and take a meal with her down-stairs or a short walk with her in the park.

Twice since her arrival Gerty had been able to be carried down when it was very fine and warm, to sit out too in the park, on an easy little couch, supported by her father's encircling arm; and as they sat alone on one of these occasions she had said to him earnestly:

'Papa darling, perhaps—in return for Julia's goodness to us, even for the kind reverential way she has with Father Walmsley, some good may come to her from being here now, though perhaps it may not be yet. It may—be good for her, papa, to see death coming like this to one like me, whom she knew only a year ago to be so healthy and lively — so fond of earth, and thinking so little of leaving it! It may make her see how—vain—it all is, the world, to see one who thought to enjoy it so long called away from it so soon— one who was never very pious either, but so very ordinary, like I am.' And the artless humility, so genuine and true, shone out in the sweet hopeful smile she raised to her father's gaze.

And so it had come to the fourth morning of Lady Hunter's stay, and she sat at breakfast with Mr. Mannering, having decoyed him to it gently while Gerty had fallen into a quiet sleep, when the letters were handed in to them as usual. There was one from Rupert, of sad anxious inquiry, and more of the affectionate notes from N—— Convent for Gerty, from her dear sorrowing Sister Teresa and her old companions, who never tired of writing to ask if it were really hopeless to pray for her recovery, if their prayers must really be only for what they could not bear to think of yet, their darling Gerty's happy death.

But there was another letter too, one for Lady Hunter, a small packet, which she glanced at and turned very pale, before she quietly began to open it on her knee. A minute later, when Mr. Mannering had read his letter from Rupert, she rose and stood close by his side.

'Mr. Mannering,' she said in a low tone which trembled audibly, 'if—if Stanley Graham, even thus late, should ever ask forgiveness for the past, and beg for leave to come to Gerty's side before the end, you— would not refuse him, would you, if she were willing—if it would make her happier and his life less full of bitter remorse than it must be now?'

He looked up quickly, almost sternly.

'Is he likely to make such a request? Does he know she—is dying?'

Then Lady Hunter told him what she had done, of the letter she had written to Stanley, of how she had felt impelled to it somehow, as to a sacred duty, not only to him, but to Gerty herself; and she showed him the note she had just received, with its enclosure. Mr. Mannering trembled visibly as he looked on the handwriting which, though he had never seen it before, seemed to bring him so near to the man who had robbed him first of his darling's heart, and who was now as it were the destroyer too of her life itself; and for an instant the devil whispered again of hatred and revenge, of how easy it would be, and perhaps wisest for his child's sake, to send back Stanley Graham's letter unopened, with a few polite words to the effect that he

was forgiven as far as he could expect, but that to give
his letter, whatever it might contain, to the dying girl
in her precarious state, which required such avoidance
of all agitation, might be fatal to her, or at least could
work no good, but only disturb her present peaceful
calm. But the temptation was rejected almost as soon
as suggested. Apart from the thought of his darling's
own happiness, apart from the knowledge of the weary
yearnings which must be ever in the poor heart, though
it hid them so bravely, could he, as a Christian and a
Catholic, set an example of such unforgiveness and scant
charity to this unbeliever, who was perhaps praying to
be admitted to a place by the death-bed which might
bring grace at last to his proud heart?

Looking at his face again, Lady Hunter saw that he
was softened, and she breathed more freely.

'Julia,' he said, for he always now addressed her so,
as Gerty did, 'how can it be done? We do not know
what it may contain. How can we give it to her without
agitating her?'

'Mr. Mannering, you see what he says: it need not
be given to her, but *read* to her first, if that is easier.
Suppose we wait until Father Walmsley comes, it
wants but an hour to his time; and if you think best,
let him read the letter first, and then break the news of
it gently to Gerty.'

'God bless you, Julia! You always know what is
best.' And Mr. Mannering grasped her hand with a
grateful pressure for a minute.

Then they sat together silently, waiting for Father
Walmsley, both feeling thankful in their hearts that
Gerty still slept on quietly up-stairs; for their agitation
was so great, that they would have had difficulty in
hiding from her that some new cause for it had arisen.

Father Walmsley came at last, and with trembling

hands and still more trembling voice, Mr. Mannering gave him Stanley Graham's letter, telling him briefly what Lady Hunter had already told himself, and his expectation of what it might contain. Calmly, with a solemn earnest look on his face, but with inward wonder and perturbation, the good priest opened the letter, and as he did so the enclosed ring, twisted in tissue-paper, fell out upon the table, to be carefully taken up by Lady Hunter, who saw at once what it was, her heart beating strangely at the sight of it. She and Mr. Mannering sat motionless while Father Walmsley stood reading the letter a little apart; and they both started as he laid it down, and turned to them again with a smile sweeter even than ordinary on his face.

'Mr. Mannering, God has chosen to work a miracle of grace in answer to the prayers of your child—to bless her with the knowledge of it before she dies. What your little Gerty might never have accomplished in life has been worked by—her coming death, in the proud heart whose love she gave up for conscience' sake, though she broke her own in the effort. Mr. Mannering, Stanley Graham is a Catholic, made to yield at last to grace by the force of the blow that brought the news of Gerty's hopeless illness; and—he writes to implore permission to see her, if only once, before the end. There is much in his letter, Lady Hunter, that you will scarcely understand, much less appreciate, which will sound strange, coming from one who so lately was not merely indifferent, as you are, and kindly disposed towards our holy religion, but who hated and despised it. But I think you should stay while I read it to Mr. Mannering—you who have been so instrumental in its arrival, and so great a friend of the writer; because, in any case, you ought to know its contents before seeing Gerty again.'

Lady Hunter seemed too bewildered and awestricken to speak; she could only make a gesture of assent; while Mr. Mannering sat down and buried his face in his hands.

Then in a low impressive voice Father Walmsley read Stanley Graham's letter, and as he paused Mr. Mannering looked up and stretched out his hand for it.

'My God! is it really so—really true?' he whispered. 'Who is to tell her, Father Walmsley? who is to break it to her? Who *can*, without agitating her, tell her that her prayers are answered; that he does not ask only to see her again and to be forgiven, but that he asks it as a Catholic like herself; that it will be no longer an infidel who has stolen her heart and her life from her father?'

Feeling somehow *de trop* now, and that Mr. Mannering would be best left alone with Father Walmsley for at least a few minutes, Lady Hunter stole from the room to inquire if Gerty were yet awake. On being answered in the affirmative, she waited yet a little longer, and then went back to tell Father Walmsley, who had, as she hoped, succeeded in restoring Mr. Mannering to outward calmness, and was ready to go up-stairs.

'Don't be afraid,' he said as he left the room; 'it will not be allowed to agitate her more than God wills, this joy for which she has prayed so long. And if it should, after *all* care has been taken, if the joy should, by God's will, shorten her life in any way, Mr. Mannering, you *could* not repine—could not grudge this last great happiness to her who is dearer than yourself;' and he turned back a minute as he spoke the last words with a strange solemnity which startled Lady Hunter, who made him promise to summon them as soon as Gerty should know all.

Gerty was sitting up in bed, having taken her slight breakfast, as Father Walmsley entered.

'You look very peaceful and happy this morning, my child,' he said to her, with his kind smile.

'Don't I always look so, father?' she asked somewhat ruefully. 'Indeed, I try to, very hard; but, you see, it is not so easy always, on account of—poor papa,' and her voice faltered.

'Gerty, could anything make you feel happier—more peaceful than you do? Is there anything you could wish for before you die—anything which could come even on earth?' and he sat down by her side, speaking in a low quiet tone.

The colour rose to her pale thin face again for a minute.

'Father Walmsley, you know what would make me happier if I could hear it before I die, if it were possible; you know what would be almost too great joy for me on earth, though I *know* it will come some day, however late.'

'To hear that—you were to see—Stanley Graham again, my child—to hear that you were not dying in vain—that he had yielded to God's grace at last?'

She sighed in assent, and then, suddenly looking up at his face, saw the strange smile upon it.

'Father Walmsley,' she whispered, with her divination too quick for the gradual telling of his news, 'if —if you know anything, don't be afraid of startling me. I am quite calm; it cannot harm me. O, tell me if you know anything, Father Walmsley, if—if there is any hope—of anything like that!'

But her quickened breath and heightened colour alarmed him so much that he said very quietly, in a tone of gentle rebuke:

'You are not going to be impatient, are you, Gerty

—to expect too much all at once?' And the kindly reproach had directly the desired effect, for Gerty was calm again in an instant, ashamed of her own impetuosity.

'I am so sorry,' she said, with her sweet rueful smile; 'but, you see—just for a minute—it seemed to be coming near, what I have been so hoping and praying for.'

'And perhaps it is not so far off either, my child,' was the quiet answer, as, looking at her very earnestly, he resumed his difficult task; 'but you must promise not to excite yourself at all while I tell you why I think so.' Then, very slowly, so slowly as to make it at first purposely only half intelligible to her, he told Gerty how Lady Hunter had written to Stanley Graham, and of the answer which had just come from him; of the wonderful news of his conversion to the Catholic Church, and deep repentance for the past.

Gerty sat motionless against her pillows, with her hands clasped, and her eyes now and then raised to Father Walmsley's face; not excited, but with a strange awe upon her, a wonder too absorbing yet for agitation, as it dawned upon her at last that Father Walmsley was not telling her what might possibly be, but what really was—that her prayer was heard, the sacrifice of her life accepted, as she had prayed it might be; that Stanley Graham was coming to her death-bed, an infidel no longer, but a Catholic now, forced, as it were, at last to yield to the grace he could no longer resist.

'Father Walmsley,' she said, in a low tone of entreaty, with a smile so beautiful on her pale face that it struck the good priest as that of one who already looked on heaven, 'may I not see the letter?

May I not read it, to convince myself it is not all a happy dream?'

Then he gave it into her hands; and with the sweet tears falling from her eyes she read it, not once, but many a time over, kissing it lingeringly as she folded it up at last.

'I may write to him myself, may I not?' she asked pleadingly, looking up again. 'Papa will be—kind to him, for—his own sake now as well as mine. Ah, Father Walmsley, when he comes, when you know him like I do, you will not wonder why I have wanted him so for God! Ah, it is almost too great joy, as if it could not be real. And yet it is true!'

She was so strangely calm amid her absorbing joy, there seemed so much more of heaven than of earth in her happiness, that Father Walmsley was not afraid to ask her:

'My child, you are sure there is no regret to overcome? no undue longing for life, which could now have been joined with his?'

She looked up with a strange happy look, and shook her head. 'Don't be afraid, father. If I had lived he might never have yielded to grace, and I—think, I trust that our Lord will give me grace not to wish to come back to earth even when—I see him; that I shall be able to—remember that I tried always to pray for him for God, not for myself.' But her voice began to tremble and her face to flush again, as if in the reaction after her strange calmness, so that Father Walmsley rose and summoned her father, who waited outside.

'Papa,' Gerty whispered as he took her in his arms for a minute, 'you must never grieve about me now, even when I am dead, because I am so happy that it seems like heaven, papa, to think of it—such joy that I hardly dared to look for it to come to me on earth!

You will so—love him too, papa, you will console each other always. And the ring, papa darling, the poor little ring that—I sent back to—him, where is it, papa? Ah, you have it! Now put it on for me yourself, so that—we can tell him *you* did it, and then he will know at once—that—you have forgiven him.' And as her father with his trembling hand placed Stanley's ring once more on her finger, as she looked at it, her voice, which had been growing more broken and agitated with every word, seemed to fail entirely all at once, and falling back on her father's arm, she fainted away.

The joy, gently as it had been broken to her, had been too much for the poor little heart when once that first wondering calm had vanished, and for a minute, in his agony, Mr. Mannering thought she was dead; but Lady Hunter and the nurse, who now came in to give their assistance, assured him that though perhaps dangerous, from the very complaint that had caused it, his darling's attack was not necessarily a fatal one. Gerty was slowly recovering when the doctor arrived on his daily visit; and when he had solemnly assured Mr. Mannering that this time the seizure would not end in her death, though he looked terribly anxious as he said so, he asked Father Walmsley in a low tone what had caused the attack. It was hardly possible to keep him in ignorance of all the circumstances now, when also Stanley Graham might be expected in a day or two; so drawing Mr. Mannering aside, Father Walmsley whispered that they must speak to him for a few minutes, and told him what the doctor had asked.

Then Mr. Mannering, speaking as quietly as he could in his agitation, told the doctor, what he had never directly done before, the nature of the trouble that had been the cause, as they felt only too surely, of his daughter's illness. He did not mention the precise reason for the separation between her and Stanley Graham, but only that such a separation had been necessary; adding that circumstances had now occurred which would enable them to come together again for the short time left to his daughter on earth, and that it was this news which, though told to her as gently as possible, must have caused her sudden attack.

The doctor listened without surprise, perhaps only to the confirmation of his own suspicions, and then said very earnestly in reply:

'Mr. Mannering, if there has been anything of this kind, you must never reproach yourself for what has been told her to-day, for consenting to let this Mr. —Graham, I think you said, come to her as he wishes, and for allowing her to read his letter. To have let her continue in ignorance of whatever has occurred would have been cruel, nay impossible, under the circumstances. And in her weak state it would in any case have become every day more difficult to ward off agitation from one of an excitable sensitive nature like hers. Some slight cause might any day now have produced an attack quite as serious as this has been, indeed, though we may not have seen it, the very hiding of the anxiety and inner feelings concerning this one matter must have been so injurious, that the joy she is feeling now can scarcely be as much so, because any day the repression might have become too strong for her, and have ended her life suddenly, and of course more painfully than it can end now, even—should another attack come soon.'

'Then—do you fear one, Dr. Baldwin?' earnestly asked Father Walmsley, seeing that Mr. Mannering could not speak.

'I will not deceive you,' replied the doctor painfully. 'Though I cannot, of course, foretell one, Miss Mannering is in that state now that you should be prepared for the worst any time, especially after the agitation, which is unavoidable, of seeing Mr. Graham when he arrives. I think you said she wished to write herself to give him the required permission ? Do not hinder her if she wishes it when she is quite recovered, in an hour or two, if she does not fatigue herself with too long a letter, because he should in justice be written to to-day, as every minute is precious that keeps him from her; and if she once recovers from the agitation of seeing him, she may be all the better for his frequent presence.'

Father Walmsley turned for a minute to Mr. Mannering.

'Would you wish to send for Rupert, Mr. Mannering? It could do no harm, and it is but fair to have him near his sister now, at least for a day or two.'

Mr. Mannering grasped the priest's hand eagerly.

'Of course, of course. I seem to think of nothing, Father Walmsley, nothing but—her. If—she—died without seeing Rupert, I could never forgive myself.' And he looked so broken down, so changed, that even the doctor was for a minute unmanned.

At once Father Walmsley wrote out a few words to be taken at once to be telegraphed to Rupert:

'Can you come home for a day or two at least? Your sister is in a very dangerous state.'

And then he followed the doctor and Mr. Mannering back into Gerty's room.

She was quite conscious now, and was talking quietly, with that sweet smile on her face, to Lady Hunter, whose arm was supporting her tenderly. When the doctor had assured himself that nothing more could be done at present, he took his leave, having quietly given directions as to what must be done in case of another attack, which, however, he did not yet apprehend. As soon as he had gone Mr. Mannering took his place again by Gerty's side, which Lady Hunter gave up to him.

'You see I am quite right again now, papa darling,' she whispered, as her hand sought his in their fond accustomed way. 'And I may—write to—him to-day, may I not, papa, to tell him—how happy he has made me—and—you, to tell him—to come, that—you *will* receive him joyfully even, papa dear?'

Even if it had been a positive enemy, one whom he personally disliked, for whom she pleaded, her father could not have resisted his darling's low eager tone of sweet entreaty, the yearning gaze of the eloquent eyes which shone now with such a joyous light.

'Tell him to come, Gerty, whenever he chooses; I am ready to receive him for your sake, because it will bring you such happiness, even if I were not ready to forgive him for God's sake, Who has called him in such a wonderful way to the faith which he has hated so long, at a—time, too, when no—hope of possessing you, my darling, can have influenced him in *any* way.'

'That is it, papa, the greatest joy of all; what I have prayed for always for him. And, papa,' she added in a low solemn whisper, holding his hand very fast, 'if —if even—the seeing—him should be too much for me, if it—killed me—you could not grieve, papa dear, because it would be joy that would have done it; your little girl would have died of joy too great for earth, and he—the cause of it, *must* be very dear to you always.' And a strange awe, which for the time seemed to render mere human grief unfitting, came over her father as she spoke, as he seemed to feel that his darling, so ripe for heaven, could not be long for earth, that God was calling for her to be given back to Him very quickly now.

No one spoke for a minute or two, Lady Hunter appearing bewildered with a feeling that showed her the world could never be the same to her again. Then Gerty asked if she might be left alone for a little while with Father Walmsley before he went.

'I should like to go to Confession, you know, papa, because I should like to receive our Lord to-morrow, to thank Him, you know, and to ask for strength to bear the—joy.' And so they left her alone again, as she wished, with Father Walmsley.

At once, as the door closed, she turned to him with an eager look.

'Father Walmsley, I could not ask you before papa, but I know you won't deceive me. Was I—very ill? was it dangerous when I fainted?'

He could not deceive her, as she had said, so he answered very earnestly and gently:

'It was dangerous while it lasted; but you are better again now, my child, and you must keep so, must you not, very calm and quiet, to be able to write your letter, so that—he may be here to-morrow?' And he smiled cheerily; but she looked still more serious as she continued:

'Then if—that was dangerous, another might come —any time, might it not, father? Tell me truly, because, you know—I ought—to be prepared, and I don't think I am afraid.'

He saw that it would agitate her more if he evaded the question, and that she was ready, with the wonderful grace God had given her, to hear whatever he might say.

'My child, you are right. Though we need not *necessarily* apprehend one, an attack might come with undue excitement; but you must not fear it or think of it, if only—for—Stanley Graham's sake, Gerty; you must live to see him.'

'But—if—it were God's will that I should not, if I were to be—taken—before—he comes, O Father Walmsley, should I be resigned to give—it up, that last joy?'

He saw what was troubling her—what he himself had thought of with much anxiety—that if God should call her away before the moment for which they all waited so tremblingly, there might be some regret, some earthly yearning, to tarnish the perfect resignation she had prayed for, and with which she wished to surrender her soul to God. Taking up the small crucifix she kept always near her, he gave it to her, as he said earnestly and solemnly:

'If God should will it, Gerty, you would, would you not? Try to make an act of *perfect* resignation, to be ready for *whatever* God wills—to live or die, Gerty. Would it be too hard, my child, too hard to give up willingly this last joy, if God saw it to be best—best for both of you?' And as he prayed silently by her side, he thought for an instant that the sacrifice would be too much, too great to be offered at once, without a struggle.

Gerty bent her face upon her clasped hands, as for a minute there rose before the poor little heart a vision of him who had been its idol, but who was gained now for God; and then with a beautiful smile she looked up as she spoke, in a voice a little above a whisper:

'Help me to pray to be quite ready for whatever is God's will, to *wish* to—die—without—seeing him if it is best. Because,' she added even still more solemnly, 'it seems somehow, father, as if it would be so; as if it would be best, even for him too, because I know I should not live long after—our meeting; something tells me the joy would be too great to bear quietly, and it would be harder for him then, than to come and find me dead already, spared the pain of parting, with his ring on my finger, the sign of our reunion. You see I am only very weak, and it might be that if I saw him some regret might come into my heart and keep me longer from God, or at least some thought too much of him and earthly love, some pain for his grief and self-reproach, that would make the parting harder for us both. And when I think of this, father, it is easy to give up this last joy of seeing him; I can almost *pray* for it to be denied, if it would make me at the last think less of God and too much of him.'

Then for a minute or two Father Walmsley knelt by her side, praying in silent thanksgiving for the great and wonderful gifts of grace God was bestowing on her, young and weak as she was, in return for the sacrifice she had made to Him of her earthly love, in return for the unselfish offering she had made of her life to gain one noble soul for His service.

In a few minutes also Gerty had made her short simple confession very quietly and calmly, now that earth was fleeing away so fast, as the good priest also felt with a strange prophetic awe. Then, in a voice which trembled slightly, but without any other sign of agitation, Gerty asked if she were not in that state which made it fitting and necessary for her to receive Extreme Unction too; and again inwardly thanking God, who made his task so easy, Father Walmsley told her gently that she had but anticipated him in speaking of it, for he had intended to tell her that he should come prepared in the morning to administer it as well as Holy Communion to her, forbearing however to tell her also that, had he known of her rapidly increasing danger, he would have come prepared to give her Extreme Unction even to-day, before he left her.

Then, when he had talked to her quietly for a little while longer, he summoned her father again into the room, and bade her a temporary adieu, promising to return late at night, bringing the Blessed Sacrament with him, to be given to her very early in the morning, before he must leave to say his Mass.

She looked so calm and happy now that her father and Lady Hunter both tried to drive away out of their hearts the fear, 'Will she be able to bear the meeting? will she even bear the inward excitement of looking forward to it all night, and perhaps nearly another whole day?' And they told her gently that they had sent for Rupert, so that he too might be here to welcome him whom God had called so wonderfully in answer to her prayers, knowing not how they betrayed to her the fear they felt—the fear which could not startle nor alarm her now, since God had made her so ready for whatever He should will.

Then they could keep her no longer from the sweet task—sweet, yet so sad—of writing herself while she had strength, to summon Stanley Graham to her death-bed; the task which must have been so difficult and agitating if she had not been so weaned from earth, so full of heavenly joy, for the sake of him whom she had once loved too strongly, with an idolatry too great to be given to any creature. With her little thin white hand trembling slightly, but without other signs of perturbation to excite alarm, she wrote to Stanley her second letter only, and her last:

'Stanley, I am so happy, so full of joy, that it is too great for earth. You have blessed me with a delight you could never have given me even as your wife, Stanley—my own Stanley now indeed—because I know now I should have loved you too much, that I *did* love you more perhaps than God, and only a short false happiness could have been ours then. But now, in dying, I love you *in* God, as we can love each other all through eternity, as you will love me too when the first grief is past, even if you should come and find me dead, Stanley, and I could not speak to you in words. And, O, never reproach yourself, now or in the future; *never* say your cruelty has killed me, for that is the only thing that grieves me now, that you should think so for one instant. Every word you call stern which you uttered that day I know to have been wrung from you in the pain of seeing what I know seemed my obstinacy, which then you could not understand, by your hatred, which I know to have been sincere and earnest, against our holy faith—yours now, Stanley, thank God a thousand thousand times! If there *was* one word that required forgiveness (though I remember none), the sight of your ring on my finger once more, to be buried with me, shall be the sign that it is forgiven joyfully, that I am your own again, more than before, in death. Do not grieve for me, Stanley; I could not wish to live now, even for your sake, because something tells me that God, who has called you so wonderfully by my death, which you are making such a happy one, wants you in some way for His service, that what He brought us together for is accomplished now, and that we must finish out His will, you on earth, and I, as soon as by prayer and pain I shall be made fit, in heaven, to meet again there as dear brother and sister in God. If they let me, and if I had strength, I could go on for hours telling you all that is in my heart of wonder and joy, and of the welcome waiting for you in my dear old home from my father, who, for your own sake now, is longing to receive you, to bid you never reproach yourself again, but rejoice with him over my happiness. If I do not live to welcome you in words, know that I do it even more in reality in prayer in Purgatory, that even on earth your noble heart may find perfect peace and contentment in the exercise of our holy religion, which you will *love* now with a strength surpassing that of the former hatred. The little crucifix which, if I can, I wish to have in my hands at the last, is to be given to you whenever I die, soon or late—the crucifix I had with me, Stanley, that night after our parting, which was with me during the last struggle, which struggle has won me now such a joyous heavenly reward—your conversion, my own beloved, your conversion to God. I am growing weak and must write no more, but even in death remain

'Your own
'GERTY.'

'Papa,' she said then, as she folded up her letter and gave it to him, 'I won't read it over; I will let it go just as it is, though it is so poor compared to what I should like to have written. He will understand—how hard it is to say fully all I want; so it may go now at once, papa.'

And they gratified her by sending it off at once, instead of letting it wait for the usual hour for posting their letters from the Grange, scarcely guessing, perhaps, her hidden reason for wishing it to be gone—that whatever should come in the interval, Stanley might receive it as sent really from herself while yet living and expecting him. They knew from his letter that he must arrive in London late that night, so that he would be able to start for Whitewell in the morning as soon as Gerty's letter should reach him.

Gerty was calmer and quieter almost than before, now that her letter was really gone and that there was nothing more outwardly to be done but to wait for Rupert's arrival, which must be late in the evening, they knew; and she lay for the most part quite still, with her eyes closed, as if in bodily exhaustion, with her hand in her father's, as he read aloud for her from her favourite spiritual books or the prayers in preparation for Communion. And Lady Hunter, though she would not weary or excite Gerty by speaking much, yet seemed unable to tear herself from the room, from the sight of that sweet peaceful resignation, the sight of which seemed to make her wonder grow less each hour, as she thought of what she could hardly yet realise—the fact that Stanley Graham had embraced the religion he had hated so long and bitterly.

Late in the evening, as they had expected, Rupert arrived, and was met in the hall by his father, who told him everything that had occurred before he went up to Gerty's room. Wonder-struck in the midst of his grief, and feeling, as they all did, that the next twenty-four hours of anticipation would prove a crisis in his sister's precarious state, Rupert went up-stairs quietly to her side, and for a minute the colour that rose to her face, and her quickened gasping breath as she greeted her idolised brother, seemed to threaten the dreaded attack of her insidious complaint; but it passed away, as she said with a sweet smile and whisper:

'Don't look so frightened, Rupert. I do not think our Lord will let me die, at least before I have received Him into my breast, to give me courage and strength to go before Him as my Judge.' And when they left her alone for a little while with her brother, she continued: 'O Rupert, is it not wonderful, is it not a grand answer to our prayers—so soon too—before I die? You will be to him like a brother, I know, Rupert, not for my sake only, but for God's; for you do not know yet what a noble soul he has, what great things he will be able to do for religion; for he is not one to turn to it weakly, or with only half a heart or coldly; it will be with *all* his heart and all his noble mind. Isn't it strange how he has been before Lady Hunter, Rupert, in turning to God, when she has *naturally* seemed always so much more inclined that way? If *she* were only gained, I should not have one more wish on earth, Rupert, except,' she added, in a lower, faltering tone, ' that for papa's happiness, that he may not be too lonely and grieve for me too heavily.'

'My dear little sister, *that* we can but leave to God's mercy, with many earnest prayers, and then do our best in a human way, my poor father! But for Lady Hunter, do not be impatient, Gerty. You see she has scarcely had such ardent, incessant prayers offered for her as have been for Stanley Graham; and in any case, Gerty dear, she was perhaps all through less likely to yield quickly and in earnest to grace, so wedded to the world as she is, and only *careless* about God and religion, than one like him who hated the very name, and whose love now will be as earnest as his former bitterness against it; one too who, by what you say, Gerty, must long have despised and been weary of the world in his heart.'

Gerty smiled so brightly that as Rupert looked at her, hope for at least her temporary recovery rose within him.

'Rupert, when he is baptised, do you know, somehow, I should like him to take the name of Xavier,' she said earnestly.

'And a proud, beautiful name too, Gerty, that he

should be happy to take for its own sake, as well as because you will ask him, dear.'

She smiled again strangely to herself without speaking, and soon after grew so visibly weak and exhausted, though without outward agitation, that they persuaded her to try to settle to sleep for the night, because she usually woke very early in the morning, and wanted this time to do so specially, so as to release Father Walmsley in time to say his Mass as usual at the church.

She was sleeping still, quietly and peacefully, with her father at his untiring watch by her side, when Father Walmsley arrived, about one or two o'clock in the morning, being unable to divest himself of the vague fear, which she herself had helped to increase, that the death-summons might come to her suddenly in her weak state, that she might be unable to fight long against the cruel disease, which must be so much augmented by the inward excitement and agitation which she concealed so bravely for their sakes. Lady Hunter and Rupert were up too, having been unable to rest in their anxiety; and drawing Rupert aside before he withdrew to wait in prayer with the sacred treasure he carried with him, he told him what Gerty had not mentioned to them yet—that he was going to administer Extreme Unction also to her this morning before leaving again. Rupert acquiesced and thanked him with quivering lips, and they separated silently.

A few hours later, between five and six o'clock, Gerty awoke, and asked at once for Father Walmsley; and while her father went to summon him Rupert arranged the little altar in her room, as it had been now three or four times since her return home from Beachdown. Impelled by some irresistible feeling, Lady Hunter begged to remain in the room, and Gerty's face was lighted up with a bright smile as she heard her decision.

'She has never been so near to God before as she will be now,' she whispered to her father and Rupert, as Lady Hunter knelt, as they did, by the bed.

Then with her father's arm supporting her, and after a few earnest prayers, Gerty received her Lord into her heart—Jesus, for Whose love she had given up so much of earthly love and joy. Father Walmsley let her pray silently for a few minutes, and then began to make aloud for her the thanksgiving after Communion, during which Lady Hunter was motionless, with her head bowed in her hands. Then suddenly, as he paused a minute, a change came over Gerty's face, which quivered in pain as she gasped for breath in her father's arms.

'Papa,' she whispered, 'it—is—coming—now, the end! I feel it—papa—kiss me—and say good-bye! Father Walmsley, I am not—to—see—him! God is —calling—me—His—will—be—done!' And then, with the deadly faint coming over her again as she struggled for breath, she lay speechless with her head on her father's breast.

Whilst they did as had been ordered, Lady Hunter carrying out the doctor's directions, as Mr. Mannering was too paralysed to do so, Father Walmsley whispered to the latter and Rupert, and a minute or two later was administering to the dying girl the Church's last holy consolation of Extreme Unction, with an inward prayer of thanksgiving that time was granted for it. She seemed to revive a little as he finished, and they knew she was conscious by the sweet smile on her pale lips.

'Father Walmsley, the crucifix—give it to me,' she said. And he placed it in her hands—the one she wished to have there at the last, the one which was to be given to Stanley Graham—asking her as he did so if she suffered much.

'A—little, but—the—joy—is greater!' she whispered, the beautiful smile breaking over her face again as she looked up for an instant at her father, and then with one gentle sigh lay back quite still in his arms. For a minute, only Father Walmsley knew that she was dead, that the pure spirit had passed away to God, to the heaven which it had so well won; then, as the rest slowly realised it too, as even Mr. Mannering, in his speechless, tearless agony was forced to do, the good priest, with trembling voice, repeated aloud the prayers for the soul just departed. Then, with only Rupert's and Lady Hunter's sobs breaking the stillness, he waited for Mr. Mannering to grow more able to realise that his darling was dead, as the little hand grew colder each moment in his grasp; and in a few minutes, still upon his knees, he spoke:

'Mr. Mannering, now that she is dead who was so dear to us all—to you more than all the world, your most precious treasure—now that God has called her to Himself while yet He dwelt sacramentally in her heart, I may tell you what, in deference to her sweet humility, I might not tell you while she lived. Months since, whilst her trouble was still fresh, when she felt her bodily health just beginning to fail, she offered up her young life for Stanley Graham's conversion, with a perfect spirit of self-sacrifice and submission to God's will, feeling, somehow, as she told me, though then I made light of it purposely, that if God heard her prayers for this conversion, He would want Stanley Graham in some way for His own service, for some nobler destiny than earthly love and marriage. Hence she, in making this offering, drove all selfish human motive from her prayer for him who had been her earthly idol, being ready to rejoice to be taken away in God's own good time. And even now, when her prayer was so wonderfully answered, when God accepted the pure offering of her innocent life, she yet made a further sacrifice, in the fear lest anything of mere earthly love and regret should tarnish her thoughts at the last; for with His other abundant graces, God gave her that of true earnest humility and distrust of herself. She prayed that if He should will, this last joy might be denied her—of living to see again the object of all her prayers; that He would make it easy and best for Stanley Graham himself to come and find that the pain of parting was spared him, his ring upon her finger to be the silent token of their reunion. Mr. Mannering, even in your terrible loss, your intense grief, you must feel what holy consolation is yours, to know that you have reared a little angel for God, that you have this day given back to Him another sweet saint for heaven; for I seem to feel, almost with certainty, that this last sacrifice was enough, sufficient to purify whatever of earthly stain remained, and that our little Gerty is already in heaven with God!'

And now, from even the parched-up eyes of that bereaved father, that bowed old man, lately so hale and strong, the tears flowed freely—the kind, relieving tears—as he gazed on his darling's peaceful dead face, with a feeling in his heart, broken almost as it was with its grief, that he could not have called her back, that he could cherish no selfish yearning to have his treasure again on earth, away from her eternal rest in the blessed home with God, where she was praying for and awaiting him.

CHAPTER XXVIII.

A FEW hours later they had made her ready for the grave, three young girls from the village, who had been special favourites of Gerty's, having come with many tears to beg to be allowed to help in the sweet sad work, bringing with them choice beautiful flowers to be laid about her remains, which they persisted instinctively in reverencing as those of a saint, even before they knew anything of the secret of her death. They put a wreath of the purest white roses upon her brow, and on her breast and about the pillow they placed lilies, fitting emblems of her maidenhood and sweet virginity. And while they were yet engaged silently and tearfully at their task, Father Walmsley came to them, and bade them also to let the ring they observed upon her finger be left conspicuously to view, so as to be seen at once by any one entering the room. They obeyed him, and then in a few impressive words he rewarded them by telling them what was no longer a secret now, but a beautiful edifying fact, the story of their dear young lady's love and self-sacrifice; of the wonderful conversion granted, as if by miracle, to her prayers; and that he who was to have been her husband, but whom she had renounced for God's sake, was coming that very day, to find her dead, with his ring upon her finger—the silent token of the forgiveness she might not speak in words. Then, when all the household had visited her, their sweet little saint laid ready for her last resting-place, when her father had prayed long and silently by her side for strength and resignation, the spirit of agitating expectation seemed to come upon them all, as though they could do nothing now but wait for the arrival of him to whom the blow of her death meant so much more than even to that bereaved father.

It needed all Lady Hunter's sweet persuasion, all Rupert's holy consolation, to calm Mr. Mannering's agitation, as he moved restlessly about the rooms so desolate to him now, looking every minute at the clock to see if the hour drew near at which they expected Stanley Graham.

'Rupert,' he said two or three times that long afternoon, 'pray that when I see him the spirit of unforgiveness may not rise again in my heart, that the thought of my darling's holy death may help me to feel kindly towards him, as she would have wished.'

About six that evening, when the bright August day was beginning to decline, they heard the sound of wheels through the closed blinds, and a minute or two later Stanley Graham was shown into the breakfast-room, where Lady Hunter, with heart beating terribly, had gone first alone to receive him. He had seen the drawn blinds as he drove up, but refused yet to realise what they must mean; meeting Lady Hunter's gaze with one of almost wild entreaty, 'Lady Hunter! I am not too late?' and the hollow, agonised tone struck to her beating heart.

'My poor Stanley!' and she held out both her hands, taking his own into them for a moment.

Then with a terrible groan he turned away, and leaned upon the mantelpiece in his old attitude, with his head bowed upon his hand.

U

'When was it?' he asked at last, still with that hollow tone.

'This morning, about six o'clock, very happily and *so* peacefully, Stanley,' she replied in a broken voice.

'My God! am I not punished too heavily?' he groaned, as he leaned there still in that bowed-down position.

Father Walmsley entered just then, in time to hear that agonised exclamation, and approaching Stanley, he laid his hand gently upon his arm.

'Mr. Graham,' he said kindly and solemnly, 'you are a Catholic now already in heart, by God's mercy granted to *her* unceasing prayers; you can understand how that which, in your present bitter grief, seems so cruel, may yet be to you a source of holiest consolation.'

'Consolation!' burst quickly from Stanley, heeding and knowing not who spoke, as he looked up with the old sternness on his face; then seeing it was a priest who addressed him, he at once changed his look and attitude to one of respect and attention, while Lady Hunter gently explained:

'It is Father Walmsley, Stanley, her confessor and best friend.'

'Father Walmsley,' he continued then respectfully, but with the bitter pain ringing in every word, 'you do not know, as I do, how I tried to tempt her to eternal ruin; you did not hear her plead for her religion, to meet only with a stern refusal to believe that she could love me sincerely unless she gave it up at my bidding; you did not see her face that night as I let her leave me, carrying with her the cold cruel words that broke her heart, or you would not speak to me of consolation.'

And as Father Walmsley listened to his words, as he looked on the noble face, its beautiful features so

stamped with stern anguish, he understood still more
fully how Gerty must have loved him, how he had won
such a deep idolatry from the sensitive heart now so
still up-stairs in its hard-won rest; he felt clearly, old
man as he was and detached from all mere earthly
affection, what it must have cost her to make her sacrifice so promptly and willingly. There was silence for
a minute, and then Lady Hunter gently went closer
again to Stanley.

'Stanley,' she whispered, 'you must not think it
was all that, that alone which caused her death. The
doctors say that she was never really strong; that she
inherited her mother's delicacy; that she would not have
been long-lived, even if she had been always perfectly
happy. If she had become your wife, Stanley, you
might have lost her very soon, by the first illness that
came to her. And as it was, Stanley, she begged so
hard that you might never be let to reproach yourself.'

The anguish on the pale proud face softened somewhat, and Father Walmsley, seeing it, said very kindly:

'Come and see her, Mr. Graham, now at once. You
will be better, more able to bear it, when you have
looked on her face, so sweet and peaceful in its last
sleep.' And Stanley followed him quietly, while Lady
Hunter remained behind, knowing he would like best
to be alone with the priest when he first entered the
presence of the dead. They met no one on their way
up-stairs, as for the first time Stanley treaded the pass-
ages of the dear old home which Gerty had so loved to
describe to him, and silently they went together into
the room, her own pretty little room, where she lay in
her beautiful rest, ready for the grave. For a minute
Stanley stood motionless as he gazed at her, at the
dead sweet face which he had last looked upon that

night in the library at Nethercotes in its life and bloom, when she had torn herself from his embrace, away from his perilous presence. Then he went a step nearer and saw his ring upon her finger, as she had promised him he should see it, and the little crucifix in her hands, which he knew from her letter, that he carried near his heart, to be the one given to him when she should be laid in her coffin. And as he gazed, there was something so pure and holy in the very air about that lovely corpse that, with the anguish softening still more upon his face, he fell upon his knees by the bedside as he whispered aloud:

'My God! I was not worthy of her, never should have been worthy to possess her! She was too pure, too ready for heaven, ever to be given to me or any earthly spouse.'

And already Father Walmsley felt that Gerty had been right, that it was easier for Stanley to see her again thus, with the pain of parting past, and all of earth for ever over between them, than it would have been if he had even only once more heard her voice and held her in his arms, meeting the old look of love and life.

'Mr. Graham,' he said gently, but with solemn earnestness, 'perhaps when you have heard what I may tell you now, as I have to-day told to the rest, you will say so still more; you will be able to *thank* God even for her holy death; because, as a Catholic now, you know and believe how much merit suffering and self-sacrifice can gain for a human soul. Mr. Graham, the sweet life which has passed to-day from our midst was offered up willingly and freely for your conversion months since, when her illness was suspected only by herself, and then only slightly and at intervals. There was a feeling upon her that God wished and asked for the sacrifice, and she made it joyfully, because now there could be no fear of selfish earthly motive in her prayer for you. She kept her secret well and humbly; for after she had once told me what she had done, half fearing I might blame her as she did so, she never spoke of it again until she knew her sacrifice was accepted; and yesterday, once more, when the joyful news came to her that the *object* of it was granted already, that her prayer was heard so fully even while she was yet on earth. And knowing, as you do now, the sanctity to which God must have brought her by His wonderful grace in so short a time, you will learn without surprise that, fearing lest aught of earth with its mere human love and yearning should tarnish her perfect resignation at the last, she prayed that the joy of seeing you again might be denied her, and that it might be made easier for you to come and look upon her in death, knowing that she had died reunited to you in heart, than it would have been to part with her in life, as with her cruel complaint must have been very, very soon. And I know, Mr. Graham, that you will not grudge her this last sacrifice, which has already perhaps gained for her her eternal reward; that you would not selfishly call her back to your arms, thereby keeping her longer when she came to die from the presence into which nothing defiled can enter, nothing of earthly stain or imperfection, however small it may be.'

Stanley was still on his knees by the bed, with his head bowed down upon his arms, as he sobbed now with a vehemence that made Father Walmsley turn aside in his emotion—that painful emotion, which only the sight of a proud man's tears can call forth. He had wept last years ago at his mother's death-bed, but then he had been little more than a boy, now he was a man; and mingled with his grief were wonder and self-abasement in the presence of such sweet holiness, with an overwhelming sense of unworthiness of the sacrifice which had been made for him—of unworthiness of the innocent, costly price which God had been pleased to accept in return for the precious grace of his conversion.

'My God! what did I ever do to deserve it, that her sweet life should be offered up and accepted for my soul, proud unbeliever as I have been?'

'Mr. Graham, it has made *her* happy and gained heaven for her thus early; let this thought make *you* happy too, as you cease to reproach yourself for what has been so plainly God's blessed will;' and then Father Walmsley left him quietly alone with the dead.

And already, as Stanley stayed there, bowed down by her side, the peace and holiness of his lost darling's dead presence seemed to come upon his spirit, as he thanked God for her sweet virginity, safe and secure now with her Lord in heaven, as a voice from out of the future seemed to whisper to him, making already more of heaven than of earth mingle in his love for the dead.

For nearly an hour he knelt there, until a quiet footstep entered, and a gentle voice whispered in his ear:

'Mr. Graham, will you come with me down-stairs, where my father is waiting to receive you?' And as Stanley looked up he saw a young, almost boyish, face, with a sweet heavenly expression, bent towards him.

'I am Rupert Mannering, *her* brother, Mr. Graham;' and Rupert held out his hand to Stanley, who took it with his firm lips quivering.

'You do not shun me, then? You receive me as a dear friend, for her sake?' he faltered.

'Not only for her sake, Mr. Graham, sweet and precious as that is to us, but for the sake too of Him who has given you to us in her stead; who bids us, where there *is* anything to forgive, to forgive it freely, and remember it not.'

Then Stanley rose, and bending for a moment over the dead, kissed the pale forehead gently and reverentially, as he might have done that of a saint, as though a closer, more lingering pressure would profane the pure remains.

Another minute, and he had left the room with Rupert on his way to Mr. Mannering's presence, his proud heart, so changed and humbled now, beating strangely as Rupert softly opened the dining-room door and he saw a bowed, aged figure sitting alone, leaning upon the table.

'That is my father, Mr. Graham,' Rupert whispered; and then he withdrew, leaving them alone.

Mr. Mannering did not appear to have heard the door open, for he never stirred from his bowed position, and approaching him quietly, Stanley stood by his side. Then, before he could speak, Mr. Mannering looked up at him, into his face, and at once, as it were, whatever of human repugnance remained in his heart vanished strangely before the charm of that noble presence—the irresistible charm Gerty had tried to describe and prepare them for. As he looked on the face, with its noble beauty so indelibly stamped with such a keen repentance, though the anguish of it was softened somewhat now, the old man's heart yearned as a father's to a son towards this stranger, who had been so dear to his child, that she had reckoned her sweet life but a poor price by which to gain him for God—this young man whose grief, he felt, must be so much heavier than his own.

Stretching out both his hands to Stanley, he said in a trembling voice:

'Do not grieve for her, Mr. Graham, so bitterly: she is happier now than you or I could ever have made her.' And as though he should be the consoler instead of the consoled, he placed a chair for Stanley close by his side.

For a minute Stanley could not speak, as his proud heart nearly gave way again before this unexpected reception. He had looked for cold charity and politeness; he had been prepared for Christian forgiveness, but not for this kindness, little short even of affection; and at last, as he took the old man's hand and kissed it with respectful fervour, he said, his rich voice broken with emotion:

'Mr. Mannering, if already, through her sweet prayers and generous love, I had not yielded to God's grace, I must have done so at this moment, when I am received not merely with charity, but with such goodness and affection by one whose home I have made desolate!'

'Mr. Graham, never say that, never, if only for my sake. Mr. Graham,' he continued, with trembling earnestness, rising for a minute as he laid his hand on Stanley's arm, 'has it not been all plainly God's doing? must He not have brought you and my little girl together for *no* earthly end, but for her early sanctification, and that you, through her means, might receive the precious treasure of our holy faith? Can I let you say you have made my home desolate, Mr. Graham, when God has made you the instrument to enable me to give Him to-day, as Father Walmsley said to us, surely with truth, a sweet little saint for heaven?' And then, while the manly tears fell again from Stanley's eyes at intervals, wrung from them by the sight of the beautiful Christian resignation of that sorely bereaved father, Mr. Mannering went on to tell him every little detail of Gerty's death, how she had spoken so much of him after the arrival of the joyful news of his conversion, and how she had yearned and prayed that they might all love him too.

It seemed to give the old man strength, to make him merge his own grief in the other's greater one of self-reproach, thus to take upon himself to reverse their positions, and be the consoler of the very one whom once in his anguish, before grace had conquered, he had styled his darling's murderer. He was calmer now than he had yet been throughout the day, with all Lady Hunter's sweet kind efforts, and Rupert's and Father Walmsley's attempts at consolation. For an hour or more they sat there alone together, the rest purposely keeping from intruding upon this first sacred interview between those two so strangely brought together by the holy death of the one so dear to both, as they might never have been had she lived.

And surely Gerty, looking down from her heavenly home, must have smiled in rapture to see already so soon her last wish and prayer granted for that dear father left lonely upon earth; so that even with a *natural* yearning he felt he must love this stranger, who had been called in such a special way by God, for whose soul his darling had so imitated her Divine Saviour, and fulfilled the sacred saying, 'Greater love than this no man hath, that a man lay down his life for his friends.'

Four days later, on the eve of Gerty's funeral, Stanley was baptised by Father Walmsley in the little church where she had prayed for him so long and so often, taking the name of 'Xavier,' in obedience to her wish confided to Rupert during their last conversation together, though he of himself felt unworthy of so glorious a name. There had been a feeling in his heart that, if possible, he would wish to be already a Catholic, even outwardly received, when he assisted as mourner at the funeral of her whom he now revered as a saint, who had loved him with such a pure, unselfish, generous love—a love of which he had been wholly unworthy, and for which he must spend his life in thanking God.

He had not wished to intrude upon them by remaining at the Grange during the interval, but Mr. Mannering had besought him so earnestly to do so, joined, too, in his entreaties by Rupert, that Stanley could not refuse. How could he, when the request was that he would stay so near the dead, and when those who asked him were her dear ones, whose kindness and forgiveness had been so great and so unlooked for? And so every day for two hours he had gone down to Father Walmsley to receive instruction—he, proud Stanley Graham, to listen reverently to every word of the humble priest's, to become a child again, as it were, in docility and unquestioning faith. The good priest found the instruction an easy task, for Stanley had read and learned so much of himself, even while he had yet hated the faith, that it was not knowledge he had wanted so much, but only God's grace to make him see and prize it aright—to turn, as it had now done as if by miracle, what had been all darkness into glorious light. And as Lady Hunter watched him day by day, seeing the change, independent of his sorrow, in him whom she had known so long and so well, while scarcely yet able to realise it, she was filled with a strange holy envy, to which she wanted courage to yield truly and bravely, which made her often hold painfully aloof, as though divided by an indescribable barrier, from the three who were united now by a holier bond than even their love for the dead.

And when all was over—when Gerty had been

borne from her dear old home, as sweet and true a martyr as any of her ancestors—when she had been laid in the vault by her mother's side, with the simple inscription on her coffin :

'GERTRUDE MARY MANNERING,
Aged 19 *years and* 9 *months*,'

with the date of her death, there was not a dry eye in the church, even among the villagers and simple poor. They knew now, most of them, and were proud with a holy pride, of the history of their much-loved young lady's death ; for Stanley, regardless now of what might be thought of himself, wished it to be told to every one, that his darling might receive, at least after death, the honour he had not paid her in life, and that her father might have at least this holy consolation when all earthly brightness was fled.

That afternoon Lady Hunter had to bid them adieu, to return home to Nethercotes, and Stanley went alone with her to the station.

'Pray for me, Stanley!' she whispered amid her tears, as her hand rested in his at parting.

'Lady Hunter, can you doubt it?' and his voice shook with emotion. 'Can I ever cease to pray that the grace which has been given to me may come to you in God's good time?—you whom He made so great an instrument in my conversion, and but for whom my darling would have died without the knowledge of it—but for whom I might not even have looked upon her in death.' And a minute later the train bore Lady Hunter away from his sight, back to the world which had for ever lost its satisfying charm.

Then a day or two afterwards, when Rupert too was obliged to leave him, to return to his duties at the College, when he could remain no longer at present, dearer and more precious than ever as he was now, Mr. Mannering besought Stanley not to go away yet, but to stay with him at least until he had made his first Communion under Father Walmsley's direction.

'I should like to kneel by your side that morning, Mr. Graham, in our little church that she loved so much, and where she is resting. Stay with me until then, as she would have wished. We are both lonely with the same sorrow; why should we not be a little longer together, to console each other for—her loss? our—little—Gerty, who will be always our—little Gerty now, always young and girlish—as she died; who can never change to us now, even if God leaves us years yet on earth.'

'Mr. Mannering, may God heal your broken heart! may He soften your pain, as you are doing so nobly for one who is so unworthy!'

And so for three or four weeks that were to intervene before he was received to the holy table, while the news of his sudden conversion to the Catholic Church was oozing out to the astonished world, Stanley stayed quietly at Whitewell with Mr. Mannering, becoming dearer every day to the old man even for his own sake. Perhaps now more than ever there was something irresistibly winning about him, for with the old charm was blended now the sweet yet noble humility taught by the lessons of the Cross, to which he turned now with all the ardour of the great soul for which such a loving heart had so joyfully given up its life. Every morning the two figures might be seen wending their way to Mass, the tall noble one of the young man supporting the bent form of the elder, who was an older man now in appearance by years than he was in reality, but to whom God had sent consolation in so strange a manner, giving him in place of his 'little sunbeam' the very one who had robbed her of her earthly brightness, who was forgiven now, and taken as a son to the heart he had bereaved. And day by day they learned, those two, to know and love each other better than even Gerty herself could ever have hoped for; to appreciate each other as they might never have been able to do had their dear one lived.

CHAPTER XXIX.

YEARS have passed away—twelve long years—since Gerty Mannering was laid in her early grave; and he for whom she offered up her sweet young life has received the utmost plenitude of grace she ever asked for in her untiring prayers for him; that which was surely foreshadowed to her upon her holy death-bed, making it so easy for her, has come to pass; for Stanley Graham, once the proud, scornful unbeliever, is now a priest of the Society of Jesus, that glorious order which he had once so detested and maligned.

For two years after Gerty's death he had lived quietly at Briardale the life almost of a religious in the world, spending his wealth upon the Church and the poor, and employing his intellect in writing in defence of the faith to which he had been so wondrously called, visiting nowhere but at Whitewell Grange, and once or twice very quietly at Nethercotes. The world, which had been *his* world once, called him mad and eccentric, having always suspected, so it said, that he would do something peculiar one day. But if in the past he had been able to despise it in merely a human sense, the world could not frighten or shame him now, when grace had won his heart and conquered his intellect, when God had given him the victory in the struggle with pride and human respect. Then, listening to the Divine Voice, which was calling him still further, he did not shrink or resist, but, like Rupert Mannering, gave up his ancestral home and inheritance to one who was a stranger (his uncle being now dead), and became a humble novice among the sons of St. Ignatius—a Xavier truly now in his renunciation of the world and its honours, which his intellect and wealth combined might so easily have won for him. And after the years of retirement and secluded study, he comes out to the world again at times—as Father Graham now—to try and win souls for God. For though he holds an important post in one of the colleges, though his head and intellect are those of a writer and scholastic, his superiors discovered early that with these gifts God has given him the *heart* of a missionary—a heart burning to help in the sweet labour of reclaiming sinners and unbelievers for the Divine Master whose religion he himself hated so long and bitterly. And so they send him away at intervals, from his books and studies, out into the world, to assist in giving missions, often in the metropolis, where those who once knew and courted haughty Stanley Graham would, if they were to come across him now, scarcely recognise him in the humble zealous priest. For the one quality conspicuous in him above all the rest is the sweetest, most unaffected humility, so visible as to make even the poor and lowly love to approach him, to listen to his voice and look into that pale beautiful face, which they say is a sermon in itself, with its beauty so much of heaven, surpassing the old earthly attractiveness, with its smile of peace and holy calm on the lips which once could curl so scornfully, and the eyes with their saintly, often rapt expression, the eyes which never look sternly now even at the greatest sinner, but only when preaching with burning words against the sin. None in trouble ever come away from Father Graham, in the confessional or elsewhere, without receiving the consolation he seems to know so well how to impart; no stranger approaches him without meeting with that irresistibly winning courtesy which, together with the dignity which can never desert him, seems the only outward characteristic by which those who knew Stanley Graham in the past can recognise him in the ardent mortified Jesuit.

And when Father Graham thinks now of Gertrude Mannering, as he must every day when he thanks God for his conversion, it is as of a sweet saint who was sent across his path for their mutual good, who was too pure and holy ever to have been meant for his earthly possession, to whose love God led him for a time to win him to the faith, and whose innocent life was taken in its generous sacrifice, so that God's work might be fulfilled in his own soul. He rejoices as he thinks of that pure heart taken so early to its Divine Lord's embrace, having in so short a space fulfilled such long time; and he is never weary of acknowledging in the humility of his heart his unworthiness of the grace she so generously obtained for him.

And Mr. Mannering is living yet, an infirm old man, who never goes beyond the park, except down to the church or to see Father Walmsley, who still lives too, with less of age's infirmities about him than his friend. Little Gerty is a sweet beautiful memory now in the village, where she is still instinctively revered as a saint, and where those who knew her persist in asking her prayers, instead of praying for her, feeling somehow that grief for her is unfitting, even though through her death the old ancestral home must pass to a stranger. Her father can speak calmly and smilingly now to Father Walmsley of his little sunbeam, as he can call her again now that the sharp pain of her loss has passed away; he can rejoice that he will not leave her behind on earth when his own summons comes, which it must do surely soon, as he tells Rupert in his letters. For the old man longs for it strangely, as he sits in the lonely, desolate rooms, and conjures up a bright face and sylph-like figure, and is happy for a while in the life-like vision, and scarcely sad now when it goes; only weary with a patient yearning for his darling who is awaiting him, together with her mother, still earlier taken from him. He sits for hours, on days when he is too feeble to go out, alone in the old dining-room, peopling it with the shadows of the past, with the echo of children's merry voices, the children both now given in different ways to God, trying not to be weary of his desolation, but to accept it thankfully even, as the way by which he may be more quickly fitted for heaven before death comes; thanking God also with all the fervour of his truly religious heart that the relative to whom the old house must pass after him, though a stranger almost, is a Catholic good and true; that the roof which so often was a shelter to Catholics in the glorious days of persecution, will own one of the true faith still for its master. And if he can think always of his darling's holy, martyr-like death with consolation, it fills him with a sweet pride and triumph when he thinks of what it has won for Stanley Graham, whom he has never ceased to regard as a second son, whose saintly repute fills him with joy, though he has seen him but twice since his ordination—once on the happy day itself, when he left his seclusion to be present at it, and once when, in company with Rupert, Father Graham came for an hour's visit to the Grange when they were travelling together in the neighbourhood. For in his gratitude Father Graham could not neglect the opportunity of offering up a prayer of thanksgiving on the spot to which he owed his conversion and vocation, the spot which could raise no mere human feeling now, but only heavenly joy in his heart; and so, together with him who was his brother really now in religion, he went to gladden the old man by the brief visit, which he might never be able to repeat during that feeble waning life.

But one thing more remains to be told—one happy fact concerning another with whom we have travelled through these pages, and for whom many and earnest prayers were offered, more than all by those two who knew her best, Gerty Mannering and him who is now Father Graham. Lady Hunter is a Catholic also, having, about the time that Stanley quitted the world, yielded at last to the grace which had been whispering to her heart so long, first planted there even so early as the time of Gerty's visit to her in London, when she had listened to the young girl's simple but earnest defence and explanations of her faith. What had been then begun had been finished by Gerty's sweet convincing example, and the overwhelming impression of her holy death and Stanley's almost miraculous conversion; but the *courage* had been wanting, 'the flesh was weak;' the earthly heart, which dreaded the step that seemed as if it must in some measure alienate her from her beloved husband. But she gave way at last, unable to fight any longer against conscience with its never-ceasing voice—unable to resist the example of haughty Stanley Graham in quitting the world to become a humble religious novice; and the step was made easy for her by her indulgent husband, who cared only to see her happy and contented, as he knew she only would be now in this new way she had chosen.

He is dead now, poor Sir Robert, and his widow's one abiding sorrow is that she was not able to win him to the faith—kind and indulgent as he was to her. She feels at times that if she had yielded earlier and more bravely to God's grace, she might have merited that further mercy by her prayers, and her life now is one long reparation for her tardy submission. She lives quite secluded in the country house which forms part of her jointure, employing herself in works of charity and piety, only leaving home now and then to visit and cheer the old man in his solitude at Whitewell Grange. Once or twice lately she has visited London; but the gay world, in which she had formerly shone, knows her no more. She remained but a few days in its vicinity, and during those her object was to see and hear him who was once so mixed up with her life —to seek one interview with Father Graham, to beg his continued prayers, and to hear from the lips she had heard scoff so often, some of those sermons with their burning eloquence which she knew beforehand would go so straight to her heart. And as she gazed at the preacher, at the humble and ascetic though still dignified figure, she asked herself was this really Stanley Graham whom she had known so well, who had loved Gerty Mannering, who had been their companion so often at opera or ball, winning that sweet girl for his affianced wife for that brief joyous space at Nethercotes, and then in his pride trampling on her heart and his own in his hatred to the religion of which he was now so zealous a priest? And as Lady Hunter fell on her knees, able even as the rest to thank God for that sweet beautiful death and all it had wrought, surely Gerty's prayers were fulfilled beyond the measure she could ever have hoped for; surely too she had gained, by her noble example and unhesitating sacrifice, as great victories for God as any of her martyr ancestors; surely Father Walmsley's saying has come true which he spoke to her father, and by God's grace the simple little convent girl—bright merry 'little sunbeam'—has proved 'worthy of her race.'

THE END.

www.ingramcontent.com/pod-product-compliance
Lightning Source LLC
Chambersburg PA
CBHW022050230426
43672CB00008B/1128